# Made In Sicily

# Made In Sicily

Giorgio
Locatelli

with
Sheila Keating

Photographs by
Lisa Linder

Fourth Estate
*London*

First published in Great Britain by
Fourth Estate
An imprint of HarperCollins*Publishers*
77–85 Fulham Palace Road
London W6 8JB
www.4thestate.co.uk

9 8 7 6 5 4 3 2 1

Quote on page 178 from *Sicilian Food: Recipes from Italy's Abundant
Isle* by Mary Taylor Simeti, reproduced by kind permission of the
publisher Grub Street.

Quote on page 88 from *The Wings of the Sphinx* by Andrea Camilleri,
published by Picador, reproduced by kind permission of the publisher
Pan Macmillan.

Quote on page 14 from *Midnight in Sicily: On Art, Food, History,
Travel & Cosa Nostra by Peter Robb*, published by Harvill Press,
reprinted by kind permission of The Random House Group Limited.

Quotes on pages 310 and 348 from *Sweet Honey, Bitter Lemons,
Travels in Sicily* by Matthew Fort published by Ebury, reprinted by
kind permission of The Random House Group Limited.

Quotes on pages 2, 77, 182 and 338 from *The Leopard* by Giuseppe
Tomasi di Lampedusa, published by Vintage, reprinted by kind
permission of The Random House Group Limited.

Quote on page 150 from 'The Oil Jar' by Luigi Pirandello, from *The
Oil Jar and Other Stories*, published by Dover Publications, reprinted
by kind permission of Dover Publications.

Quotes on pages 84, 124 and 355 from works by Leonardo Sciascia,
reprinted by kind permission of the estate of Leonardo Sciascia.

A catalogue record for this book is available from the British Library

ISBN 978-0-00-743369-8

Designed by Joby Barnard
Typeset by Birdy Book Design

Printed and bound in Italy by L.E.G.O. SpA

To Clive Exton

who always told me I could achieve anything I wanted

What grows together, goes together.

# Contents

# A mythological island

'Sicily is Sicily – 1860, earlier, forever'

– Giuseppe Tomasi di Lampedusa

As a northern Italian, I grew up with preconceived ideas about Sicily and southern Italy. The joke was always that no one in the south did any work; it was the northern Italians who ran the country and made things happen. I grew up in Corgeno, on the shores of Lake Comabbio in Lombardy, where our family had a hotel and restaurant, La Cinzianella, and like most people in the village we went on holiday to Emilia Romagna, or maybe Liguria. It was only in the seventies that people really started to go south.

So you cannot overestimate how exciting it was that when I was about twelve years old, four friends, whom I looked up to because they were older – maybe eighteen – went off to Calabria, and from there to Sicily because one of them fell in love with a Sicilian girl (he actually ended up marrying her). Corgeno is a small place, where everybody knows everything about everyone else, and in those days when someone came back from their holidays they would be in the village square telling stories about the time they had had.

When these guys returned, they were full of talk about the fantastic life, the sun, the beautiful sea … they made Sicily sound like a Robinson Crusoe island, full of beaches with no one on them. In my mind it became an idyllic, almost mythological place that sounded like the Caribbean, populated by people who were Italians, but yet not like Italians; almost a different race. They spoke a language that was completely different to ours, and the whole island seemed to work in such a different way to northern Italy.

It was twenty years before I finally got to go to Sicily for the first time. Life got in the way: the army, cooking in Paris and London, having a family – my wife Plaxy, son Jack, and daughter Margherita (Dita) – setting up our first restaurant, Zafferano, and then later Locanda Locatelli. Then, in the late nineties, the winemaker Alessio Planeta (pictured on the previous page) invited me to look at an olive oil project he was beginning at La Capparrina in Menfi, in the south-west of the island. What was interesting was that after cooking for over two decades in London, I found myself looking at the island as much through the eyes of a Londoner as those of a northern Italian. Even after countless holidays in Menfi, where I have got to know many of the local people, there are times when I still feel as foreign as Plaxy, because when the local farmers or fishermen talk in dialect I can't really understand what is being said!

On that first visit it was early spring, just before Easter, when I arrived in Palermo, and as we drove down to Menfi I was completely blown away by the fact that the island looked so green and bright and gorgeous. I had expected something like northern Africa, and it is true that some areas are like that, but even in the middle of the motorway there were masses of big red bougainvillea, and the road cut through beautiful wheat fields and orange and lemon groves, olive groves, vineyards and fields of artichokes. The whole island was like a garden, and in a way the structure, with its funny old walls, reminded me a little of the English countryside.

I could see straight away that the northern Italian idea that the guys who lived in Sicily sat around doing nothing was completely wrong. Everywhere

you saw the hand of man, the agriculturist, over nature, in fields and groves that had been worked and tended for thousands of years.

## What grows together, goes together ...

Every time I go to Sicily, what blows me away is not only the incredible intensity of flavour that is in everything you eat, from the pale greeny-gold broccoli that punches you in the face with its taste, to the tomatoes from Pachino, which are so exquisitely sweet they almost make you want to cry, to the lemons growing everywhere, so beautiful you can just slice them and eat them with salt and olive oil. No, it is not only that. It is the absolute belief that the Sicilians have in the ascendancy of the ingredients over any kind of over-creativity or pretentiousness. Whenever I have eaten in people's houses or in restaurants, what I see is not the personality of the cook or the chef coming out in the dishes, but the personality of the land and the sea.

The first wave of people to invade Sicily, the Greeks, went there because of the abundance of the territory. In the *Odyssey*, Homer talks about the land of the one-eyed giants, the Cyclops, at the foot of Mount Etna, which, despite the fact that the Cyclops did nothing to tend the land, was so rich with produce that it amazed the hero, Odysseus, when he landed on the island. Obviously the Cyclops never existed, but I sometimes think that Homer invented the idea of them because he had found such a beautiful place he didn't want anyone else to share it: 'Don't go there; there are one-eyed giants!' Because the orchards, gardens and groves of olives, 'luscious figs', the 'vine's fruit', and the 'vegetables of all the kinds that flourish in every season' were very real, and they have remained, immovable, at the heart of Sicilian cooking no matter who has invaded or ruled over the island.

When people talk about Sicilian cooking, they always say, 'This is what the Greeks left', or 'This is what the Arabs or the Spanish brought', because Sicily's history is a complex one of two and a half thousand years of invasion and domination by foreign powers who treated the island as a colony, and often plundered their produce to feed their homelands. After the Greeks came the Romans, the Arabs, the Normans and the Spanish, and when Napoleon invaded Naples in 1798, King Ferdinand and his court took refuge in Sicily, bringing over chefs from Paris who cooked the fashionable French food of the times and were known as the *monzu*, a version of 'monsieur'. Finally, in 1860, Garibaldi, helped by the English, landed at Marsala with his band of 'redshirts' to begin his conquest of Sicily and the unification of Italy.

Historians talk about the sophisticated, baroque, baronial cooking of the Sicilian nobility on the one hand, and on the other, *cucina povera*, the cooking of the poor people who were forced to be clever with whatever ingredients they had. And we cannot forget the Mafia, which has historically controlled food prices, production and businesses. Of course, all this social history left some sort of mark, but I believe that the biggest influence on Sicilian food, and the winning force over everything, is the territory: the

land and the sea. These determine the produce, which has stayed constant and strong throughout all the cultural changes, hardships, bloodshed and extortion.

Even if the Arabs introduced oranges and lemons, sugar and spices all those centuries ago, it is the territory that ultimately decides what grows. We are talking about food from a very special, particular land, especially the volcanic area around Mount Etna (where the mythological Cyclops lived), all the way down the plain of Catania to Pachino where they produce the tomatoes that taste like no others, and the arid groves that produce the most beautiful olives and grapes. And then there is the profusion of fish and shellfish that throughout most of Sicily is prized above meat. Especially swordfish and tuna, which were once abundant around the Straits of Messina but are now sadly overfished, and the beautiful red prawns that come from the cold waters off Mazara del Vallo.

The quantity of traditional recipes that the Sicilians have is enormous, but they are all based on the same set of ingredients. As always throughout Italy, a dish with the same name will be made in a slightly different way in every town, every village and even every house, with everyone claiming the authentic version, but in Sicily these are only small variations on the same simple but beautiful combinations: broccoli and anchovies, capers, sultanas and pine nuts, olives and lemons, oranges and fish, almonds, pistachios and wild fennel, aubergines and breadcrumbs, and in desserts fresh ricotta, candied fruit and peel, and chocolate. Somebody, some day, a long time ago, put certain combinations of these ingredients together in a way that the Sicilians found pleasing, and, like the ancient Saracen olive trees that have stood resolutely on the island for thousands of years, the people have remained resilient in the face of any influences that feel false to the flavours they love.

The whole production of food has a harmony and a natural seasonal rhythm, but above all, there is this idea that what comes from the same land and sea can be put together on a plate. What grows together, goes together, as my grandmother used to say about the vegetables and herbs in our garden in Corgeno. I find it very inspiring as a chef to understand the way ingredients like swordfish, sultanas, breadcrumbs, capers and cheese can come together in something that tastes fantastic – particularly as in most of Italy we have an unwritten rule that you never put fish and cheese together, something that the Sicilians happily do all the time, and that works. The dishes are not about clever transformations, they are about conducting and expressing the taste of the ingredients to the maximum, in the simplest way.

We talk a lot about fusion these days, but in a city like London or New York, fusion means you can have ingredients from different cultures all over the world brought to you, so you can put them together on a plate. In Sicily, that idea of fusion is turned upside down, in that it is the different cultures that have come and gone over the centuries, but the ingredients have stayed still.

## Salt, pepper and a knife ...

This idea of simple meal-making with a limited set of incredible ingredients has had a big influence on the way I cook. I have always valued simplicity – and anyway the nature of Italian food is to be less complicated than other cuisines – but in Sicily you encounter a *true* simplicity that I have never experienced anywhere else.

After my visit to Planeta I returned in the summer with the family and we rented a house near Menfi, where we have been spending Easter and summer holidays ever since, close to the sea and the ruins of the Greek temples at Selinunte. Plaxy remembers seeing the place for the first time: dusty roads and tumbleweed; it was like stepping back in time, but we feel so at home there. Everyone has been so sweet and welcoming; and whenever you arrive, people are really happy to see you; and if you don't go around and say hello to everyone they will be offended. It reminds me so much of Corgeno, because everyone knows the business of everybody else. The first time I went into the butcher's shop the butcher already knew who I was and where I was staying.

On the first morning I went for a walk into the village in search of ingredients, because when we are there I cook lunch every day, and sometimes dinner, though mostly in the evening we go out to eat. That walk has now become my daily routine in Sicily. I buy a newspaper and stop for a coffee and maybe a pastry in the local bar, then I buy some vegetables, and usually some meat for Margherita, because she is allergic to fish. I go to one of the ten or twelve bakers to buy some of the beautiful local bread, and then home.

On that first holiday I had no preconceptions about what I was going to cook, and I was in that relaxed holiday mood of not having to organise a restaurant kitchen, or prepare dishes according to a menu. I had no time to build up a larder with spices or condiments, but I had a kitchen full of fresh ingredients – of course, I bought way too much, because I couldn't resist the boxes of artichokes and tomatoes and peppers – and I had some salt and pepper and a knife. That was it.

In London we live in such an organised way, with so many ingredients at our fingertips, but in a Sicilian village you don't leave home with a list, you just have to go out and see what there is. It limits you in a way, but it also makes you feel so free and inspired, because it is such a natural way of cooking, and it has become something I look forward to every time I go there. The ingredients are in charge. You see what ingredients you have, and they decide what it is that you are going to cook. This is the Sicilian way.

Very little in this book is complicated, because in Sicily the ingredients are so special, they speak for themselves. If you have been to Sicily you will understand. If you haven't been to Sicily, then you must go ...

# Antipasti

… soon a saucer of green olives and anchovies was sitting on the table, and some bread, and some mineral water. A small woman with dark hair and dark eyes and precise features whirled up like a woodland bird. She perched lightly at the table and rattled off a long list of antipasti, first courses and seconds, and every single one of them came out of the sea. This was Palermo in summer for you.

– Peter Robb, *Midnight in Sicily: On Art, Food, History, Travel & Cosa Nostra*

The best way to have a good meal in a restaurant in Sicily is not to ask for the menu; just let them bring you whatever the guys in the kitchen want to prepare for you, which of course will begin with the antipasti.

Everyone everywhere in Italy eats antipasti, the plates of shared food that arrive with the bread, before the pasta. They are the signal to relax, eat, discuss and enjoy, and the quality of the antipasti is a sign of what is to come. If the antipasti sets a high tone, you can be hopeful that more good things will follow with the pasta course, the fish or meat, and finally, the fruit or dessert. But what I see in Sicily, which marks it out from other regions of Italy, is that the abundance and the kinds of dishes that are put down also owe something to the influence of the Arabs who occupied the island from the ninth century. When the antipasti comes out I am reminded of a mezze: suddenly the table is full of little plates, and people hate the idea that they have not put out enough food. Whenever I have eaten out in Lebanese restaurants, if there is some food left at the end of the mezze, the waiter says nothing, but if all the plates are empty, they are anxious to know if they can bring you some more, and the same philosophy seems to apply in Sicily.

That generosity carries over into the Sicilian home. Even if you don't have as many dishes to share when family and friends are around the table, if a little bit of food is left over you can congratulate yourself that you made enough. And nothing will be wasted. Whatever is left over will be used again, maybe in a different way, for the next meal.

The production of food, in the Sicilian mind, never seems to be a problem; I never felt that anyone was thinking, 'I have to cook for all these people', perhaps because there is no pretension to Sicilian food. Instead there is an understanding that you will feed people with whatever you have, which is summed up by the Sicilian word *companatico*, which translates as 'what you have to go with the bread'. And since most of Sicily is a vast garden, what you have most abundantly is vegetables, and, because it is an island, there is a greater emphasis and pride in fish, rather than meat.

As someone who comes from northern Italy, where the antipasti is much more about cured hams and salami, it feels very different to sit around a table filled with bowls of *caponata*, the sweet and sour vegetable dish that you find made slightly differently everywhere; plates of beautiful *gamberi rossi* (red prawns, eaten raw with just a little olive oil and salt), *sarde a beccafico* (stuffed sardines), perhaps some *polpettine* (little balls of tuna or swordfish), deep-fried squares of *maccu* (the most delicious paste of broad beans and wild fennel), baked aubergines with sultanas and pine nuts, chargrilled artichokes under oil, octopus salad, *parmigiana di melanzane* (see page 140), served at room temperature, or perhaps fried courgette flowers, stuffed with ricotta, again served cold.

Because *verdure* (vegetable dishes) feature so strongly in Sicilian eating, I have given them a chapter all on their own, which follows this one; however, all of them are fantastic served as part of the antipasti.

**Insalata di mare**
Seafood salad

This is a typical antipasto all over the island, and will reflect what has been fished at any one time, so there might be more, or less, mussels, squid and octopus. Sometimes there will also be pieces of tuna or swordfish. Any fish goes, as long as it doesn't have any bones. I have seen people adding things like apple, or carrot, or spring onions, to add a bit of crunch, but I think the best *insalata di mare* is this simple one, just with celery, which is very important to the flavour, parsley, garlic, lemon and oil. If you only have one kind of fish, you can make the same salad. One day we had boxes and boxes of *seppia* (cuttlefish) come into the kitchen at Locanda, too much to use up in the pasta, so we made this salad, but with cuttlefish only. Serve it at room temperature, not chilled, or something of the flavour will be lost.

Ask your fishmonger to clean the octopus and squid for you, and to give you the body and the tentacles.

Serves 4

1 octopus (about 330g), fresh or frozen (and defrosted), cleaned, with tentacles
330g squid, cleaned, with tentacles
450g medium prawns
600g mussels, clams or both
80ml white wine
2 celery stalks (preferably with leaves), chopped
50ml lemon oil (see page 63)
sea salt and freshly ground black pepper
1 tablespoon parsley and garlic (see page 60)

If the octopus is fresh, beat it with a meat hammer to tenderise it and rinse it very well under cold running water, with the help of a clean sponge, to remove any excess saltiness. If it has been frozen, you don't need to do this, as freezing has the effect of tenderising it.

Bring a large pan of water to the boil and add the octopus, but don't season it, or it will toughen up. Cover with a lid, turn down the heat and let it simmer gently for about 20–30 minutes, or until tender.

While the octopus is cooking, bring another pan of water to the boil and drop in the squid bodies and tentacles. Simmer for about 10 minutes, then remove with a slotted spoon and drop the prawns into the same water for about 2 minutes, until they have changed colour and are just cooked. Peel most of the prawns, reserving a handful for decoration. Drain and keep to one side with the squid.

Scrub the mussels and/or clams separately (pulling any beards from the mussels) under running water and discard any that are open. Put the mussels and/or clams into a large pan with the white wine over a high heat, cover, and cook, shaking the pan from time to time, until all the shells have opened. Remove from the heat, strain off the cooking liquid and reserve this. Discard any mussels and/or clams whose shells haven't opened. Take the rest out of their shells and throw the shells away.

Remove the octopus from its cooking liquid and cut it into small pieces. Cut the squid bodies into strips.

Arrange the octopus, squid, mussels and/or clams with the celery in a shallow serving dish. Whisk 50ml of the strained cooking liquid from the mussels and/or clams into the lemon oil, season to taste and drizzle over the seafood. Scatter with the parsley and garlic and serve.

### Insalata di gamberi ai pomodori
Warm prawn salad with sun-dried and fresh tomato

This is a Sicilian dish that we refined a little for the menu at Locanda. The bread dressing is something I first made a long time before I fell in love with Sicily, when I started out cooking with Corrado Sironi at Il Passatore in Varese – but the use of breadcrumbs, lemon juice and olive oil has a very Sicilian feel to it, and when you combine it with tomatoes and sun-dried tomatoes, I feel it brings a little bit of the island to our menu at Locanda.

Serves 4

120g sun-dried tomatoes
olive oil
4 large tomatoes
sea salt and freshly ground black pepper
1 teaspoon parsley and garlic (see page 60)
12 big prawns, unpeeled
a handful of lettuce
2 tablespoons Giorgio's dressing (see page 64)

For the prawn cooking liquor:
2 tablespoons olive oil
1 carrot, chopped
1 onion, chopped
2 celery stalks, chopped
½ leek, chopped
450ml white wine
300ml white wine vinegar
10 peppercorns
2 bay leaves

For the bread dressing:
2 handfuls of breadcrumbs (see page 45)
juice of ½ lemon
3 tablespoons extra virgin olive oil
1 tablespoon garlic oil (see page 60)
a little white wine vinegar, to taste

To make the cooking liquor for the prawns, heat the olive oil in a large pan and add the chopped carrot, onion, celery and leek. When they start to colour, add the white wine, the vinegar and 500ml of water, along with the peppercorns and the bay leaves. Bring to the boil, then turn the heat down and let it simmer for 15 minutes.

With a pestle and mortar, or using a blender, blend the sun-dried tomatoes with a tablespoon of olive oil until creamy.

To make the bread dressing, mix the breadcrumbs with the lemon juice, extra virgin olive oil and garlic oil. Taste, and if you like a little more sharpness, add the wine vinegar.

Cut the tomatoes into wedges, put them into a bowl, season and toss with the bread dressing and the parsley and garlic.

Bring the cooking liquor for the prawns to the boil, put in the prawns and cook for 3–4 minutes. Lift out and peel them while hot. Add them to the bowl of tomatoes, mixing well.

Spoon the tomatoes and prawns on to plates. Dress the lettuce with Giorgio's dressing and arrange on top, and drizzle some of the sun-dried tomato dressing around each plate.

### Insalata calda di polpo
Warm octopus salad

Serves 4–6

1kg octopus, fresh or frozen (and defrosted), cleaned, with tentacles
sea salt and freshly ground black pepper
1 tablespoon white wine vinegar
750g potatoes, cut into 2.5cm cubes
75g whole green and black olives in brine
4 tablespoons extra virgin olive oil, plus a little extra for finishing
1 tablespoon chopped flat-leaf parsley, plus a little extra for finishing
juice of 3 lemons
1 chilli pepper, finely chopped (optional)
1 carrot, cut into matchstick pieces
1 celery stalk, chopped

If the octopus is fresh, beat it with a meat hammer to tenderise it and rinse it very well under cold running water, with the help of a clean sponge, to remove any excess saltiness. If it has been frozen, you don't need to do this, as freezing has the effect of tenderising it.

Bring a large pan of water to the boil and add the octopus, but don't season it, or it will toughen up. Cover with a lid, turn down the heat and let it simmer gently for about 20–30 minutes, or until tender. Remove, drain and chop into pieces about 2.5cm long.

While the octopus is cooking, bring a pan of salted water to the boil, add the white wine vinegar, add the cubed potatoes and cook until tender, then drain.

Drain the olives and pat dry. With a sharp knife, make three or four cuts in each olive from end to end, then cut each segment away from the stone as carefully as you can.

Pour the extra virgin olive oil into a bowl. Add a good pinch of salt and pepper, the chopped parsley, the lemon juice and the chilli, if using. Mix well, then add the octopus and potatoes.

Finally add the olives, carrot and celery and toss everything together. Finish with a little drizzle of extra virgin olive oil and some more chopped parsley.

## Calamari fritti
Fried squid

One day when I was in the kitchen of my friend Vittorio's restaurant in Porto Palo, he said, 'Do some calamari fritti for me,' so I dutifully sliced up the squid, dusted it in flour and put it in the fryer, got some kitchen paper ready in a container, and when the calamari was golden I lifted it out on to the paper to drain off the excess oil, as we always do if we fry anything in Locanda. Vittorio looked at me as if I had landed from another planet:

'What are you doing?'
'I'm drying them, so the people don't eat so much oil.'
'This is not a Michelin-starred restaurant,' he said. 'People like oil. That's why they eat fried fish.'

And then he throws Trapani sea salt, which is a little moist and a bit grey, over the top, literally throws it – fingers into the pot and bang – so you can see the grains. But his food never tastes over-salted, because the quality of the salt is so high; it really makes all the difference to a calamari fritti.

Serves 4

about 400g plain flour
500g calamari, cleaned and cut into rings or strips
vegetable oil for deep-frying
sea salt
finely chopped flat-leaf parsley

Have the flour ready in a shallow plate. Dip the calamari rings into the flour and shake off the excess. Heat the oil in a deep pan, making sure it comes no higher than a third of the way up the pan. It should be 180°C. If you don't have a thermometer, put in a few breadcrumbs, and if they sizzle straight away the oil is ready. Fry the calamari until golden, and drain, season with salt and scatter with chopped parsley.

**Fritto misto alla piazzese**
Mixed fried vegetables, with anchovies or sardines

Sicilians love *fritto misto*, so much so that in the summer people set up stalls
or park vans or three-wheelers with gas burners and big pots on the back,
and deep-fry vegetables or fish for you there and then.

Serves 4

4 baby artichokes
juice of 1 lemon
1 tablespoon salt
1 small cauliflower, cut into florets
500g cardoons, tender heart only
1 apple, peeled and cored
vegetable oil for deep-frying
500g fresh anchovies or small sardines, cleaned

For the *pastella*:
250g plain flour
150ml water
1 large egg, beaten
10g fresh yeast

Peel the tough outer leaves from the artichokes, stopping when you reach
the tender leaves, then cut in quarters vertically. With large artichokes, you
need to cut out the hairy choke, but with baby ones, the choke will not
have developed properly, so there is not much to remove. Put them into a
bowl of water with a little lemon juice squeezed into it, to keep them from
discolouring, until you are ready to use them. Drain, and dry.

Bring a pan of water to the boil and add the salt. Put in the cauliflower and
cook for a couple of minutes, until just tender, then lift out and drain. Put
the cardoons into the same water and cook for about 7–8 minutes, until they
too are just tender, but still retain some bite. Drain and keep to one side.

Combine the flour, water, egg and yeast to make a *pastella* (batter) with
a fluid consistency. Slice the apple, and cut the cardoons into strips. Heat
several inches of oil in a high-sided pan (make sure it comes no higher than
a third of the way up the pan) to 180°C. If you don't have a thermometer,
put in a few breadcrumbs, and if they sizzle the oil is ready.

Immerse the artichokes in the *pastella* and deep-fry until golden. Lift out
and drain on kitchen paper. Repeat with the cardoons, cauliflower and
apple, then the anchovies or sardine fillets, and arrange everything together
on a warm serving plate.

## Polpettine di tonno o pesce spada
Tuna or swordfish balls

As well as putting these out as part of an antipasti, you can also add the tomato sauce on page 75 and serve them with pasta.

Serves 4

olive oil
400g yellow fin tuna, bonito or swordfish, cut into cubes
50g pine nuts
sea salt and freshly ground black pepper
1 teaspoon dried oregano
a handful of flat-leaf parsley, chopped
200g breadcrumbs from stale bread (see page 45)
50g pecorino cheese, grated
2 eggs
zest and juice of 1 lemon
a little vegetable oil, to oil the tray

Heat a good couple of tablespoons of olive oil in a large frying pan and add the fish and pine nuts. Season lightly and sauté for a minute or so, until the fish is coloured on all sides and the pine nuts are golden.

Remove from the heat and transfer to a bowl. Leave to cool for 5 minutes, then add the oregano, parsley, breadcrumbs, pecorino, eggs, and the lemon zest and juice. Mix everything together well, then moisten your hands with water and form the mixture into smooth balls, slightly bigger than a golf ball. If the mixture is very sticky, add a few more breadcrumbs.

Lightly oil a baking tray with vegetable oil, lay the fish balls on top, then put into the fridge for an hour to rest and firm up.

Heat a little more olive oil in a clean frying pan. Add the fish balls and fry in batches, shaking the pan to move them around, until they are golden brown all over.

### Chiocciole a picchi pacchi
Snails in tomato and chilli sauce

When we go to Castelvetrano in the spring and early summer, we usually see the old guys who sell land snails in the square outside the walls of the old city. The snails come out after the rain, and are best around May, when there is a chance of eating green grass that hasn't yet been burnt in the heat. Because of the association with rain, there is a belief that if there is an abundance of snails in the spring it will be a good year for crops.

If it has been very wet, the old people will go out and if they are lucky they might collect up to ten kilos of snails, some to cook themselves, and the rest to put into boxes and sell to anyone who wants to buy them. Even if families no longer need to gather and eat snails to survive, they are still a big thing in Sicily, and sometimes you can choose between snails that have just been gathered, and those that have been collected a couple of days earlier and have already been purged for you. Snails always have to be purged, or purified, before cooking, in order to remove any dirt, grit or chemicals that get into their system from the leaves they eat.

In Italian we call snails *chiocciole* or *lumache*, but in Sicily they are sometimes known as *munachedde* (after the sisters in a closed convent, who never come out!). The Sicilians also distinguish four different types of snail, and each of them has a string of different names in dialect. *Ciocco* or *vaddareddi* are the small, light brown ones. The white ones that have a brown line running around the shells are *babbaluci*, and these are the ones that are used in this recipe – the smaller ones are often known as *picchi pacchi*, which is a kind of sweet, kind of rude kids' expression for 'little bottoms'. The third type are dark brown, found on the branches of trees, and because the snails always seem to be closed inside the shell they are mainly called *ntuppateddi*, which means 'corked'. The fourth category are the wine snails. These are the biggest, with browny-green shells with brown circles on them, and they live near vines. These ones are known throughout Sicily, so they have even more names, but the main ones are *barbaniu, crastuni* or *muntuni*.

Traditionally snails would be purged, then blanched in boiling water, then put into a fresh pan of boiling water and simmered for an hour. Then they would be drained and eaten either with *zogghiu*, a light sauce of garlic, mint, lemon juice and olive oil (see page 66), or alternatively just with olive oil, parsley and garlic; or olive oil with lemon juice or vinegar, seasoned with sea salt, freshly ground black pepper and a little oregano.

The whole Sicilian pleasure seems to come from sucking the snails from the shells, and licking the greasiness from the shell. I remember when some English people were sitting in Vittorio's restaurant, delicately trying to eat with toothpicks and forks. Ever the showman, he went over and said, 'No, you don't do it like that.' He picked up a snail, cracked a little hole with his teeth on the other side of the snail from the opening, so that the air would come through, then sucked the snail straight out. He was so proud

of his trick and everybody loved it. But I did see him behind the restaurant afterwards spitting out bits of shell!

This recipe is originally from Palermo, where snails are the traditional street food served on the feast day of St Rosalia, the patron saint of the city.

Serves 4

a little flour, wheat or oats
900g small edible land snails (*Helix aspersa*)
4 ripe plum tomatoes
2 tablespoons olive oil
1 medium onion, thinly sliced
sea salt and freshly ground black pepper
a pinch of dried chilli flakes (optional)
2 tablespoons chopped flat-leaf parsley or basil

If the snails have not already been purified, put them into a large basket with a net over the top that will let them breathe, but stop them escaping. Put some flour, wheat or oats into the basket. The snails eat this, and if you leave them for 24–36 hours, anything from the ground they have been eating will pass through their systems and they will excrete all the impurities. Wash them carefully, then put them into a pan, cover them with cold water and bring to the boil. Once they have boiled, take the pan off the heat and drain the snails in a colander.

Put the tomatoes into a pan of boiling water for 10 seconds, then drain them under cold water and you should be able to peel them easily. Cut them in half, scoop out the seeds with a teaspoon, and chop the flesh.

Heat the olive oil in a pan and cook the onion gently until soft but not coloured. Add the snails, still in their shells, and stir them around a little, then add the tomatoes, salt, black pepper, chilli flakes if using, and parsley or basil. Stir carefully, cover with a lid and cook for 30 minutes.

Northern Italians pride themselves on producing the rice that feeds Italy; however, rice was actually introduced to Europe through the Arabs in Sicily and Spain. There were paddy fields around Sambuca and Sciacca, where the river Verdura gave good swampy conditions, until the Spanish transferred the major production to northern Italy where there was more water and the perfect habitat.

*Arancini*
Rice balls

The paddy fields are not there any more, and there is very little rice in Sicilian cooking. Risotto, the staple of northern Italy, with its technique of making a base of onions, toasting the rice, adding wine, stirring in the stock ladleful by ladleful, then beating in cheese and butter, doesn't really figure at all, perhaps because rice cooked in this way is more of a warming food against the colder weather in the north. The only traditional kind of risotto you are likely to see in Sicily is a seafood one (see page 306). However, Sicilians love *arancini*: balls of rice, made golden with saffron, moulded around a filling of fish or meat and peas, and deep-fried. The name, which means 'little oranges', comes from their shape and golden colour, and they have that sturdiness and self-contained look of an orange that conceals its beauty inside.

There is an idea that *arancini* reflect the Arab influence, in that this is the way they would have eaten, taking some rice with their hands, and using it to scoop up some meat or fish, but I can also imagine that as time went on the *arancino* fulfilled the same function as the Cornish pasty: it was a meal inside a casing, one that was easy to transport with you when you went to work in the fields or on the fishing boats, and it was easy to eat too … so these *arancini* would have been quite big. However, if you are making them at home, especially as an antipasto, you don't want to spoil everybody's dinner, so it is best to make little ones.

As always all over the island you will find variations in the filling. Mostly you would just use whatever you had, such as chopped leftover roast meat and vegetables, but traditionally in Catania they like to use *ragù*, with peas and a little cheese – my favourite. In Enna, *arancini* might be filled with chicken livers in a white wine and tomato sauce, and in Ragusa they mix some tomato sauce into the rice, and then put cheese and peas inside – these are known as *arancini rossi*.

In my region of Italy, Lombardy, we have adopted *arancini*, but we make them with leftover saffron risotto, whereas the Sicilian way is to boil the rice in water with saffron added. It is just a different way of arriving at a similar result. When you make a risotto, you are constantly moving the grains of rice around the pan and by doing this you scratch the surface and help to release the surface starch, known as amylopectin, which makes the rice creamy and can sometimes change the shape of the grains. The way

the Sicilians do it, the starch stays inside a bit more, and the rice retains its 'soul', its inner shape, but by boiling it in the right quantity of stock or water it will absorb all the liquid as it cools down gently, and by the time it is completely cold it will be very sticky – it is a similar idea to Thai sticky rice, made with jasmine rice.

The 'due zie', the two aunties in the Planeta family (our friends at the wine and olive oil estate), who are in charge of the cooking for big events, and are really accomplished, very knowledgeable and academic cooks, insist that it takes two days to make good *arancini*. You must cook the rice and the meat one day, and the rice must cool down naturally and rest for at least twelve hours so that it becomes glutinous.

One time when I was at Planeta I asked one of the aunties: 'What is the right ratio of water to rice?' She took down the big pan that is always used for *arancini* and, pointing at it, she said, 'This much rice, and this much water.' 'But have you never tried to weigh it, so you know how much water you need?' 'No, why would I?' she asked. 'This is the only pan we ever use.' What is more, sometimes they cook for 600 people when they are entertaining at Planeta, and if they are making *arancini*, do they use lots of pots? No, the same one, about twenty-five times!

Note: The Sicilian way is to dip the *arancini* into *pastella* (batter) before dusting them with breadcrumbs, which gives them a really crunchy outside once they are deep-fried. I know a kilo of breadcrumbs for coating the *arancini* seems a lot, and you won't use them all, but you really need a big mound of them in order to roll the *arancini* in them and get them properly encrusted.

## Arancini al sapore di mare
Seafood rice balls

Makes about 10

It's best to cook the rice the day before you want to use it – once it has cooled, keep it in the fridge.

1.6 litres fish stock or water
500g arborio rice
5g salt
a pinch of good-quality saffron threads (about 15)
60g pecorino cheese, grated
about 1kg fine breadcrumbs (see page 45)
vegetable oil for deep-frying

For the filling:
5 plum tomatoes
2 tablespoons olive oil
1 garlic clove, finely chopped
½ medium onion, finely chopped
225g mixture of small pieces of white fish (swordfish, if you can find it, otherwise cod or haddock), pieces of cleaned squid or cuttlefish, and small prawns (or chopped larger ones)
120ml dry white wine

For the *pastella*:
350g plain flour
1 egg

Bring the stock or water to the boil in a pan, add the rice, salt and saffron, bring back to the boil and cook very slowly for at least 15 minutes, until the rice is tender and the liquid has been absorbed. Remove from the heat, leave to rest for a minute, then quickly beat in the pecorino. Set aside to cool completely.

Prepare the filling: put the tomatoes into a pan of boiling water for 10 seconds, then drain them under cold water and you should be able to peel them easily. Cut them in half, scoop out the seeds with a teaspoon, and chop the flesh.

Heat the olive oil in a large pan and cook the garlic and onion gently, until softened but not coloured. Add the seafood – the pieces of fish first, then the squid and lastly the prawns. Stir until the prawns change colour. Pour in the white wine and bubble up to let the alcohol evaporate, then add the tomatoes and cook for about 5 minutes. The mixture should be soft but not soupy. If it is a bit too liquid, cook for a little longer, to reduce and thicken it. Remove from the heat, then crush the fish lightly with a fork. Leave to cool.

To make the *pastella*, beat the flour, egg and water in a bowl. Have ready the breadcrumbs in a separate shallow bowl. Wet your hands to stop the rice from sticking, then take a tangerine-sized ball of rice mixture and press your thumb in the centre to make a hollow. Spoon in a little of the seafood filling, then close the rice around it and form it into a ball. Dip each one into the *pastella* and then into the breadcrumbs, making sure they are completely covered in crumbs and pressing them lightly, to make sure the crumbs cling.

Heat around 8cm of vegetable oil in a large pan, making sure the oil doesn't come any higher than a third of the way up the pan. The oil must be hot, but not smoking, before you add the *arancini* (if you have a thermometer it should be around 170°C, otherwise test it by putting in a few breadcrumbs – if they sizzle gently the oil is ready). Working in batches (being careful not to crowd the pan or you will lower the temperature of the oil), fry the *arancini* for about 4–5 minutes, moving them around until they are golden all over. Drain well on kitchen paper and serve hot.

**Arancini di carne**
Rice balls with meat and peas

If you have any kind of leftover minced beef or pork in sauce, you can use it as a filling, rather than making it from scratch as in the recipe below.

Makes about 10

1.6 litres chicken stock or water
500g arborio rice
5g salt
a pinch of good-quality saffron threads (about 15)
60g pecorino cheese, grated
about 1kg fine breadcrumbs (see page 45)
vegetable oil for deep-frying

For the filling:
olive oil
1 medium onion, finely chopped
1 carrot, finely chopped
1 celery stalk, finely chopped
400g minced beef (not extra lean) or pork
sea salt and freshly ground black pepper
120ml red wine
1 x 400g tin of chopped tomatoes
50g cooked peas
100g *tuma* (Sicilian unsalted sheep's milk cheese) or mozzarella, cut into small cubes

For the *pastella*:
350g plain flour
1 egg

Bring the stock or water to the boil in a pan, add the rice, salt and saffron, bring back to the boil and cook for about 15 minutes, until the rice is tender and the liquid has been absorbed. Remove from the heat, leave to rest for a minute, then quickly beat in the pecorino. Set aside to cool completely.

While the rice cools, prepare the filling. Heat a little olive oil in a pan, add the onion, carrot and celery and cook gently until soft, but not coloured. Add the meat, season with salt and pepper, cook for few minutes, then add the wine and bubble up to evaporate the alcohol. Add the tinned tomatoes and cook gently for 1 hour. You need the sauce around the meat to be quite thick. Set aside to cool down, then stir in the peas and the cubes of cheese.

To make the *pastella*, beat the flour, egg and water in a bowl. Have ready the breadcrumbs, in a separate, shallow bowl. Wet your hands to stop the rice from sticking, then take a tangerine-sized ball of rice mixture and press your thumb in the centre to make a hollow. Spoon in a little of the meat filling, then close the rice around it and form it into a ball. Dip each one into the *pastella* and then into the breadcrumbs, making sure they are completely covered in crumbs and pressing them lightly, to make sure the crumbs cling.

Heat around 8cm of vegetable oil in a large pan, making sure the oil doesn't come any higher than a third of the way up the pan. The oil must be hot, but not smoking, before you add the *arancini* (if you have a thermometer it should be around 170°C, otherwise test it by putting in a few breadcrumbs – if they sizzle gently the oil is ready). Working in batches (being careful not to crowd the pan or you will lower the temperature of the oil), fry the *arancini* for about 4–5 minutes, moving them around until they are golden all over. Drain well on kitchen paper and serve hot.

## 'Bread is life'

You cannot overestimate the importance of bread to Sicilian life; bread *is* life, it is right at the heart of society. There is an old proverb, '*chi mi da il pane mi é padre*', which means, 'who gives me bread is my father'. Even if the money that your father makes is blood money, he is still your father because he gives you bread. And bread is the most important thing. When I was staying near Mount Etna, where bread was so revered and so essential to the old diet of the mountain people, I heard a story about a brigand in the time of the Bourbons who was put in prison for contrabanding wheat, but there was a woman who set him free – this woman was described as very beautiful, but 'a little overproved', so even in describing the beauty of a woman a little past her youth, they use the terminology of bread.

What is exceptional is that even in the small villages you still have two, three, four bakers, and they all make a living. Where we stay, outside Menfi, we are down by the beach, with a few little roads – not even roads, really, more like tracks, leading up to a 'square' – not even a square, really, just where the roads meet. And even here, there is a fantastic bakery, run by an English woman who is married to a Sicilian. The first time we went in and heard her speak English, we asked her where she was from, and she told us she grew up in Norwood, in south London. It seemed so strange to find her there in the middle of nowhere, where the wind blows tumbleweed down the streets some days, as if you are in a spaghetti western. Yet here she was baking beautiful bread over the embers of olive branches in a wood-burning oven. Imagine how much it would cost you in London to make your barbecue with olive wood – but here, where there are olive trees all around that must be trimmed, it is readily available. The olive branches give a special aroma to the bread, and when you take it home and unwrap it, it smells incredible. In parts of Italy, such as Lentini, where there are almond trees all around, they use the shells of the nuts in the wood-fired ovens, which gives a different character to the bread.

Theirs is a lovely, well-organised little bakery where they bake more than 400 kilos of bread every day; and what is amazing is that they bake twice a day, in the afternoon as well as at dawn. The bread they bake is typically Sicilian, made with *farina di semola rimacinata* (semolina flour), which is milled from hard durum wheat, the wheat that is used to make dried pasta. When you break the kernel of the wheat it shatters into semolina, which is then milled again into flour for bread. Like sourdough, the bread is made without commercial yeast, using a *criscenti*, or 'starter', 'ferment', or 'mother', whatever name people prefer to call it, according to their culture. In northern Italy we call it a *biga*. The name *criscenti* means 'something that is allowed to grow'. For the first bread you bake, you cultivate your own natural yeast by mixing flour and water with something sweet and sugary, such as a pear, or grapes, then allowing it to ferment and grow over several

*Pane*
Bread

Famiglia Mulé

weeks. Then, when you make your first batch of dough, you keep back a piece, and this is added to the next batch of dough, and so on, building up the strength and flavour of the dough. Some bakeries have *criscenti* going back over generations.

The baked bread is a beautiful golden-yellow colour, from the semolina, and quite heavy. In texture you can compare it to soda bread, but with a thick crust that typically has sesame seeds embedded in it. It is a bread that if you were to rub a sweet juicy tomato across, and sprinkle with olive oil, it would hold up and absorb the juices without becoming soft and disintegrating.

In the days of the barons, as happened in most cultures throughout Europe, white bread became fashionable and was considered more refined among the wealthy. What everyone else ate, although it was looked down on by the aristocracy at the time, was far tastier and more nutritious, and it is the bread that is treasured today in most communities, especially the small towns and villages, even if people buy it these days instead of making it at home. At one time everyone made their own bread, and if you didn't have your own oven you could take your *criscenti* and flour down to the bakery, knead the dough in wooden tubs, called *madie*, then shape it into loaves and carve your initials into them, so that you would know they were yours. Then the baker would bake them for you to carry home, wrapped in cloths.

Between Agrigento and Trapani lies Castelvetrano which is also famous for the round *pane nero di Castelvetrano*, the local black bread, which is one of the many, very particular Sicilian foods, including other breads, that are being supported by the Slow Food movement. It is traditionally made by mixing stoneground semolina (which is less fine than semolina flour) with *tumminìa*, an ancient, local variety of wheat, which must also be stoneground. Again, the bread is quite dense and yellow, but when it comes out of the oven it has a magnificent, thick, chewy crust that is very, very dark, almost black.

One day we were invited to see the bread being made by the Mulé family who have a farmhouse and a piece of land in the valley behind Menfi, where the father and the sons grow beautiful courgettes, artichokes, potatoes and other vegetables, which they bring to the local restaurants. Like a lot of the elderly people in the area, the mother and father also have a little house down by the beach, in what used to be the swamp. In the garden they have a shed, with a big chimney sticking out of it, and inside is a wood-burning oven, where, every so often, they make a bit of a ceremony of baking the black bread.

As always, they use all the branches and clippings from the olive trees, which they have in square bales, stacked up outside. The oven is made with *refrattario* (refractory) bricks, the ones that are used for pizza ovens, so when the branches are lit, it will reach about 480–500°F. When the roof of the oven turns white, they sweep out all the ashes but they don't throw them away, they put them down in a different part of the garden, ready to grill some bacon and cheese and salami, to have with the fresh bread. The oven is capable of baking around twelve kilos of dough – about twenty-four loaves – so whenever they bake bread, inevitably all the brothers and sisters, aunts and uncles, cousins and friends will turn up, to eat some, and take some away with them.

When the floor of the oven is swept out, the round loaves, scattered with sesame seeds, are put inside, and the smell from the olive branches is incredible. The door is closed, and after five or six minutes they check the bread, and from the way it looks, they are able to decide how long they are going to bake it for, which is about twenty to thirty minutes, as the oven slowly cools down.

As well as the semolina bread, in the local bakeries – around a dozen in my area alone – you can find pizza, topped with anchovies, olives and tomatoes (see page 51), and various stuffed breads made with a softer, focaccia-like dough, such as *schiacciate* (see page 58), which are like pies, made with a thick piece of dough underneath and a thinner one over the top, and inside all kinds of fillings, from cauliflower and sausage, to ricotta, sardines, anchovies, tomatoes, onion, eggs, ham and peas. You find them in the bars too, with a slice cut out of them so that you can see what the filling is, and you order a piece with your drink.

There is one baker who makes *sfincione*, which is more of a Palermo speciality. When I was there, outside one of the best bakeries, so many people were waiting for the *sfincione* that the baker spent all morning shouting, 'Not till eleven o'clock!' (when they would be ready). Even if the people just happened to be walking down the street, he would shout it anyway. *Sfincione* is like a pizza, but made with a quite deep, spongy dough and topped with ricotta and onions, sometimes sausage, sometimes anchovies or sardines. The famous one is the *sfincione di San Vito*, the one made by the nuns at the convent of St Vito in Palermo, which must have been such an incredible powerhouse of baking. It is topped with tomatoes, olives, potatoes, sausage and cheese.

The other thing that is done with bread dough is *mpanata*, another sort of pie, which takes its name from the Spanish *empanada* and is half-moon-shaped, like a Cornish pasty. The *mpanate* can be savoury or sweet – at Easter they are made with lamb – and on the west coast of Sicily they are often done with swordfish (see page 297).

On special saints' days and on the feast of San Giuseppe, which is Father's Day, on 19 March, breads are made in elaborate shapes, and at Easter the shops are filled with special breads for children, shaped like little bags, or doves, which hold hard-boiled eggs: a reminder of times when people could not afford chocolate, and these, made at home for the children, would be a special treat.

### 'Every crumb is sacred'

*Pangrattato*
Breadcrumbs

Bread is sacred. If the people see you throw it away, they will really tell you off because the crumbs are so valuable in cooking – as a coating for fish, a thickener in things like *polpettine* (balls of meat or fish), or in stuffings. It is such a bad thing, that it used to be said that if you dropped even a crumb, you would spend hundreds of years in purgatory, picking up crumbs with your eyelashes. When times were harder and you had no cheese, you would sprinkle breadcrumbs over your pasta instead, with a little bit of garlic and parsley. I have even seen meat being grilled in the restaurants in Palermo, dusted with some very fine crumbs, garlic and parsley, just to give a little crunch to the outside.

In the old days families would have grated or crushed every piece of unused bread to make breadcrumbs in different sizes, because each size has its own purpose. Some would be left large, some sieved fine or medium, and then they would be kept in separate containers, in the way that my grandmother used to keep her breadcrumbs in big jars. Nowadays, most people don't need to do this all the time, because when you buy your bread in the bakery, you can always pick up a kilogram bag of breadcrumbs at the same time. Whatever bread the bakery doesn't sell in a day is put into the top of the ovens for two days to dry it out, then grated into breadcrumbs for people to buy. We make our own the same way at Locanda, with the *michette*, the puffed-up bread rolls 'with five faces', which are baked freshly every day in the kitchen, along with all our other breads. Those *michette* that are left over sit on top of the big bread oven overnight. Even when it is switched off, it retains enough heat to dry the bread and give us all the breadcrumbs we need.

At home making breadcrumbs is such an easy thing to do. If you have cooked something in the oven, when you switch it off, cut your stale bread into slices, put it on a baking tray and leave it in the oven overnight to dry out. Or you could just set your oven to 80°C and put the bread in for an hour. Of course, you need good bread, not the remains of a doughy, sliced loaf – those are only good for the ducks. When the bread has dried out, it is ready for grating. You could also put the bread into a blender and just press the pulse button very quickly, until you have the fineness you want, but I prefer to use a grater, which somehow seems to give an extra fluffiness to the crumbs.

What I also like about grating the crumbs is that they will all be different sizes, much less uniform than if you make them in a machine. These random-sized crumbs, which often have bits of crust mixed in with them, are what I call large crumbs, and are mostly used as a thickener, or in stuffings. If you put them through a fine sieve, they will become medium, and these are the

ones that are used to coat fish or meat. If you want fine breadcrumbs, put them through a sieve yet again. Fine crumbs are used to give crunch to the *arancini* on page 35, or the timbales on pages 237 and 245.

Medium breadcrumbs are also often toasted dry in the oven, or in a little olive oil in a pan, and these are the ones that are used to scatter over pasta. As I read in one Sicilian cookery book, they need to be toasted until they become *'il colore di una tonaca di monaco'*, the colour of a monk's tunic, which helps you to understand how dark they should be – not just golden, but brown.

**Cáciù all'argintéra**
Fried cheese

This is very similar to a dish from Palermo known as *formaggio all'argentiera*, or the cheese of the silversmith. The story goes that the silversmith invented the dish because when it was cooking it smelt very like rabbit – although he was too poor to eat rabbit, he didn't want his neighbours to know it.

When you read 'fried cheese', you might not think this sounds very enticing, but it is only when you make it that you understand how the typically Sicilian flavours work together to give you something really tasty.

Serves 4

25ml white wine vinegar
25ml white wine
50g sugar
200g breadcrumbs (see page 45)
½ tablespoon garlic oil (see page 60)
2 teaspoons chopped fresh oregano
450g caciocavallo or pecorino cheese (see page 242)
1 egg, beaten
vegetable oil for deep-frying

To make the sauce, put the vinegar and wine into a pan with the sugar and bring to the boil, stirring until the sugar dissolves. Take off the heat and keep to one side. Put the breadcrumbs, garlic oil and oregano into a blender and whiz until the herbs are finely chopped and the breadcrumbs are infused in the oil. Cut the cheese into pieces about 1cm thick. The thickness is important, otherwise the cheese won't melt.

Have the beaten egg and herby breadcrumbs ready in two shallow bowls, then pass the strips of cheese through the egg and dip them into the breadcrumbs, turning to coat them. Repeat this three times for each strip, so that you end up with quite a thick coating of breadcrumbs.

Heat some oil in a pan (make sure the pan is big enough so that the oil comes no more than a third of the way up). It should be 180°C. If you don't have a thermometer, test that it is hot enough by putting in a few breadcrumbs. If they sizzle straight away, the oil is ready. Deep-fry the cheese strips, in batches if necessary, for 2 minutes, until golden on all sides, and serve with the sauce.

**Ramacché**
Prosciutto and cheese fritters

When you go to the beach on Sundays you see families with boxes of these little fritters, which are eaten cold, along with things like peppers or cauliflowers, dipped in *pastella* (batter) and deep-fried.

Serves 4

30g unsalted butter
a small pinch of salt
150g plain flour, plus more as needed
3 large eggs
150g prosciutto crudo, diced
100g caciocavallo or pecorino cheese, grated
2 tablespoons parsley and garlic (see page 60)
sunflower oil for deep-frying

Put the butter and salt into a pan with 220ml of water and bring to the boil, then remove the pan from the heat and stir in the flour with a wooden spoon. Put the pan back on the heat and work the mixture continuously with the spoon until it comes together in a solid ball of dough. Take off the heat again and let it cool, then put the dough into a food mixer with a paddle, add the eggs one by one and mix until they are all incorporated.

Add the prosciutto, cheese and the parsley and garlic, and continue to mix. The dough will be quite soft.

Heat several centimetres of oil in a pan (make sure the oil comes no higher than a third of the way up). It should be 180°C. If you don't have a thermometer, test that the oil is hot enough by dropping in a little bit of the dough. If it sizzles the oil is ready.

Moisten a dessertspoon with water, then scoop out little mounds of dough, slide them carefully into the oil and let them fry gently for about 2 minutes, turning them so they are golden on both sides, and reducing the heat if they start to brown too quickly. Remove the *ramacché* with a slotted spoon, drain on kitchen paper, and serve hot.

## Pizza alla siciliana
Sicilian pizza

In every bakery all over Sicily, there is freshly made pizza, cut into pieces, ready for people to take home. I always buy some, along with the different breads, to have as an antipasto. And if you go into the local bar and have an *aperitivo*, they will give you a little pizza to eat with it.

The difference between these pizzas and the ones we are more familiar with elsewhere in Italy is that there is not much use of mozzarella. There are no buffalo on the island because they need to wallow in mud and water, so the *mozzarella di bufala* is always brought in from Campania, just outside Naples. There are also very few herds of cows, so the production even of cow's milk mozzarella is fairly small. Instead, the concentration is on typical Sicilian ingredients, such as olives, anchovies and tomatoes, scattered with *tuma*, the local fresh, unsalted sheep's milk cheese.

You need to choose good-quality black olives, with the stones still in, then pit them yourself – because the intense olive flavour is concentrated around the stone. You must remember that black olives aren't actually black at all, but a deep purple-brown, depending on the variety. They are olives that have started out green but have been allowed to mature on the tree. As their colour darkens, their flavour becomes more intense and they become softer and more oily. Avoid the shiny jet black ones that you find on many commercial pizzas, or in jars in the supermarket, which are something different completely. These are actually green olives that have been put into a water bath with oxygen running through it, to turn them black, so that manufacturers can market them as a black olive that has the firmness of a young green olive. They just taste insipid, and nothing like a real 'black' olive.

The Sicilian black olives we use in the kitchen are mature *nocellara* and *cerasuolo*. These are the olives that are picked green and pressed to make our oil, but sometimes if a tree bears only a little fruit, the olives are left on the branches to ripen until they become 'black'.

When you are making the pizza dough, the order in which you mix the ingredients makes a difference. It is best to dissolve the yeast in water and mix it into the flour before adding the salt, as the salt burns the yeast and makes it less effective. Once you have added the salt, the small quantity of sugar helps the fermentation. The oil is added last, as if you put it in at the beginning of mixing it acts like a skin, stopping the salt and yeast penetrating properly.

There are three stages that help get a great, crispy base to a pizza. First, rest the dough in the fridge but bring it to room temperature for three hours before shaping it. This is the system we have developed, because we are a restaurant not a bakery, so we have no proving room. If you can, rest it for twenty-four hours, as the longer it has to relax the more stretchy and pliable it will be, which makes it easier to get a good, thin base. Next, don't overload the topping, as this will stop the base from crisping quickly; and finally, try to recreate the atmosphere of a dedicated pizza oven, in which the temperature is 260°C/500°F. The pizzas go straight on to the hot brick base and hot air cooks the topping at the same time. At home, have the oven at its highest temperature – usually 250°C/475°F/gas 9 – then put as many terracotta pizza bases, or upturned baking trays, as you can fit into the oven so that they get really hot, before carefully sliding a pizza on to each one. If you are making six pizzas, you will surely still have to bake them in batches, but as each one only takes ten minutes, no one will have to wait too long! Remember that leaving the door open lowers the temperature. In with the pizzas, as fast as you can, then shut the door.

Makes 6 pizzas (25–30cm)

7g fresh yeast
550g '00' flour, plus extra for the bowl and rolling out
15g sea salt
6g sugar
60ml milk
30ml olive oil

For the topping:
24 good whole purple-black olives in brine
18 anchovies, either salted or in oil
2 tablespoons tomato sauce (see page 75)
1 medium onion, thinly sliced
100g *tuma* (Sicilian unsalted sheep's milk cheese) or pecorino, grated
1 teaspoon dried oregano
freshly ground black pepper
1 tablespoon extra virgin olive oil

Dissolve the yeast in 300ml of water in a small bowl. Put the flour into a large bowl and mix in the yeast mixture. Add the salt and sugar, then the milk, little by little, followed by the oil, until all the ingredients are incorporated in a dough – this will take about 10 minutes. Scrape the dough into a floured bowl and fold it in on itself a few times. Cut it into 6 equal pieces and roll each one into a ball. Put the balls of dough on a tray, cover with clingfilm and leave to rest in the fridge for 24 hours.

Bring the dough out of the fridge and into room temperature 3 hours before you want to use it.

When ready to make the bases, preheat the oven to 250°C/475°F/gas 9, or as high as possible, and put in one or two terracotta bases or upturned baking trays (or however many you can fit in your oven).

Lightly flour a work surface, then, using your fingertips, press each ball of dough lightly into a thin round, about 25–30cm. You want the base to be about 3mm thick, but with a slightly thicker rim. If the dough feels too hard to shape easily, leave it to rest for 5 minutes and then come back to it.

Drain the olives and pat dry. With a sharp knife, make three or four cuts in each olive from end to end, and then cut each segment away from the stone as carefully as you can and roughly chop.

If using salted anchovies, rinse and dry them. Run your thumb gently along the backbone to release it, then you should be able to easily pull it out. If using anchovies in oil, drain them.

Chop the anchovies roughly and put some of the pieces on to each round of dough, pressing them in so they don't get burned and bitter by being on top of the pizza. Spread some tomato sauce over each anchovy-studded base, then scatter with onion, cheese, olives and oregano, season with pepper and drizzle with a little extra virgin olive oil.

Slide the first pizza(s) on to the preheated base(s), and bake for about 10 minutes, or until the dough is golden and crunchy underneath. Repeat until all the pizzas are baked.

**Pizza arrotolata**
Rolled pizza with sausage

These rolled pizzas are made with the same dough as in the previous recipe, but rather than being floured, it is oiled at various stages, to keep it pliable enough to roll. Traditionally, the filling would be made with *strutto*, pure pork fat, but you can substitute olive oil.

Makes 4 rolls

7g fresh yeast
550g '00' flour
15g salt
1 teaspoon sugar
60ml milk
30ml vegetable oil, plus more for oiling

For the filling:
4 tablespoons melted *strutto* or olive oil
450g fresh sausage meat, crumbled
6 tablespoons chopped pancetta
2 medium onions, chopped
120g pecorino cheese, grated
freshly ground black pepper

Dissolve the yeast in 300ml of water in a small bowl. Put the flour into a large bowl and mix in the yeast mixture. Add the salt and sugar, then the milk, little by little, followed by the oil, until all the ingredients are incorporated in a dough – this will take about 10 minutes. Scrape the dough into a bowl that has been lightly oiled with vegetable oil, and fold it in on itself a few times. Cut it into 4 equal pieces, shape each one into a rough square shape and rub with a little more oil. Put the squares of dough on a tray, cover with clingfilm and leave to rest in the fridge for 24 hours. Bring the dough out of the fridge and into room temperature 3 hours before you want to use it.

When ready to make the pizzas, preheat the oven to 220°C/425°F/gas 7 and put in one or two baking trays to get hot. Lightly oil a sheet of baking parchment and roll out the dough into squares measuring roughly 25–30cm, and 3mm thick. If it feels too hard, leave it to rest for 5 minutes.

Spread each square of rolled-out dough with 1 tablespoon of melted *strutto*, or olive oil. Scatter the sausage meat and pancetta over the top, followed by the onions and cheese, season well with black pepper, then roll up and place on the baking tray/trays. Bake in the preheated oven for 15–30 minutes, or until golden. Cut each roll into thick slices and serve.

**Torta di sambuco**
Meat pie with elderflower

This is another unusual 'pie' which is made in the spring, when the elder-flowers are blossoming, and which is cut up and served with the antipasti. *Guanciale* is a bacon made from pork jowl, cured in wine, herbs and black pepper. If you can't find it, use some good lardons or cubed pancetta.

Serves 6

For the dough:
30g fresh yeast
500g semolina flour, plus more as needed
500g '00' flour
1 teaspoon sugar
20g sea salt
80ml olive oil
1 egg, beaten, for brushing

For the filling:
4 tablespoons olive oil
300g *guanciale*, chopped
400g rustic salame, roughly chopped
300g *tuma* (Sicilian unsalted sheep's milk cheese) or pecorino, chopped
50g elderflowers, chopped

Mix the yeast with 400ml of water. In a food mixer with a dough hook, mix the flours and sugar, add the yeast and water, and mix. Add the salt and when it is incorporated, add 2 tablespoons of the olive oil. Mix until soft and elastic, then emulsify the rest of the olive oil with another 50ml of water and add it to the dough a little at a time, with the motor turning, until the dough is soft. Turn out into a bowl and leave to rise in a warm place for at least 2 hours.

Preheat the oven to 180°C/350°F/gas 4.

To make the filling, heat 2 tablespoons of olive oil in a pan, put in the *guanciale* and cook until golden brown all over, then lift out and drain on kitchen paper. Mix, in a bowl, with the salame, cheese and elderflowers.

Rub the dough with another tablespoon of olive oil. Cut in half, and roll one half into a sheet large enough to line a tart tin. Scatter with the *guanciale* mixture and drizzle with the remaining tablespoon of olive oil. Cover with the other half of the dough, pressing around the edges to seal. Brush the top with the beaten egg and bake in the oven for 40 minutes, until golden. Slice and serve hot.

## Schiacciata con salsiccia
Schiacciata with sausage

This is typical of the area around Agrigento, another very rich pie that is cut up and served as an antipasti … very moreish, but also very filling.

Serves 6

4 whole black olives in brine
sea salt and freshly ground black pepper
1 head of cauliflower, cut into small pieces
2 tablespoons olive oil, plus a little extra for greasing and finishing
200g 100 per cent pork sausages
1 large potato, peeled and cut into large chunks
1 medium onion, sliced
60g caciocavallo or pecorino cheese, diced

For the dough:
500g semolina flour, plus more as needed
500g '00' flour
30g fresh yeast
80ml olive oil
20g sea salt
5g sugar
1 egg, beaten, for brushing

First make the dough. In a food mixer with a dough hook, mix the flours, yeast, 2 tablespoons of the olive oil, 400ml of water, the salt and the sugar. Mix until soft and elastic, then emulsify the rest of the olive oil with another 50ml of water and add it to the mixer bowl a little at a time, with the motor turning, until the dough is soft. Turn out into a bowl and leave to rise in a warm place for at least 2 hours.

Drain the olives and pat dry. With a sharp knife, make three or four cuts in each olive from end to end, then cut each segment away from the stone as carefully as you can.

Bring a large pan of salted water to the boil. Put in the cauliflower and blanch for a minute then drain.

Preheat the oven to 180°C/350°F/gas 4 and brush a baking dish with olive oil. Remove the skins from the sausages and break the sausage meat into pieces.

Heat the olive oil in a pan and brown the sausage meat. Lift out and drain on kitchen paper. Add the potatoes to the pan in which you cooked the sausages, season, and sauté until golden and just tender. Lift out and drain on kitchen paper, then put the onion into the same pan and cook gently until soft but not coloured. Add the cauliflower and season with salt to taste.

Put the sausage and potatoes back into the pan of onion and cauliflower, along with the olives, and season well with black pepper. Stir everything together for a minute or so, then take off the heat.

Dust your work surface with flour, and roll out the dough to about 6mm thick. Divide it into two: you need one piece big enough to line a shallow baking dish, and the other to put over the top. Line the dish with the bigger sheet of dough, then spoon in the sausage mixture. Scatter the cheese over, then cover with the other sheet of dough and seal the edges all round. Brush with a little more olive oil.

Put into the preheated oven and bake for 20–30 minutes, or until the top is golden.

**Prezzemolo e aglio, oli e condimenti**
Parsley and garlic, oils and dressings


**Prezzemolo e aglio**
Parsley and garlic

This is just a way of preparing parsley and garlic that brings out the maximum flavour in both, and is something I've always done. Every morning in the restaurant we prepare it. To 1 garlic clove we use about 4 handfuls of flat-leaf parsley. We put the garlic cloves on a chopping board and crush them with the flat of a kitchen knife, so that they become a paste. Then we put the parsley on top and chop it finely, so that we are chopping through the garlic at the same time, and the two flavours mingle.


**Olio all'aglio**
Garlic oil

It is a very Sicilian thing to make fresh garlic oil; I don't remember going into anyone's house and seeing a bottle that had been bought from a shop. Make it in small batches and use it up quickly.


Makes about 50ml

2 garlic cloves, finely chopped
50ml olive oil


Mix together and leave for a day in the fridge before using. It will keep, refrigerated, for up to 3 days.

When you spoon it out, you should have about 75 per cent oil and 25 per cent chopped garlic.

**Olio di limone**
Lemon oil

This is the simplest combination of oil and lemon juice, but when it is made with the juice of Sicilian lemons the flavour is brilliant. It should be used immediately after making, otherwise the flavour of the lemon will change, so adjust the quantities according to how much you need.

Makes about 200ml

a pinch of salt
3 tablespoons fresh lemon juice
150ml extra virgin olive oil

Put the salt into a clean, screw-topped bottle or jar, then add the lemon juice and leave for a minute until the salt dissolves. Add the oil and shake really well to emulsify. Use straight away.

**Olio di peperoncino**
Chilli oil

Like all the countries that face the Mediterranean, Sicily favours the chilli pepper, much more than the rest of Italy, especially the north. As well as fresh chillies, you will find little strings of dried ones that are often just crumbled into dishes.

I like the kick of spice that chilli brings to a broccoli and almond salad (see page 116) or some green vegetables, simply blanched and tossed in olive oil with chilli and garlic. How hot Sicilian chillies are is a bit of a lottery; they can be quite gentle and sweet, or they can be explosive.

Makes about 50ml

½ fresh red chilli, finely chopped
½ fresh green chilli, finely chopped
50ml olive oil

Mix together and leave for a day in the fridge before using. It will keep, refrigerated, for up to 3 days. When you spoon it out, you should have about 75 per cent oil and 25 per cent chopped chilli.

## Giorgio's dressing

As I explained in my previous book, *Made in Italy*, there is nothing mysterious or special about this, it is just the label we used to put on the bottle of vinaigrette in the kitchen when I was cooking at Zafferano, to help out a young chef who otherwise could never remember which dressing was which. I like a high ratio of oil to vinegar, but you can vary it as you like. Naturally, since we started making our own oil in Sicily, that is the one we use, and now we also add some white wine vingar. You will find that Sicilian oils are generally very fresh, grassy, fruity and fragrant. Make up a bottle of this and keep it in the fridge.

Makes about 375ml

½ teaspoon sea salt
3 tablespoons red wine vinegar
2 tablespoons white wine vinegar
300ml extra virgin olive oil, preferably Sicilian

Put the salt into a bowl, then add the vinegars and leave for a minute until the salt dissolves. Whisk in the olive oil and 2 tablespoons of water until the vinaigrette emulsifies. Pour into a clean bottle and store in the fridge for up to 6 months. It will separate out again, but just shake it well before you use it.

**Salsetta, salmoriglio e pesto**
Light sauces and pesto

Sicilians are not keen on heavy cooked sauces; however, light, fresh *salsette* and *salmoriglio* – a dressing made with oil and lemon or vinegar, plus garlic and herbs – along with pesto are at the base of their cooking and eating. I like the idea of putting a few of these out in bowls with the antipasti, so that they can be spooned on to vegetables or fish or seafood.

If you say pesto to most people, they think of *pesto genovese* (named after Genoa), made with Parmesan, pine nuts and basil; but if you say pesto to a Sicilian, they think of *pesto trapanese* (named after Trapani), made with almonds and tomatoes (see page 73). The word 'pesto' comes from the verb *pestare*, which just means to crush or grind, and it simply refers to a sauce that is traditionally pounded with a pestle and mortar, so the combination of ingredients can be very localised.

As well as working well with vegetables, meat or fish, the pesto-style sauces are obviously perfect tossed through pasta. Of course, you can make pesto by putting all the ingredients into a blender and pressing the pulse button, rather than working it in a pestle and mortar, but doing it by machine will give you a smoother, more refined texture than the more rustic sauce that is the result of using a pestle and mortar.

## Salsa salmoriglio
Oil, lemon and herb sauce

*Salmoriglio* is almost always on the Sicilian table, ready to spoon over vegetables, grilled fish or meat, and there are many different variations: sometimes chopped, sun-dried tomato might be added, sometimes lemon zest along with the lemon juice, or different herbs. You could vary the one below by using 40ml of white wine vinegar in place of the lemon juice, or substituting marjoram for the oregano. Marjoram is a herb that is used a lot in Sicily – our friends at Planeta grow it in huge pots on their terrace. It is the same family as oregano, but a little lighter and slightly more bitter.

Makes about 150ml

120ml olive oil
juice of 2 lemons
30g flat-leaf parsley, chopped
1 garlic clove, finely chopped
10g dried oregano
sea salt and freshly ground black pepper

Whisk together the olive oil, lemon juice and a dessertspoonful of warm water. Gradually whisk in the parsley, garlic, oregano, salt and pepper until thickened slightly.

## Zogghiu
Garlic, mint and lemon sauce

This is another light sauce used for grilled fish, or traditionally for dipping boiled snails into, or spooning over grilled meat.

Makes about 150ml

2 garlic cloves, chopped
sea salt
50g mint, chopped
3 tablespoons fresh lemon juice
6 tablespoons olive oil

Using a pestle and mortar, crush the garlic into a paste with 2 pinches of salt, add the mint and continue to crush, then finally work in the lemon juice and the olive oil, a little at a time.

**Salsa verde**
Green sauce

Again, this is a great sauce for grilled fish.

Makes 300g

1 salted anchovy
3 whole green olives in brine
1 garlic clove
100g flat-leaf parsley, chopped
30g pine nuts
15g salted capers, rinsed and well drained
1 slice of good white bread, soaked in vinegar
yolk of 1 large hard-boiled egg
120ml extra virgin olive oil, plus more as needed
15ml white wine vinegar, or to taste
sea salt and freshly ground black pepper

Rinse and dry the anchovy. Run your thumb gently along the backbone to release it, and you should be able to easily pull it out.

Drain the olives and pat dry. With a sharp knife, make three or four cuts in each olive from end to end, and then cut each segment away from the stone as carefully as you can.

Grind the garlic, anchovy and parsley using a pestle and mortar until you have a green paste, then add the pine nuts, capers and olives and pound for a few more minutes. Add the bread and pound again. Work in the hard-boiled egg yolk, and finally add the oil, a little at a time, working it in well as you go. Taste and add vinegar, and/or salt and pepper as you wish. If you like a thinner, creamier sauce, add a little more extra virgin olive oil.

### 'A symbol of good fortune'

Almonds are so important throughout Italy, in cakes, amaretti biscuits and amaretto liqueur, and are a symbol of good fortune: sugar-coated almonds, known as *confetti*, are traditional at Italian weddings and baptisms. In Sicily they are also used in savoury dishes, in pestos (see page 73), and in salads (see page 116 – broccoli, almond and chilli salad), but what is sad is that whereas the pistachios of Bronte (see page 194) have been recognised as special, and command high prices, almonds have been left behind.

*Mandorle*
Almonds

Many people in the countryside have an almond tree in their garden. However, where once you would see almonds being grown commercially all over the island, the nuts have had to fight in the market place with cheaper ones produced around the world, and have ended up being priced out. So many people have pulled up their almond groves, and planted grapes and olives instead, and while almonds are used as much in Sicilian cooking as ever, especially in the beloved almond paste, or marzipan, the nuts are often not home grown, but cheaper imports.

However, there is hope for the most famous almond groves, in the Siracusa area, between Noto and Avola, where Slow Food are now championing three old varieties of almond: the squat-shaped, perfumed and quite intense Romana, the longer, more elegant, pointed Pizzuta d'Avola, and the Fascionello, which is a good all-round almond.

### Pesto trapanese
Tomato and almond pesto

Use this with fish or meat, or toss through pasta.

Makes about 600g

75g almonds
500g plum tomatoes
4 garlic cloves
sea salt and freshly ground black pepper
40g fresh mint, shredded
50ml olive oil

Heat the oven to 180°C/350°F/gas 4. Lay the almonds in a single layer on a baking tray and put into the oven for about 8 minutes. As long as they are in a single layer you don't need to turn them. Keep an eye on them to make sure they don't burn, and when they are golden, take them out and chop them.

Put the tomatoes into a pan of boiling water for 10 seconds, then drain them under cold water and you should be able to peel them easily. Cut them in half, scoop out the seeds with a teaspoon, and chop the flesh.

Grind the toasted almonds with the garlic, using a pestle and mortar, until you have a paste. Add the tomatoes, salt, pepper and mint and pound again very briefly, just to crush the tomatoes a little. Then add the olive oil a little at a time, working it into the paste.

**Salsetta di mandorle e acciughe**
Almond and anchovy sauce

The touch of cinnamon in this is a reminder of the Arab influence in Sicily.
Use this like a pesto, with vegetables, fish or pasta.

Makes about 350g

6 salted anchovies
90g almonds
60g breadcrumbs (see page 45)
10 mint leaves, chopped
a pinch of ground cinnamon
1 tablespoon white wine vinegar
1 tablespoon fresh lemon juice
140ml olive oil, or as needed

Preheat the oven to 180°C/350°F/gas 4.

Rinse and dry the anchovies. Run your thumb gently along the backbone to
release it, then you should be able to easily pull it out.

Spread the almonds over a baking tray and the breadcrumbs over a separate
tray. Put both in the oven to toast for about 8 minutes until golden, keeping
an eye on them to make sure they don't burn, then remove and chop the
almonds.

Using a pestle and mortar, pound the toasted almonds, then add the
breadcrumbs and anchovies and pound some more. Add the mint leaves,
cinnamon, vinegar, lemon juice, and enough olive oil to pound to a creamy
sauce.

### Salsa di pomodoro
Tomato sauce

I was staying in a small, very simple hotel in Piazza Armerina in the province of Enna, and in the morning the woman asked, 'How was the food last night?' I said that it was fantastic, very natural in its flavours, especially the tomato sauce, and she was so happy. She told me, 'I can cook tomato sauce like no one else. My cousin even steals my tomatoes, but she can't make the sauce as good.' Everybody in Sicily is so proud of *their* sauce, which gets passed from grandmother to mother to daughter. Usually people are also sworn to one kind of tomato, whose acidity and sweetness they understand.

In Vittorio's kitchen, every morning, one of the women comes in, peels a whole case of tomatoes, and starts the sauce. Then at 9.30am Vittorio's son-in-law, Ignazio, arrives and the sauce is bubbling away, so he tastes it, adds a bit of salt and puts the lid on the pan. At 10-10.30am Vittorio arrives, tastes it and puts in a bit of salt and sugar. At 11am Vittorio's son, Michelangelo, arrives, and says the sauce needs something else. It is like a son with a thousand fathers, that sauce.

The sauce below is the one we make at Locanda with very ripe tomatoes, but tinned tomatoes are fine when you can't find good fresh ones. Remember, when you use fresh tomatoes, don't be scared that the sauce is going to be too dry. Tomatoes are about 70 per cent water, and only 30 per cent fibre, so you have to let them cook slowly and the liquid will come out. Don't panic and add half a litre of water, because then you will have soup.

The olives give a little bitterness and edge, and you can add a pinch of dry oregano if you like as the sauce cooks. In Modica, around Easter time, I had some quite sweet tomato sauces balanced with wild fennel, that went with *ravioli di ricotta* – this was one of the few times I ever ate filled pasta on the island, as dried pasta is much more typical. That Sambuca-like flavour is something I never thought would work with tomato, but it goes perfectly.

10 whole black olives in brine
2 tablespoons olive oil
1 medium white onion, finely chopped
1.5kg ripe, fresh tomatoes or 1kg tinned chopped tomatoes
sea salt and freshly ground black pepper
a little sugar if needed

Drain the olives and pat dry. With a sharp knife, make three or four cuts in each olive from end to end, and then cut each segment away from the stone as carefully as you can.

Heat the olive oil in a pan, add the onion and cook until soft but not coloured. Add the olives and cook for 2 minutes, then add the tomatoes and simmer for 30 minutes. Season to taste, adding a little sugar if the tomato is too acidic, and pass through a fine sieve.

## 'A city that leaves you breathless'

At the heart of Sicily's history is its food, and at the heart of its food is its history, but what comes through it all is a character that is only Sicilian. Giuseppe Tomasi di Lampedusa wrote, 'Sicily is Sicily – 1860, earlier, forever' (1860 was the year of the unification of Italy), and that is what I feel. Sicily is Sicily, and like nowhere else, even though it is an island of great contrasts: in the way it looks, from the humble to the baroque, and in its food, so full of different, bold and vibrant flavours that you expect to be discordant, but somehow they come together and bowl you over.

In Palermo I love the street food: the guys outside the restaurants grilling fish for people to take home, the vendors selling sea urchin with lemons, *panelle* – fantastic little fritters of chickpea flour (see page 98) – and all kinds of tripe, such as *quaruma* (veal or beef entrails) or *mascellato* (pieces of jaw); *stigghiola*, intestines of sheep or goat, soaked in wine, then wound around sprigs of parsley and barbecued; or *pane con la milza* – sandwiches filled with beef spleen, which is boiled, and kept warm in a big pot like a wok. The pieces of spleen are put inside soft white focaccia-like buns, known as *guasteddi*, with a sprinkling of salt and a squeeze of lemon, and the flavour is delicious. Sometimes fresh ricotta and grated caciocavallo cheese are added, and the sandwich is called *maritatu* – it is said that this is what Garibaldi ate when he landed in Palermo in 1860.

Palermo doesn't feel like a European city. It leaves you breathless from the noise and the beauty of the Arabic sense of colour and abundance in the markets, the bakeries and crazy cake shops, the *gelaterie*, bars and cafés full of every shade and flavour of ice cream and *granite*.

It is so different to the south-west coast, only an hour and a half's drive away, where you see more of the ancient, classical influence. If you go out with the fishermen and look back to the Valley of the Temples, further around the coast, between Sciacca and Mazara del Vallo, you can see where once there was a Greek city on the flat plain above the swamps, where people were scared of malaria.

In the villages the shops are sometimes so small, they are little more than holes in the wall; there is no heavy industry, and everyone is dedicated to fishing, or the production of grapes and olives. Old men sit around on their chairs in the village square, as if the street is just an extension of their houses, just sitting and talking and watching. The first time we went on holiday, Jack was saying: 'Why are they sitting on the street? Don't they have houses?' Sometimes, if the men have an affiliation to a political party, they will put their chairs outside their office, or maybe outside the confraternity of olive pickers. And when they are talking, I am sure it's about food, because everyone talks – or argues – about food: who makes the authentic version of a pasta, whose mother had the best recipe.

Dramatically different again is the eastern side of the island, where Noto was rebuilt after Mount Etna erupted, and Modica was rebuilt after the

earthquake of 1693. Everything is very elaborate, very baroque. Then, as you travel upwards through the plain of Catania, towards Mount Etna, you meet people who speak in a different dialect to the people who face the sea, and they seem to talk in proverbs. If anything, they appear to be even more resilient, even more *Sicilian*, because they live in the shadow of the mountain the ancient people called the monster with a hundred heads. It is not just one volcano, but a series of them, and every so often it shoots up its 'bombs' of molten lava, and when people find them, they write their names on them.

When you go up the mountain you see the fields of lava and the hills it formed when it erupted and fell and hardened like honeycomb, and it is incredible to think that the mountain both kills and nurtures ... whole communities have been destroyed by it, but there is nothing that won't grow in the soil enriched by the volcanic ash.

In Palermo you can see the layers of history in the buildings – churches, synagogues, Arabian mosques – and like most of the world's cities, you see the extremes of rich and poor, though slowly they are reclaiming the poorer areas. And in the late night eating you see the Spanish and Arab influence. The shops open late, people work until the early evening, go home, relax a bit, then come out for dinner, or eat at home, and then meet friends at a bar or café. I like to sit outside on a hot night at one of the places overlooking the sea, where you can eat *pasta con le sarde* (see page 215), or *involtini di pesce spada*, and ice cream. Always ice cream.

In so many places you see the old ladies preparing food in the way they have done for centuries, with the same ingredients, but there are also some young chefs who are taking the same ingredients and combinations, but interpreting and proposing them slightly differently; not only in Palermo, but in the cities on the other side of the island: Noto, Modica, Messina ... In one Michelin-starred restaurant, La Gazza Ladra in Modica, the chef, Accursio Craparo, makes artistic creations such as watermelon salad with sea urchin sorbet; 'linguine' with a cream of anchovies, candied orange and wild fennel flowers; and a clever little mini 'burger' of beautiful tuna: some of the *ventresca* (the fat belly) is mixed with some of the back and formed into little 'buns' that are part steamed, then fried, and filled with a slice of raw tuna, and a 'mayonnaise' of anchovies, lemon, sea urchin and fish liver, with herbs scattered on top.

Palermo is a loud city; from the swallows that wake you up in the morning to the sellers in the market, everyone seems to be shouting. No wonder tourists get scared – and these guys are only trying to sell snails! People say Palermo is dangerous, but I don't see it as threatening; I find it warm and welcoming. And I like the hustle and bustle and noise. But of course there have been times when, unseen by the outsider's eye, it *has* been a dangerous place, because the city is in the heart of Mafia territory.

### 'Nobody sees; everybody knows'

If you look hard enough in Palermo, you can still see some of the white stickers that appeared one night all over the city, with a message that translates as: 'there is no dignity in a people that pays the *pizzo*' – the protection money demanded by the Mafia. The stickers were an invitation to join the newly formed *addio-pizzo* movement, an alliance of restaurants, bars, shops and businesses that display the *addio-pizzo* sign in their windows, which tells you they are refusing to pay.

You cannot talk about food without talking about the Mafia, because the roots of the Mafia are in the land, and when you control the territory, you can control the production of the food, its transportation, and its price. But food also brings people together, and slowly, slowly, a change is happening in Sicilian society and it is being determined by a young generation of restaurateurs and bar owners and food producers who are finding strength in numbers and the courage to stand up to the might of the Mafia.

In the late 1980s, when I was already cooking in England, the Mafia seemed to be always in the newspapers and on the TV news: the wars between the rival families, the drug trafficking, the money laundering, the murders of anti-Mafia politicians, judges and the investigating magistrates Giovanni Falcone and Paolo Borsellino, the kidnappings, the trials. I was fascinated by it all, but I never seemed to see any explanation as to 'why?' For a northern Italian it was difficult to understand the power of the Mafia, the way it had infiltrated every organisation, so much so that during the trials, it was said that the only safe place to talk in the Palace of Justice was in the lift. So for an Anglo-Saxon person, I imagined, it would be almost impossible to understand.

Then I read *Cosa Nostra, A History of the Sicilian Mafia*, by John Dickie, Professor of Italian Studies at University College London, a brilliant, compelling, but also very scholarly work, which had a very big impact on me. Dickie told the story in a way that had nothing to do with folkloristic *Godfather* images of 'Men of Honour', the kind of glorification that brings busloads of tourists every year to Bar Vitelli in Savoca, near Taormina, where they filmed the wedding festivities of Michael Corleone in Francis Ford Coppola's movie of the Mario Puzo novel.

Since then I must have devoured a whole library of books on the Mafia, and every time a new one is written, I have to read it. So I have done a lot of searching over the years, to try and understand. You have to think about the history of Sicily: the Greeks and Romans came and left, the Normans came and left, the Spanish came and left, then suddenly Garibaldi arrived and everyone was Italian. But the promises that were made, that the land would be redistributed, didn't happen. Instead the balance of economic power shifted to the north of Italy, where industry and production increased, and in the south and in Sicily many people just became more poor. So in the vacuum between rich and poor, the state and the people, rose the Mafia.

The roots were already there in agriculture under Spanish rule, because the barons who owned the big estates were away in Palermo and in their absence they appointed managers, middle men known as *gabelotti*, who took a foothold of power, and whose ruthless henchmen were known as *campieri*. Out of this grew the Mafia, tapping into the Sicilian idea of *Cosa Nostra*, the sense of family, of looking after one another, all bound up with a sense of fate, maybe inherited from the Greeks, that somehow made the people trust in the Mafiosi, because they were their own, even though they ruled by fear and brutality.

What is interesting is that in the east side of the island the Mafia didn't take hold in the same way, because there, under the Spanish, the land was allowed to be inherited by a son, and so there were small tenements, rather than baronial estates, and not the same need for the powerful 'middle men'.

It is only when you spend time in the western side of the island, and get to know the people and the way the place is run, that you can begin to understand that the Mafia is everywhere, but there is no way you can tell who is the Mafia. It is an undercurrent. It is there, and it is not there. Nobody sees; everybody knows. The prices are controlled, and the territory is controlled, centimetre by centimetre.

For a long time, the existence of the Mafia as a structured organisation was denied, right up to the trials of the eighties. Even now there are people who will say it doesn't exist or, 'They are good people. They make things work.' Yes. But it has been proven that the Mafia is bad for business, because its presence has slowed down the development of Sicily in comparison to other regions of Italy.

What I feel is that *Cosa Nostra* is *inside* the people; you cannot defeat it on the streets, or in the courts of justice alone; you have to do it in heads and minds. In *Midnight in Sicily*, Peter Robb quotes the writer Leonardo Sciascia, who summed up perfectly the complicated relationship that exists between the community and the Mafia: 'Take this Sicilian reality I live in: a lot of things that make it up I disapprove of and condemn, but I see them with pain and *from inside* … It hurts when I denounce the mafia because a residue of mafia feeling stays alive in me, as it does in any Sicilian. So struggling against the mafia I struggle against myself. It's like a split, a laceration.'

I see some pessimism, but a lot of optimism. Pessimism because not everyone believes in change, and because some say that when the Mafia appears quiet it is at its most dangerous; and optimism in a new-found strength and pride among restaurateurs and food producers, boosted by organisations like Slow Food, which is helping the people to understand that there is a different way to market their food. And then you see the Libera Terra farming projects, in which land confiscated from convicted Mafia bosses is being given to co-operatives of young people to grow crops or make wine. The most famous is the Terre di Corleone, where a vineyard has been planted on the land of the imprisoned Salvatore 'Toto' Riina, near the town whose name Mario Puzo borrowed for his family in *The Godfather*. Ironically, he chose it just because he liked the sound of the name (which means Lionheart), with no idea of how notorious Corleone was to become as a Mafia town a decade later. When you see these agricultural projects, you have real hope that at last the people will begin to accept that they can work this beautiful land for themselves, and come out from under the cloud of *Cosa Nostra*.

# Verdure
# Vegetables

'What did you eat?'

Then he understood. Livia was trying to be there with him, at his house in Marinella. She was imagining him the way she had seen him so many times before, trying to annul the distance by picturing him as he performed the customary acts he did every evening. He suddenly felt overwhelmed by a feeling that was a mixture of melancholy, tenderness, regret and desire.

'*Caponata*,' he said in a choked-up voice.

How on earth was it possible to get a lump in one's throat simply by uttering the word 'caponata'?

– Andrea Camilleri, *The Wings of the Sphinx*,
an Inspector Montalbano mystery

The first time we stayed in Sicily on holiday I got up early one morning and walked to the square, where I found all these old guys with their little three-wheeler Ape Piaggio trucks parked up. In the back were boxes of tomatoes, aubergines, artichokes and all kinds of other vegetables. The way things work is that if a local family has a small piece of land, the men get up at about five in the morning, pick their produce, then pack it into boxes and drive to the square. Then at about 7.30 a.m. a bigger truck comes along from the greengrocer's in town and the driver buys one box from this guy, two from the next … and that is how the local people make a living.

Later in the day, you see these same guys driving around the village with more vegetables in the back of their Apes, tooting their horns, so you can come out of your house and buy them in your street. Sometimes when I drop in on my friend Vittorio, in his restaurant kitchen in Porto Palo, he will say to me: 'Drive towards Menfi, and just before you get to the village, on the corner of the last road on the right, you will see a box of tomatoes.' He will have called someone he knows and said, 'I need more tomatoes,' and the guy will have said, 'OK, I'll leave them on the corner of the road for you.' Such a funny, fantastic way to run a restaurant.

But what it shows you is the freshness of the ingredients, always. That's what strikes me every time I go to Sicily. Even if you don't grow your own vegetables, every day you can buy ones that have been harvested by someone else in your village that morning – each vegetable seems to have many different seasons, which keeps them going almost all year round. And the flavour! You can see why Sicilians don't elaborate their dishes, when a tomato or even celery delivers so much taste all by itself. I remember picking up a head of celery in the market, to put into a chicken stock, and the guy selling it said, 'No, have this one, it is much better' – and gave me a very woody-looking one instead. Back at the house I put about two stalks into the pot, as I would usually, and the stock turned out to taste only of celery – that aniseed flavour you get from celery, which is usually quite subtle, was huge – so sometimes you have to balance what you do, because of the unexpected strength and richness of flavour in the vegetables.

What I see everywhere is a great love of greens: so many recipes with broccoli, especially with anchovies and pasta, but the broccoli is different. Known as *sparaceddi* or *sparacelli*, it is bigger, quite leafy, with greeny-gold heads, the colour of the sprouting broccoli we see in the UK when it flowers, and with a sweeter, less grassy flavour.

Also, they have something I never saw in Italy before: *tenerumi*, which is the curly tendrils, stalks and leaves of the *zucca trombetta*, or trumpet pumpkin. This is a long, curvy, pale green kind of cross between a courgette and a squash or pumpkin that is hard on the outside and soft inside, with seeds. It is one of the squashes that is often candied and used to decorate *cassata* and other desserts.

The first time I saw *tenerumi*, which tastes of courgette, but is somehow 'greener', I was embarrassed that I didn't know what it was. Fortunately the guys in the market didn't know I was a chef when I asked them what to do with it! They told me blanch it briefly, then heat some olive oil in a pan, add some garlic, chilli and chopped tomatoes, put in the *tenerumi*, let it wilt like spinach and serve it with pasta, and it was so good. Traditionally, *tenerumi* was also just boiled and then some broken-up bits of spaghetti were added to the pan, along with some sautéed garlic and tomato – so the dish ended up more like a *brodo* (soup). Or it was put into a fish soup, with clams, calamari and mussels.

This simple way of blanching and then sautéing is used for every kind of greens, such as chard (which are smaller and less aggressive in flavour than the ones we get in the UK), cardoons and chicory – not spinach so much, because it is too fragile. They prefer the sturdier greens with stalks, which can be chopped up and blanched first, followed by the leaves. When the drained leaves are quickly tossed in oil, garlic and chilli, they can be put out as antipasti, cold or hot, or eaten with fish or meat. If the greens are to be eaten with pasta, when they are lifted from their boiling water to drain, the pasta goes straight into the same cooking water, so that it takes on some of the colour and flavour of the greens. When the pasta is drained it is just mixed with the sautéed greens, and the flavour of the vegetables is so intense you don't need anything else.

The Sicilian use of cauliflower is amazing, too, especially the purple '*bastardu*' cauliflower that grows in the volcanic soil below Mount Etna, and has its own sweet, delicate flavour. What do we do in Britain with cauliflower? Cover it with cheese, and that is about it. There, they use it in so many sweet and sour combinations of vegetables, or make a fantastic salad with cauliflower and black olives (see page 115). In the bakers' shops you can buy *schiacciata* (see page 58), which is a kind of baked pie made with a focaccia-like dough that is rolled out into two rectangles, one thicker than the other. The thicker one is covered with pieces of cauliflower, together with the likes of sausage meat or anchovies, raisins, olives, caciocavallo or pecorino cheese, oregano, and sometimes tomatoes. Then the thinner rectangle is put on top, pressed down to seal, and the whole thing is baked, then cut up into pieces.

The other vegetable that is synonymous with Sicily is the aubergine (see page 134). One of the most famous dishes is *pasta alla Norma*, that brilliant, vivid combination of aubergine, tomato and salted ricotta (see page 186), and most of the aubergine dishes are variations on similar combinations of ingredients. In one restaurant I ate a beautiful dish of pan-fried aubergine, which was rolled up around a filling of ricotta, marjoram, *ricotta salata* (which is the hard, aged, and quite salty ricotta that can be grated), then covered in tomato sauce, topped with caciocavallo cheese, and baked. In another place they served something similar, but the slices of aubergine were layered on a big plate, with tomato sauce, basil and *ricotta salata*, then cut up in slices, and you ate them just as they were, cold, as an antipasto.

Equally famous outside of Sicily is *caponata* (see page 124), the mix of fried aubergine and other vegetables in a sweet and sour sauce, made with

Tenerumi

vinegar and sugar, that owes much to the Arabs, who introduced the growing of sugar cane to the island. Until then honey was the only sweetener. As always, you would make *caponata* with whatever vegetables you had, and there are so many different recipes, four of which I have included in this chapter.

When you look at old books on Sicilian food, no mention is made of what a recipe would be served with; there is just a feeling that you would make it and put it on the table with whatever else you had, so all of these vegetable dishes would make a great addition to the antipasti, but they would also be brilliant with grilled fish or meat.

Although the dishes in this chapter are predominantly made with vegetables, this is the food of Sicily, so it is inevitable that anchovies manage to find their way into many of the recipes!

## Insalata di olive verdi schiacciate
Salad of crushed olives

When you look at the ingredients of this salad, you will probably think, as I did, that it is too simple to be very exciting, but it is unbelievable the way the celery takes up the flavours and combines with the olives and mint, so that the whole thing tastes really fresh and fantastic.

Serves 4–6

450g good whole green olives in brine
about 6 celery stalks, with leaves if possible, all finely chopped
the leaves from about 10–12 stalks of mint, finely chopped
40ml Giorgio's dressing (see page 64)
sea salt and freshly ground black pepper

Drain the olives and pat dry. With a sharp knife, make three or four cuts in each olive from end to end, then cut each segment away from the stone as carefully as you can. Put the pieces into a bowl and add the celery, the celery leaves, and the mint leaves. Toss with the dressing, season and serve.

### 'A herb that people would love forever'

*Menta*
Mint

Mint is a very Sicilian herb, and something you rarely see in other regions of Italy. The story is that Mentha was a Greek nymph who was loved by the god Pluto. His wife, Persephone, was so jealous of Mentha that she crushed her into the ground, but Pluto turned her into a herb that people would love forever.

There is an incredible number of different mint varieties, but the one that is most often found in Sicily is *Mentha viridis* (spearmint), which grows everywhere. It is one of the herbs that is said to stimulate the appetite, so it is often used in dishes that appear with the antipasti: in an olive salad (see page 94), or with fresh peas and artichokes. Coming from the north of Italy, where basil is the beloved herb, I have been surprised and entranced by the way a few leaves of mint can change the whole nature of a simple salad; and whenever I am in Sicily, I also make tea out of it. The important thing to remember with mint, though, is that it must always be freshly picked and used immediately, as it is a herb that loses its flavour the moment it is cut.

**Panelle di ceci**
Sicilian chickpea fritters

*Panelle* is the quintessential street food. In Palermo you see vendors frying
the thin fritters of chickpea flour in oil on street corners, or in the Vucciria
market, and in the smaller towns and villages you see guys driving around in
their little three-wheeled Ape Piaggios, with a gas burner on the back. They
stop where they feel like it, fire up the burner underneath a big wok-like pot
of olive oil, and start frying.

Serves 4

250g chickpea flour
a pinch of salt
a handful of flat-leaf parsley leaves, finely chopped
a little olive oil
vegetable oil for deep-frying
sea salt

Pour 500ml of cold water into a heavy pan, then add the chickpea flour in
a steady stream, whisking constantly to avoid lumps.

Add the salt and cook over a medium heat, stirring constantly with a wooden
spoon, until the mixture thickens and pulls away from the sides of the pan.
Add the parsley.

Rub a cold surface (marble if possible) with olive oil, spoon out the mixture,
and spread it out thinly (about 3mm) with a rolling pin or spatula. When it
cools down, cut it into squares or triangles.

Heat the vegetable oil in a deep pan, making sure it comes no higher than
a third of the way up the pan. It should be 180°C. If you don't have a
thermometer, put in a few breadcrumbs, and if they sizzle straight away the
oil is ready. Deep-fry the fritters until golden, about 1–2 minutes. Drain on
kitchen paper, sprinkle with sea salt and serve warm.

Making *panelle* and *sfincione*

### 'A flavour that feels only Sicilian'

*Finocchietto selvatico*
Wild fennel

If I had to identify a flavour that feels only Sicilian, then it is wild fennel. If basil represents the north of Italy, then wild fennel represents Sicily.

There are three types of fennel: the bulb, or Florence fennel, that Sicilians use in *caponata* and raw in salads; then there is the *sativa*, which is the intensely flavoured one that makes the seeds that Americans put in everything Italian. You go to America and you have to say, 'Can I have something to eat that is *without* fennel seeds, because not all Italian food has fennel seeds in it!' In Sicily the seeds are used in some sauces and breads. But mostly, they use wild fennel, because it grows everywhere.

Sometimes it is called *finocchietto di montagna*, fennel of the mountains, but you don't need to go near a mountain to see it. When I walk out of the house where we stay in Sicily near the sea, it is growing all along the path. So I might go into the village and buy a big fish, maybe a *branzino* (sea bass), or a gilt-head bream, then I will take some sliced potato, a couple of slices of lemon, put in some wild fennel, and maybe some mint, with the fish on top, add a little olive oil and bake it in the oven. When it cooks the fish takes on the fantastic aniseed flavour, which is more aromatic and grassy and less overpowering than the seeds can be: it just seems to produce a very fine note in the background to whatever you are cooking. It is a key ingredient in one of the island's most famous dishes, *pasta con le sarde* (pasta with sardines, see page 215), it is put into the cooking water for broad beans, and picked fresh, it really helps the flavour of a tomato sauce and gives it another dimension, if you put it in at the last minute.

You can't come back from Sicily without big bunches of wild fennel. It is impossible. The boys in the kitchen at Locanda would never forgive me. On the road towards the airport it grows all along the verges, so the last thing you do before you come home is get out of the car and pick some, and when you arrive to check in you see you are not the only one with the idea!

## Panelle di fave
Broad bean fritters

These are similar to the *panelle* made with chickpea flour, but this time they are made with dried broad beans. Broad beans have a big significance in Sicily. The ancient Greeks believed the souls of the dead lived in fava beans, and they are still associated with All Souls' Day on 2 November, when special biscuits are made in the shape of the beans. They are also meant to be a good omen, especially on Good Friday. When I was in Ragusa over the Easter holiday, we ate at a restaurant and we were each given three cooked (dried) beans, with a little salt and olive oil, to represent the Trinity, before the start of the meal.

The best are the beans of Leonforte, now supported by a Slow Food Presidium. When the young beans are harvested they are eaten fresh with spring onions and cheese, or added to *frittedda* (see page 111) and spring stews (see page 114), but the dried beans are equally popular. They have a very different flavour to the fresh ones. You can buy them whole with the skins on, or already skinned and split, in Turkish and Jewish stores. If they are whole, once cooked put them through a sieve to lose the rough skins.

The beans are cooked with wild fennel (see page 101), but you could use a teaspoonful of fennel seeds, soaked for an hour or two in a tiny bit of water.

Serves 4

900g dried broad beans
½ medium onion, sliced
a few fronds of wild fennel, or 1 teaspoon of fennel seeds soaked in water
a pinch of dried chilli flakes (optional)
a little olive oil
vegetable oil for deep-frying
sea salt

Soak the dried beans in water overnight, then drain. The next morning put them into a pan with the onion and fennel, and the chilli flakes, if using. Add enough unsalted water to cover and bring to the boil. Turn down the heat and cook gently for 2–3 hours, adding a little water if necessary until the beans break down to form a very thick purée, then season to taste with salt. Keep stirring to avoid sticking, then pass through a sieve. Grease a work surface, preferably marble, with olive oil and pour the mixture on to it. Roll out to a thickness of about 5mm and allow to cool. Cut into 5cm strips.

Heat a few inches of vegetable oil in a pan, making sure it comes no higher than a third of the way up. It should be 180°C. If you don't have a thermometer, put in a few breadcrumbs and if they sizzle the oil is ready. Deep-fry the strips until golden, about 1–2 minutes. Drain on kitchen paper and serve warm.

*Fave*, dried broad beans

### Maccheroni nel 'maccu' fritto
Pasta and fava (broad bean) cubes

This is another of those surprisingly delicious dishes born out of *cucina povera*. *Maccu* comes from the old Italian word *maccare* (to crush) and this is a simple purée of dried fava beans that you would make to eat on its own, with pasta or thinned down with water, to make a soup. If any purée was left over, you could leave it to harden, then cut it up and fry it the next day. In Palermo they traditionally mixed the purée with cooked squash, instead of fennel, and in the Madonie mountains, south-east of the city, they would add chopped tomato.

I also like the purée just served with onions, sautéed in olive oil, then mixed with a little salt, sugar and vinegar, on top, or some chicory, blanched quickly in boiling water, drained, then sautéed gently in olive oil with a little chopped garlic and chilli. The sweet and sour of the onions, or the bitterness of the chicory, make a great contrast with the *maccu*, which is quite sweet.

Serves 4

360g dried fava or broad beans
1 sprig of wild fennel or 1 teaspoon of fennel seeds, soaked in a little water
400g small macaroni
sea salt and freshly ground black pepper
extra virgin olive oil
4 tablespoons plain flour
vegetable oil for deep-frying

Soak the dried beans overnight. Next day, drain and put them into a pan with enough unsalted water to cover, bring to the boil, then turn down the heat, add the fennel and cook gently for 2–3 hours, stirring regularly to stop the beans from sticking, until they form a thick purée. Season with salt.

Cook the macaroni in plenty of boiling salted water for about 6 minutes, or until al dente. Drain and season generously with pepper. Mix with the broad bean purée. Grease a rectangular baking tray with extra virgin olive oil and spread the bean and macaroni mixture in a layer no more than 1.5cm thick. Put into the fridge overnight to solidify.

Next day, slice the *maccu* into small squares and dip them into the flour, shaking off any excess. Heat 2.5cm of vegetable oil in a deep pan, making sure it comes no higher than a third of the way up the pan. It should be 180°C. If you don't have a thermometer, put in a few breadcrumbs and if they sizzle the oil is ready. Deep-fry the squares until golden on all sides. They can be eaten hot or cold.

### 'Black from the ashes, smoky, tender, delicious…'

The truly Sicilian way with artichokes is to bury them in the ash of a wood-burning stove after the bread has been made, or in the embers of the barbecue, and roast them slowly until they are black on the outside from the ashes, but smoky, tender and delicious inside.

*Carciofi*
Artichokes

In Sicily there is a big production of artichokes. It is not unusual for me to drop into Vittorio's restaurant and find him and his wife, Francesca, or one of the women who helps him, working their way through five boxes of them, brought in that morning.

In spring and summer, if you buy artichokes from the local guys or in the stalls in the market, they come in bunches, some big, some small, usually with one or two baby artichokes attached. They are put into everything from *frittedda* (see page 111) and spring stews (see page 114), made with fresh peas and broad beans, to *caponata* (see pages 124–33), or they are simply blanched, then put under oil, perhaps with a little chilli, as an antipasto; or chopped and tossed in a salad with some olives and slices of lemon.

But my favourite way is this roasting in the ashes, usually of olive branches. There is even a special kind of *graticola*, an iron grill, enclosing a series of 'cones' for the purpose. Instead of peeling the tough outer leaves as you would normally do before cooking the artichokes, what you do is lay each artichoke on its side on a table and roll it, pressing down gently, to loosen the leaves; then you hold it by its stalk and press the tips down on the table, just enough to open out the leaves a little, so that the hot air can circulate through the artichokes as they cook.

Next you put them, stalk first, into the iron cones and push the grill into the ashes, leaving the tops of the artichokes showing, sprinkle them with salt and oil, and leave them for about forty minutes, so they boil from the inside, but char on the outside. Then you simply peel off the blackened leaves and eat them just as they are.

**Carciofi ripieni**
Stuffed artichokes

Serves 4

1 salted anchovy
8 small spiny artichokes
3 tablespoons grated pecorino cheese
5 tablespoons breadcrumbs (see page 45)
2 teaspoons garlic oil (see page 60)
1 tablespoon chopped flat-leaf parsley
6 big mint leaves, chopped
salt
olive oil, if needed
juice of 1 lemon
extra virgin olive oil for finishing

Rinse the anchovy and dry it. Run your thumb gently along the backbone to release it, and you should be able to easily pull it out. Chop the fillets.

Hold each artichoke upside down, by the stem, then knock the tips of the leaves against your work surface to open out the leaves and give you space to put in the stuffing.

In a bowl, mix the pecorino, breadcrumbs, chopped anchovy, garlic oil, parsley and mint with a pinch of salt until smooth. If the mixture looks too dry, add a little olive oil.

Trim each artichoke stem close to the base, then spoon some stuffing into the centre and between the leaves of each one.

Pack the artichokes upright in a deep frying pan or sauté pan. Mix the lemon juice with a litre of water and pour this around the artichokes in the pan. It only needs to be about 2cm deep, just enough to cover the base of the artichokes.

Place the pan on the heat and bring the water to the boil, then turn down the heat, put a lid on the pan, and cook gently for 20–30 minutes, depending on the size of the artichokes. Keep checking the water level as the artichokes cook, to make sure the water doesn't evaporate.

To check if the artichokes are cooked, insert a cocktail stick into the bases. It should go through without any resistance. Transfer the artichokes to a serving dish and drizzle with extra virgin olive oil.

**Frittedda**
Fried spring beans, peas and artichokes

This is a springtime dish, to make when all these vegetables are young and at their most sweet.

Serves 4

6 artichokes
juice of 1 lemon
olive oil
1 medium shallot, finely sliced
200g fresh shelled peas
300g fresh shelled broad beans
100ml white wine vinegar
sea salt and freshly ground black pepper
extra virgin olive oil for finishing

Prepare the artichokes by slicing off the tough tips, and then, working down towards the base, snapping off the tough outer leaves. Stop when you get down to the tender ones. With a small paring knife, peel away the stringy outside of the stalk, and then peel the base of the artichoke where it meets the stalk. Cut in half lengthways, and if the hairy choke has formed, scoop this out with a spoon. Cut the artichoke again lengthways into thin slices and put into a bowl of water with some lemon juice squeezed into it, to stop the artichokes from discolouring, until ready to use.

Heat some olive oil in a pan, add the shallot and cook gently until soft, but not coloured. Add the artichokes, peas and beans. Add the vinegar, and bubble up to let it evaporate. Add boiling water, a ladleful at a time, letting the vegetables absorb it, before adding some more, until they are just tender. By the end of cooking the liquid should have almost disappeared, but the *frittedda* should not be dry. Season to taste.

Serve drizzled with extra virgin olive oil.

**Stufato di verdure primavera**
Stew of spring vegetables

Serves 4

6 artichokes
juice of 1 lemon
60ml olive oil
1 small onion, finely chopped
60g pancetta or prosciutto, diced
200g fresh shelled peas
200g fresh shelled broad beans
sea salt and freshly ground black pepper
200ml vegetable stock
40ml white wine
extra virgin olive oil for finishing
1 tablespoon finely chopped fresh basil
1 tablespoon parsley and garlic (see page 60)

Prepare the artichokes as on page 111, cutting them into thin slices and putting them into a bowl of water with some lemon juice squeezed into it until ready to use.

Heat the olive oil in a large pan, add the onion and cook until soft but not coloured. Add the pancetta or prosciutto and stir. After a few minutes add the peas, broad beans and artichokes and season. Add the wine and turn the heat up to high for a few minutes until the alcohol evaporates. Add the stock, cover with a lid and cook over a low heat, stirring from time to time, for 20 minutes. When the vegetables are tender, drizzle with a little extra virgin olive oil if needed, and sprinkle with the basil and the parsley and garlic. Toss through, and serve hot.

**Insalata di rinforzo**
Cauliflower salad with black olives

The cauliflower in Sicily is closer to broccoli; the heads are more green-looking, and less tight and neat than we are used to in the UK – they are more of an explosion, and they have an incredible flavour.

Serves 4

1 head of cauliflower
sea salt and freshly ground black pepper
6 salted anchovies, or 12 fillets in oil
about 40 good whole black olives in brine
1 tablespoon olive oil
1 teaspoon white wine vinegar
1 teaspoon dried chilli flakes, or to taste
2 spring onions, chopped
2 hard-boiled eggs, chopped
2 teaspoons parsley and garlic (see page 60)

Cut the cauliflower into florets. Bring a pan of boiling salted water to the boil, add the florets, blanch for 2 minutes, then drain and leave to cool.

If using salted anchovies, rinse and dry them. Run your thumb gently along the backbone to release it, and you should be able to easily pull it out. If using anchovies in oil, drain them.

Drain the olives and pat dry. With a sharp knife, make three or four cuts in each olive from end to end, and then cut each segment away from the stone as carefully as you can.

To make the dressing, whisk the olive oil and vinegar in a small bowl and add the chilli flakes and anchovies. Put the spring onions and olives into a serving bowl, add the cauliflower, and toss with the dressing. Sprinkle with the chopped hard-boiled eggs and the parsley and garlic, and serve.

## Insalata di broccoli, mandorle e peperoncino
Broccoli, almond and chilli salad

Serves 4

200g whole blanched almonds
sea salt
2 heads of broccoli, separated into florets
2 tablespoons chilli oil (see page 63)
1 tablespoon garlic oil (see page 60)
50ml Giorgio's dressing (see page 64)
2 fresh chillies (1 red and 1 green), cut into fine strips

Preheat the oven to 180°C/350°F/gas 4.

Lay the almonds in a single layer on a baking tray and put into the oven for about 8 minutes. As long as they are in a single layer you don't need to turn them. Keep an eye on them to make sure they don't burn, and when they are golden, take them out and chop them.

Bring a pan of salted water to the boil, put in the broccoli and blanch for 2–3 minutes, depending on the size of the florets. Drain and put into a bowl of iced water to stop it cooking, and to keep the bright green colour.

Drain the broccoli on kitchen paper, patting to dry off the excess moisture. Put the chilli oil and garlic oil into a pan and heat until the garlic pieces in the garlic oil turn golden, then put in the broccoli and toss until warmed through. Transfer to a serving dish, toss with Giorgio's dressing and the strips of red and green chilli, and scatter with the toasted almonds. Serve at room temperature.

**Insalata d'acciughe, fagiolini e mandorle**
Anchovy, green bean and almond salad

One of the few times I have seen potatoes eaten in Sicily is in a salad with tomatoes and green beans, as in this recipe.

Serves 4

1 large onion
80g whole blanched almonds
200g waxy new potatoes
sea salt and freshly ground black pepper
200g green beans
12 anchovies, either salted or in oil
200g Pachino or cherry tomatoes, chopped
1 teaspoon chilli oil (see page 63)
Giorgio's dressing (see page 64)

Preheat the oven to 180°C/350°F/gas 4. Put the onion, still in its skin, on a baking tray and put into the preheated oven for about 20–30 minutes, until it becomes slightly caramelised and soft. Remove, and when cool enough to handle, take off the skin and cut the onion into cubes.

Lay the almonds in a single layer on a baking tray and put into the oven for about 8 minutes. As long as they are in a single layer you don't need to turn them. Keep an eye on them to make sure they don't burn, and when they are golden, take them out and chop them.

Meanwhile, put the potatoes into a pan of salted water, bring to the boil, and cook until just tender. Lift out, drain and leave to cool. Drop the beans into the same water and blanch for a minute or so, until they too are just tender. Drain and put into iced water, to stop the cooking and help them to keep their bright green colour.

If using salted anchovies, rinse and dry them. Run your thumb gently along the backbone to release it, and you should be able to easily pull it out. If using anchovies in oil, drain them.

Put the tomatoes, potatoes and beans into a serving dish, add the chilli oil and toss together, then add the cubes of onion. Chop the anchovies and add them to the bowl. Toss with Giorgio's dressing, season to taste and sprinkle with the toasted almonds.

**Insalata di fagioli verdi**
Green bean salad

Again, this is very, very simple, but really flavoursome. Use long banana shallots if possible – they are sweeter.

Serves 4

2 shallots, finely chopped
2 tablespoons extra virgin olive oil
2 tablespoons white wine vinegar
400g green beans
salt
50–80g pecorino or Parmesan cheese, grated, to taste

Put the shallots into a bowl with the oil and vinegar.

Blanch the beans in boiling salted water for about a minute, then drain and toss with the shallot mixture and plenty of grated pecorino or Parmesan. Taste and season with salt if necessary (remember, the cheese will be quite salty).

**Insalata d'estate**
Summer salad

Serves 4

a handful of whole black or green olives in brine
sea salt and freshly ground black pepper
100g green beans
100g fresh shelled broad beans
12 anchovy fillets, either salted or in oil
300g Pachino or cherry tomatoes, chopped
1 small red onion, finely chopped
1 tablespoon salted capers, rinsed and drained
1 tablespoon chopped fresh mint
2 tablespoons lemon oil (see page 63)

Drain the olives and pat dry. With a sharp knife, make three or four cuts in each olive from end to end, then cut each segment away from the stone as carefully as you can and chop.

Bring a pan of salted water to the boil, put in the green beans, and blanch for about 2 minutes, until just tender. Lift out (keeping the cooking water) and drain under cold running water, so that they keep their bright green colour. Blanch the broad beans in the same water for 2–3 minutes, depending on their size, and also drain under cold running water, then peel.

If using salted anchovies, rinse and dry them. Run your thumb gently along the backbone to release it, and you should be able to easily pull it out. If using anchovies in oil, drain them.

Chop the anchovies and put them into a serving bowl with the olives, beans, tomatoes, onion, capers and mint. Mix well, toss with the lemon oil and season to taste.

**Insalata di Natale**
Christmas salad

You don't have to wait until Christmas to make this, of course!

Serves 4–6

80g pine nuts
10 whole green olives in brine
sea salt and freshly ground black pepper
600g chicory leaves
450g celery, chopped
450g fennel, thinly sliced
100ml olive oil
juice of ½ lemon
2 tablespoons salted capers, well rinsed and drained
2 oranges, segmented, for garnish
seeds from 1 pomegranate, for garnish

Preheat the oven to 180°C/350°F/gas 4. Lay the pine nuts in a single layer on a baking tray and put into the oven for about 8 minutes. As long as they are in a single layer you don't need to turn them. Keep an eye on them to make sure they don't burn, and when they are golden, take them out and chop them.

Drain the olives and pat dry. With a sharp knife, make three or four cuts in each olive from end to end, and then cut each segment away from the stone as carefully as you can, and roughly chop.

Bring a large pan of salted water to the boil. Put in the chicory, blanch for a minute or so until tender, then lift out and drain. Repeat with the celery. Mix the two together in a serving dish, with the sliced fennel, olive oil, lemon juice, capers and olives, and season to taste. Decorate with the orange segments and sprinkle with the pomegranate seeds and toasted pine nuts.

**Asparagi selvatici in umido**
Braised wild asparagus

When the hunters go out looking for rabbit in the mountains in April and May, in among the spiky grass they can often find wild asparagus. It also likes to grow in the olive groves under the trees, so you can find it in the markets for its short season. It is thinner than most English asparagus, its stalks have a purple tinge, and the tips are more loose and open, a bit more broccoli-like than we are used to seeing in the cultivated English variety. Also the flavour is a little more bitter. Even though it is very slender, the lower part of the stalk can be too woody, so only the tips are used, either braised as in this recipe, or blanched and added to a frittata.

Wild asparagus can be grown in the UK (you can buy the seeds and grow them in the garden), or, as a substitute, you can use 'sprue', which is the very finest, spindly grade of English asparagus.

Serves 4

60ml extra virgin olive oil
1 tablespoon garlic oil (see page 60)
400g fine asparagus tips (about the top 6cm of the stalks)
100ml white wine
2 tablespoons tomato sauce (see page 75)
sea salt

Heat 3 tablespoons of the olive oil in a pan, then add the garlic oil. Lower the heat, put in the asparagus and stir with a wooden spoon, to coat with the oils. Add the wine, with a few tablespoons of water and the tomato sauce. Season with salt. Cover the pan, so that none of the aroma will be lost, and cook for about 5 minutes, until the asparagus is just tender, checking to make sure the mixture doesn't get too dry (add more wine and a tiny amount of water if necessary). When the asparagus is just ready, drizzle with the remaining olive oil and serve warm.

**Cardi fritti**
Stuffed fried cardoons

Serves 4

12 cardoon stalks
juice of 1 lemon
sea salt
around 12 anchovy fillets, either salted or under oil
120g pecorino cheese, cut into short strips
plain flour, for dredging
3 large eggs, beaten
300g breadcrumbs (see page 45)
vegetable oil for deep-frying

Trim the cardoon stalks of any leaves and remove the stringy outsides, as you would with very stringy celery or rhubarb. Cut them into an equal number of lengths, about 7–8cm each, and drop them into a bowl of water with a little lemon juice squeezed into it, to stop them from discolouring, until you are ready to use them.

Bring a pan of lightly salted water to the boil, put in the cardoons, and blanch for about a minute. Drain well, dry and allow to cool. Lay the pieces of cardoons in pairs, then lay an anchovy fillet and some strips of cheese on to one of each of the pairs, and put the other one on top to make a kind of cheese and anchovy sandwich. When the cardoons are dry they are quite sticky, so the pieces will cling together.

Have the flour, beaten egg and breadcrumbs ready in separate shallow dishes. Dip the cardoon 'sandwiches' in flour, then shake off the excess and dip them in the beaten egg and finally into the breadcrumbs, pressing them in all around until the 'sandwiches' are well coated and will hold together.

Heat some oil in a deep pan, making sure it comes no higher than a third of the way up. It should be 180°C. If you don't have a thermometer, test that the oil is hot enough by dropping a few breadcrumbs in carefully. If they sizzle, the oil is ready. Put in the stuffed cardoons and deep-fry until golden on all sides. Lift out, drain on kitchen paper and serve hot.

### 'A hungry man's dream'

Something that is recurrent all over the Mediterranean basin is the idea of *agrodolce* (sweet and sour). In his fantastic book *Midnight in Sicily*, Peter Robb quotes the Sicilian writer Leonardo Sciascia, who, when describing the famous painting of the Vucciria market in Palermo by his friend the artist Renato Guttuso, talked of '…certain sweet and savoury dishes that contain everything, where the savoury merges into the sweet and the sweet into the savoury, dishes that seem to realize a hungry man's dream …' Guttuso is the artist who created the brilliant illustrations for Elizabeth David's first edition of *Italian Food*.

*Caponata*

This is exactly what *caponata* is about: a truly Sicilian combination that brings a little bit of the island's sumptuous baroque history to the kind of vegetables that grow in abundance all over the island, in order to produce an explosion of sweet and sour flavours that just make you want to eat more and more of it. They almost think of it as a chutney.

In every house and in every restaurant you will find a different version and an opinion. I have been in the market and said to the guy selling vegetables 'I am making caponata: which are the best courgettes?' And been told, categorically, 'You don't put courgettes in caponata!' The truth is it is made with whatever vegetables the people have, depending on the time of the year, but the principle is always the same: the vegetables are fried, each one separately, to retain the integrity of each flavour, then combined in a sweet and sour sauce. When we make *caponata* at Locanda, because people are aware of eating too much fried food, and want something lighter, we grill the vegetables, but in truth, I prefer the oiliness that comes from the fried ones!

From all the different versions, I have chosen four favourites that I have eaten in Sicily: the classic summer one, a winter one, a colourful Christmas one, and one that is made primarily with artichokes, when they are in abundance.

# Caponata d'estate
Summer caponata

Summer caponata, made with aubergines, courgettes, celery, fennel, tomatoes, olives, sultanas and pine nuts, when all the vegetables are at their best, is the most famous, outside Sicily. Often some chunks of good bread are added, and then the dish is called *pane a caponata*.

Serves 4

1 large aubergine
sea salt and freshly ground black pepper
100g whole black olives in brine
50g pine nuts
400g country bread, cut into cubes of about 2cm (optional)
olive oil for frying
1 onion, cut into 2cm dice
2 celery stalks, cut into 2cm dice
1 tablespoon tomato passata
1 tablespoon caster sugar
5 tablespoons good-quality red wine vinegar
vegetable oil for deep-frying
½ fennel bulb, cut into 2cm dice
1 courgette, cut into 2cm dice
3 fresh plum tomatoes, cut into 2cm dice
a bunch of fresh basil
50g sultanas
about 100ml extra virgin olive oil

Cut the aubergine into 2cm dice, sprinkle with salt and leave to drain in a colander for at least 2 hours. Squeeze lightly to get rid of the excess liquid.

Drain the olives and pat dry. Then crush them lightly and take out the stones.

Heat the oven to 180°C/350°F/gas 4. Lay the pine nuts in a single layer on a baking tray and put into the oven for about 8 minutes. As long as they are in a single layer you don't need to turn them. Keep an eye on them to make sure they don't burn, and when they are golden, take them out and chop them. Spread the cubes of bread (if using) on a separate baking tray and toast for 5–10 minutes, until golden. Set the pine nuts and bread aside.

Heat a little olive oil in a pan. Add the onion, celery and olives and cook until soft but not coloured, then add the tomato passata. Mix the sugar and vinegar together in a cup and add to the pan. Bring to the boil, then take off the heat and transfer the contents of the pan to a big bowl.

Heat about 4cm of vegetable oil in a deep pan, making sure it comes no higher than a third of the way up the pan. (If you have a thermometer the temperature should be 180°C, otherwise, to test if it is hot enough, sprinkle in a little flour or breadcrumbs; if the oil is ready, the flour will fry.) Add the fennel and deep-fry for 1–2 minutes, until tender and golden. Lift out and drain on kitchen paper. Wait until the oil comes up to the right temperature again, then repeat with the aubergine, followed by the courgette.

Add all the deep-fried vegetables to the bowl containing the onion, celery and olives, together with the diced tomatoes. Tear the basil leaves and add them to the bowl, along with the sultanas, the toasted pine nuts and the extra virgin olive oil. Season well, and mix together gently. Cover the bowl with clingfilm while the vegetables are still warm and leave to infuse for at least 2 hours at room temperature.

Mix in the toasted bread, if using, and leave to infuse for another 20 minutes before serving. Don't be tempted to put the bowl into the fridge, because it is during the process in which the vegetables steam a little under the clingfilm, and then come down in temperature very slowly, that 'the savoury merges into the sweet and the sweet into the savoury'.

## Caponata d'inverno
Winter caponata

At one time parsnips were used to give sweetness to winter *caponata*, though you rarely see parsnips in Sicily nowadays, and carrots have taken their place in this dish, which is put into the oven briefly, once the vegetables have been fried separately in the usual way, and served hot, topped with hard boiled eggs.

You might think it odd to blanch the spring onions in this recipe, before frying them, but I have noticed that Sicilians often like to do this (even though in this recipe it is only the spring onions and not the white onions that are blanched). Sometimes they will put onions into a frying pan with just a couple of teaspoons of water and start to cook them, then, the moment all the water has evaporated, they add some oil and fry them. The feel of the onions is a little slimier, but rather than taking away some of the flavour, as I expected, this process actually seems to concentrate the taste, and in some recipes the texture really seems to make a difference.

Serves 4

12 small artichokes
juice of 1 lemon
100ml white wine vinegar
2 carrots, sliced to the thickness of a £1 coin
2 celery stalks, chopped
6 spring onions, sliced
16 whole green olives in brine
olive oil
6 medium onions, sliced
60ml tomato purée
salt
2 tablespoons sugar
60g salted capers, rinsed and drained
6 large eggs, hard-boiled and chopped

Preheat the oven to 180°C/350°F/gas 4.

Prepare the artichokes as on page 111, cutting them into thin slices and putting them into a bowl of water with some lemon juice squeezed into it until ready to use.

Bring a pan of water to the boil with 70ml of the vinegar. Put in the artichokes and blanch them for about a minute, then lift them out and drain them. Add the carrots for a further minute or so, then drain, and repeat with the celery and spring onions.

Drain the olives and pat dry. With a sharp knife, make three or four cuts in each olive from end to end, and then cut each segment away from the stone as carefully as you can.

Heat about 1.5cm of olive oil in a frying pan that will transfer to the oven. Put in the artichokes and sauté them gently until softened, but not coloured. Drain and set aside. Repeat with all the other blanched vegetables. Now put the sliced onions into the pan and sauté gently until golden. Add the tomato purée and salt to taste.

Mix the sugar and remaining vinegar together in a cup and add to the pan. Stir for a minute or so, then add all the sautéed vegetables, along with the olives and capers. Stir, take off the heat, and put into the oven. Bake for about 5 minutes until hot all the way through, then scatter with the hard-boiled eggs.

# Caponata di carciofi
Artichoke caponata

Serves 4

30g pine nuts
8 artichokes
juice of 1 lemon
100ml white wine vinegar
sea salt and freshly ground black pepper
1 celery stalk, chopped
1 tablespoon olive oil
1 tablespoon garlic oil (see page 60)
30g raisins, soaked in warm water and drained
a few mint leaves
1 tablespoon sugar

Preheat the oven to 180°C/350°F/gas 4. Lay the pine nuts in a single layer on a baking tray and put into the oven for about 8 minutes. As long as they are in a single layer you don't need to turn them. Keep an eye on them to make sure they don't burn, and when they are golden, take them out and chop them.

Prepare the artichokes as on page 111, cutting them into quarters and putting them into a bowl of water with some lemon juice squeezed into it until ready to use.

Bring 3 litres of water to the boil with 70ml of the vinegar and a pinch of salt. Add the artichokes and blanch for a couple of minutes until al dente, then remove, drain, and set aside. Add the celery to the same water and blanch for a minute or so until tender, then drain.

Heat the olive oil in a pan and sauté the celery until lightly golden. Add the artichokes to the pan along with the garlic oil, raisins and mint. Season with black pepper and stir for a few minutes. Mix the sugar and the remaining vinegar together in a cup and add to the pan, then bring to the boil. Turn down the heat, add the toasted pine nuts, then take off the heat – you can eat the caponata straight away, but to really help the flavours to develop, cover with clingfilm and leave to cool down before serving.

## Caponata di Natale
Christmas caponata

Serves 8

375g almonds
450g whole green olives in brine
sea salt
1 large head of celery, chopped
120ml olive oil
300g salted capers, rinsed and drained
375g raisins
60g sugar
120ml white wine vinegar
seeds of 1 pomegranate (optional)

Preheat the oven to 180°C/350°F/gas 4. Lay the almonds in a single layer on a baking tray and put into the oven for about 8 minutes. As long as they are in a single layer you don't need to turn them. Keep an eye on them to make sure they don't burn, and when they are golden, take them out and chop them. Keep to one side.

Drain the olives and pat dry. With a sharp knife, make three or four cuts in each olive from end to end, and then cut each segment away from the stone as carefully as you can. Chop the olives.

Bring a large pan of salted water to the boil. Add the celery and blanch for about a minute, until just soft, then drain. Heat the olive oil in a large pan and sauté the celery, olives and capers until the celery is lightly golden. Add the raisins and cook for a few minutes. Mix the sugar and vinegar together in a cup, add to the pan, bring to the boil, then add all but 2 tablespoons of the toasted almonds and take off the heat.

You can eat the caponata straight away, but to really help the flavours develop, cover with clingfilm and leave to cool down before serving sprinkled with the remaining almonds and the pomegranate seeds, if using.

### 'The apple of craziness'

The favourite Sicilian aubergine is the 'Tunisian' aubergine, which is fat and round, changes colour from deep purple, through violet, to white, and has a spongy and marshmallowy texture that lends itself to frying, and especially grilling. It has a slightly sweeter flavour than the purple ones we are more used to in the UK, and a thinner skin, which makes it better for dishes like *parmigiana*, in which rounds of fried or grilled aubergine are layered up. It also makes an amazing purée, if you bake it whole in foil in the oven. By doing it this way, and not cutting the aubergine before baking, you prevent oxidation, which turns the flesh darker, so the colour is a fantastic golden-green. When the aubergine is completely soft you mix it with a little extra virgin olive oil, chopped garlic and oregano – and some chopped chilli if you like – and serve it as an antipasto.

*Melanzane*
Aubergines

Aubergines were first introduced to Sicily by the Arabs, and at some point apparently the Capuchin Fathers played a big part in diffusing the growing of the fruit all over the island ... wherever they went, they scattered the seeds. But aubergines weren't always so loved. At first all Europeans were suspicious of these extraordinary-looking purple fruits brought in by the Arabs from India, which they called *melanzane*, which means 'the apple of craziness'. The first aubergines were more seedy and bitter than they are now, which is why old recipes always say to salt and soak them for a long time, to draw out the bitterness. With the modern strains of aubergine, some of them almost seedless – especially the Tunisian aubergine – you don't have to do that. A couple of hours' salting, just to remove some of the moisture, and firm up the flesh if you are going to fry or grill it, is all you need.

All over Sicily aubergine is used in so many ways: fried and kept under oil for an antipasto; as a shell, with its own flesh puréed and mixed into a stuffing; sprinkled over a pasta sauce made with tuna and tomato, with some almond pesto on top (see page 73); or in the famous *pasta alla Norma* (page 186).

It is also used in the equally famous dish of *parmigiana*, in which slices of grilled or fried aubergine, overlapping each other, are covered in tomato sauce and then topped with cheese. It is a dish which is made all over Italy, and everyone assumes it owes its name to Parmesan cheese, which it is usually made with, and so has its roots in the north, in Parma. However, a different story is told by Mary Taylor Simeti, in her book *Sicilian Food*. Simeti is an American who went to Sicily after she finished college, married a Sicilian, and lives on a farm there. She has done an amazing job of researching the history of Sicilian food and discovering old recipes, looking at everything through ancient manuscripts, novels and poetry, and her book is very charming.

According to Simeti, Sicilians claim to have made the dish first, with caciocavallo cheese. She suggests that the original name was *palmigiana*, which means 'shutter', and that the person who made it first was reminded of a shutter as he overlapped the slices of aubergine. Because Sicilians have difficulty pronouncing the letter 'l', the word changed into *parmigiana* and it has been known by that name ever since.

Note: You can often find the violet variety of aubergine in the UK. When you buy any aubergines, check around the stalk. If it is tender and green, then it is good. Avoid stalks that are dark and shrivelled, and choose aubergines that are heavy, as this usually means they have more flesh and fewer seeds.

## Melanzane a beccafico
Twice-cooked aubergine and anchovy parcels

Serves 4–6

170g anchovies, either salted or in oil
1 large aubergine
salt
olive oil
200g *tuma* (Sicilian fresh unsalted sheep's cheese) or mozzarella, cut
into small cubes
a bunch of fresh basil
4 large eggs, beaten
300g breadcrumbs (see page 45)

If using salted anchovies, rinse and dry them. Run your thumb gently along
the backbone to release it, and you should be able to easily pull it out. If
using anchovies in oil, drain them. Chop the anchovies.

Cut the aubergine into slices widthways, about 6mm thick. You need an
equal number of slices that will fit together in pairs. Sprinkle with salt and
leave to drain in a colander for at least 2 hours. Squeeze lightly to get rid of
the excess liquid.

Heat a little olive oil in a pan and sauté all the aubergine slices in batches, on
one side only. Lay out half of the slices, sautéed side down, on a board, and
divide the cheese, anchovies and basil leaves between them. Cover each with
another similar-sized slice of aubergine, placing it sautéed side up. Secure
these 'sandwiches' with cocktail sticks.

Have ready the beaten egg and breadcrumbs in separate shallow dishes. Coat
the 'sandwiches' with egg, then dip them into the breadcrumbs, pressing
them in gently so they are well coated.

Heat about 1.5cm of olive oil in a sauté pan over a medium heat and fry the
'sandwiches' in batches, turning them very carefully, until they are golden
brown on all sides. Remove the cocktail sticks and serve hot.

## Involtini di melanzane
Aubergine rolls

Serves 4

2 medium aubergines
sea salt and freshly ground black pepper
olive oil
1 onion, finely chopped
2 garlic cloves, finely chopped
15g sultanas
15g pine nuts
15g pecorino cheese, grated
bay leaves
2 tablespoons breadcrumbs (see page 45)
juice of 1 lemon

Cut the aubergines into slices lengthways (about 5mm thick), sprinkle with salt and leave to drain in a colander for at least 2 hours. Squeeze lightly to get rid of the excess liquid, then bring a large pan of water to the boil, add the slices of aubergine, and blanch for a minute. Drain and set aside.

Preheat the oven to 180°C/350°F/gas 4. Heat a little olive oil in a pan, add the onion and garlic and cook gently until soft, but not coloured. Add the sultanas and pine nuts and cook for a minute, then take off the heat, cool and then add the pecorino, mixing well and adding a little more olive oil until you have a dense, moist mixture.

Lay the slices of aubergine out on a board. Spoon a little of the onion mixture on to each slice, then roll up. With wooden skewers, secure the rolls, four at a time, with a bay leaf in between each roll and at either end. Arrange the skewers in a baking dish, scatter with the breadcrumbs and bake in the oven for 10 minutes, until golden. Squeeze a little lemon juice over the top before serving.

## Parmigiana di melanzane
Baked aubergine with cheese

Serves 4

4 large aubergines
sea salt and freshly ground black pepper
olive oil
16 ripe plum tomatoes
1 tablespoon garlic oil (see page 60)
1 tablespoon sugar
4 large hard-boiled eggs, cut into quarters
150g *tuma* (Sicilian fresh unsalted sheep's cheese) or mozzarella, cut
into small cubes
a bunch of fresh basil
50g caciocavallo or pecorino cheese, grated

Cut the aubergines into slices lengthways, about 6mm thick. Sprinkle with salt and leave to drain in a colander for at least 2 hours. Squeeze lightly to get rid of the excess liquid.

Preheat the oven to 180°C/350°F/gas 4 and grease a baking dish with olive oil.

Put the tomatoes into a pan of boiling water for 10 seconds, then drain under cold water and you should be able to peel them easily. Cut them in half, scoop out the seeds with a teaspoon, and chop the flesh.

Heat 2 tablespoons of olive oil in a pan and add the garlic oil. When the pieces of garlic in the oil turn golden, add the tomatoes and cook until reduced to a thick sauce. Stir in the sugar and cook for a couple of minutes.

Heat about 2.5cm of olive oil in a pan and sauté the aubergine slices until they are golden and crisp. Lift out and drain on kitchen paper.

Spread a few tablespoons of tomato sauce over the base of the baking dish, then start to layer up the ingredients: begin with some of the aubergine, followed by some of the eggs, and the *tuma* or mozzarella. Scatter with some of the grated caciocavallo or pecorino. Spread some more tomato sauce over the top, add the basil and layer again as before. Finish with a layer of aubergine, and scatter with the last of the cheese.

Put the dish into the preheated oven and bake for about 10 minutes until heated through, and the cheese on top has melted and turns golden. Allow to cool to room temperature before serving.

## Zucchine fritte
Crispy courgettes

This is the sort of thing I do for Margherita when we are in Sicily if I find guys selling courgettes on my morning walk to the shops. I just put a big bowlful out with some salami or ham as an antipasti, or to have alongside some pasta or meat. Margherita loves the sweetness, and the crunchiness that you get from the durum wheat flour coating when you deep-fry the courgettes.

Serves 4

4 courgettes
sea salt
'00' flour for dusting
vegetable oil for deep-frying

Cut the courgettes into fine strips, ideally with a mandolin. Put them into a bowl and sprinkle with sea salt. Leave in the fridge for 1 hour. Don't rinse them, as the salt will draw the moisture out of the courgettes, so that they will crisp up better when you fry them.

Have the flour ready in a shallow dish. Take the courgettes from their bowl – don't squeeze them, as you want them to be a little moist so that the flour clings to them – and dust them with the flour.

Heat some oil in a large pan (no more than a third full). It shouldn't be more than 180°C, as you don't want the courgettes to brown too quickly (if you drop in some flour it should start to sizzle very gently).

Lower the courgettes into the oil and fry until golden and crispy. Lift out and drain on kitchen paper.

## Peperoni in agrodolce
Sweet and sour stuffed peppers

Peppers, because of the shape they have, are natural vessels that lend themselves to stuffing. The northern Italians like to stuff them with meat, the Sicilians prefer to stick to their favourite sweet and sour flavours of anchovies, raisins and capers or just roast them, strip off their skins and serve them, tossed with olive oil and herbs, as part of an *antipasto misto*.

Don't expect to find perfectly shaped shiny peppers, the kind British supermarkets love, in the markets in Sicily. They are simply the shape they are, and that is that: some squareish, some short, some crooked, some streaked with red and green, but the flavour! Because they grow under such intense sun they have an amazing sweetness.

The condiment *vincotto* ('cooked wine') is usually made from the must of grapes that have been left to dry out a little on the vine and intensify in sweetness. The must is heated and reduced very, very slowly until it becomes syrupy.

Serves 4

150g whole black olives in brine
8 baby or pointed peppers (red or yellow)
140g crustless stale bread, crumbled
140g breadcrumbs (see page 45)
2 garlic cloves, chopped
60g chopped flat-leaf parsley
75g sultanas
75g salted capers, rinsed and drained
olive oil
50ml *vincotto*

Preheat the oven to 180°C/350°F/gas 4.

Drain the olives and pat dry. With a sharp knife, make three or four cuts in each olive from end to end, and then cut each segment away from the stone as carefully as you can. Chop the olives.

If using baby peppers slice off the tops, reserving these 'lids', and with the tip of a sharp knife remove the seeds and inner membrane, taking care not to break the peppers. Put the bread, breadcrumbs, garlic, parsley, sultanas, capers and olives into a bowl and mix in enough olive oil to bind.

Stuff some of the mixture inside each of the peppers and if using baby peppers put the 'lids' back on. Grease a roasting tin with a little more olive oil, put in the peppers, packing them together snugly so that they stay upright in the case of baby peppers or on their side if using pointed ones. Drizzle a little more oil over the top. Cover the tin with a sheet of foil and cook in the oven for 15–20 minutes, or until the peppers are tender, adding more olive oil if necessary.

Lift out the peppers and put them on a serving dish, put the roasting tin on top of the stove, and add the *vincotto* to the pepper juices. Bubble up, stirring, to make a little sauce. Add some water if it is too thick, then spoon over the peppers.

## Peperoni ripieni
Stuffed peppers with cheese

Serves 4

4 baby red peppers
4 baby yellow peppers
4 salted anchovies
4 ripe plum tomatoes
olive oil
1 red onion
15g salted capers, rinsed and drained
185g crustless white bread, crumbled
185g breadcrumbs (see page 45)
60g fresh basil, chopped
120g caciocavallo or pecorino cheese, grated
sea salt and freshly ground black pepper

Preheat the oven to 180°C/350°F/gas 4.

Slice the tops off the peppers, reserving these 'lids', and with the tip of a sharp knife remove the seeds and inner membrane, taking care not to break the peppers.

Rinse and dry the anchovies. Run your thumb gently along the backbone to release it, and you should be able to easily pull it out. Chop the anchovies.

Put the tomatoes into a pan of boiling water for 10 seconds, then drain under cold water and you should be able to peel them easily. Cut them in half, scoop out the seeds with a teaspoon, and chop the flesh.

Heat a little olive oil in a pan and add the onion, capers and anchovies. Cook for a minute, then take off the heat and put into a bowl with the bread, breadcrumbs, tomatoes, basil and cheese. Season, mix in enough olive oil to bind, then stuff some of the mixture inside each of the peppers and put the 'lids' back on. Grease a roasting tin with a little more olive oil, put in the peppers, packing them together snugly so that they stay upright, and drizzle with a little more oil. Cover with a sheet of foil and cook in the oven for 15–20 minutes, until the peppers are tender, adding more olive oil if necessary. Serve at room temperature or cold.

## Peperoni con aglio e basilico
Peppers with garlic and basil

Serves 4

4 medium red peppers
4 medium yellow peppers
150ml olive oil
sea salt
2 teaspoons garlic oil (see page 60)
½ medium white onion, thinly sliced
1 tablespoon white wine vinegar
12 big leaves of basil, chopped

Preheat the oven to 180°C/350°F/gas 4.

Put the peppers into a baking dish, brush them with the olive oil and sprinkle with salt. Put into the oven and bake for about 15 minutes, or until the peppers are soft, turning them halfway through the cooking, then take them out, wrap them in clingfilm and leave until they are cold. They will steam inside the clingfilm and this will make them easier for you to peel.

Once they are cold, peel them, halve them, remove the seeds, and cut the peppers into strips about 1cm wide.

Heat the garlic oil in a pan. Add the onion and cook until it is translucent, then add the peppers and stir until heated through. Add the vinegar and let it bubble up and evaporate. Scatter with the chopped basil, toss everything together and serve.

**Cicoria e aglio**
Wild chicory and garlic

Serves 4

550g wild chicory, cleaned
2 teaspoons garlic oil (see page 60)
2 teaspoons chopped fresh chilli (green and red)
sea salt and freshly ground black pepper

Bring a pan of salted water to the boil. Add the wild chicory, blanch for about 2 minutes, drain, then cut into chunky pieces.

Heat the garlic oil in a pan, add the chilli, stir for a minute or so, then add the chicory. Cook for a minute, just to warm the chicory through, season to taste and serve.

# Polpettine di cavolfiore
Cauliflower balls

Serves 4

1 head of cauliflower
sea salt and freshly ground black pepper
25g caciocavallo or pecorino cheese, grated
70g white bread, soaked in milk, then squeezed dry
a pinch of grated nutmeg
1 large egg
100g breadcrumbs (see page 45)
vegetable oil for deep-frying

Trim the outer leaves off the cauliflower, then cut into florets, put into a pan of lightly salted water and bring to the boil. Cook until tender, about 7–8 minutes (the cauliflower needs to be soft). As soon as it is ready, drain the florets, chop them into small pieces, put them into a bowl, and leave to cool. Add the cheese, bread, nutmeg and a little pepper. Work the ingredients well to bring them all together, then shape into little balls, about 2.5cm in diameter.

Beat the egg in a shallow bowl and season with a little salt. Have ready the breadcrumbs in a separate shallow bowl. Dip the cauliflower balls into the egg, then roll them in the breadcrumbs, making sure they are well coated. Heat about 5cm of oil in a pan, making sure it comes no higher than a third of the way up. It should be 180°C. If you don't have a thermometer, test that the oil is hot enough by putting in a few breadcrumbs – if they sizzle, the oil is ready. Put in the cauliflower balls and deep-fry until golden. Lift out, drain on kitchen paper and serve hot.

### Torta di bietole e ricotta
Baked Swiss chard and ricotta

Serves 4

2 tablespoons olive oil, plus a little extra for oiling the dish
550g Swiss chard, cut into large pieces
280g ricotta
sea salt and freshly ground black pepper
2 large eggs, beaten

Preheat the oven to 180°C/350°Fgas 4 and grease a baking dish with olive oil.

Peel off the stringy outside of the Swiss chard and bring a large pan of water to the boil. Add the chard and cook for about 5 minutes, until tender, then drain well.

Put the ricotta into a bowl and crush with a fork, then season lightly and mix in the beaten eggs.

Heat the 2 tablespoons of olive oil in a pan and add the chard. Cook until the stalks are golden, and the leaves are totally wilted. Season lightly and add to the bowl of ricotta. Mix together, then transfer to the oiled baking dish, put into the preheated oven and bake for 10 minutes, until heated through.

**'Uncle Dima Licasi … was a crooked old man, with knotty arthritic joints, like an old stump of Saracen olive tree …'**
**– Luigi Pirandello, *The Oil Jar***

Towards the end of his life, Luigi Pirandello, writer of poetry, essays, plays and novels, and winner of the Nobel Prize for Literature in 1934, wrote that the olive tree was the key to understanding the Sicilian character. Pirandello was born on a farm near Agrigento, in a place with the brilliant name Càvusu, which means Chaos, surrounded by ancient olive trees, and when I look at those trees that have stood on the island for thousands of years, I know what Pirandello means. They call the oldest trees Saracens (one of the oldest is on the other side of the island, in Noto), and their gnarled, complicated and tangled trunks have witnessed thousands of years of turbulent history, but their roots are strong and powerful, and they are still able to bear the precious fruit that makes the oil the ancient Greeks called liquid gold.

In a way they are a metaphor for the complex Sicilian character: passive yet resilient and generous in the face of everything. For most Italians the gift of olive oil is an emotional thing, but for Sicilians it seems to touch something even deeper. When you think about it, it is the ultimate co-operation between man and nature, something ancient and very special. My head chef, Rino, who comes from Sciacca, says that there are two things you expect every family to have in their house: olive oil and wine, and if you don't have any oil, or you don't drink wine, they want to know what is wrong with you. You have to remember that what crude oil does now, olive oil used to do a couple of thousand years ago: it was the all-purpose oil used for lighting, medicine, everything. These days Sicilians still deep-fry using olive oil, which at home or at Locanda I would never do. I would always use vegetable oil, because olive oil has a lower smoking point and changes its nature at a very high heat and it loses some of its goodness. But to a Sicilian the only oil is olive oil.

Olives and olive trees feature often in Pirandello's novels, but he is not the only writer to draw inspiration from the territory and olive groves around Agrigento. Another is Andrea Camilleri, famous for his Inspector Montalbano novels, set in the fictional town of Vigàta, based on Camilleri's home town of Porto Empedocle, close to Agrigento and the Valle dei Templi, the valley of the Greek temples which date from the fifth century BC. Inspector Montalbano, the hero of the novels, also has an immense appetite and love of food – a favourite dish is *pasta alla Norma* (see page 186) – and when he needs to think he seeks out the branches of a great Saracen olive tree in the Valle dei Templi. In *The Scent of the Night*, Montalbano reacts with true Sicilian horror when he discovers his favourite tree torn up to make way for a new villa. 'I don't like to talk when I eat' is a favourite Montalbano expression that all Italians say these days.

Saracen olive tree

Olive oil was a late discovery for me, because I grew up in a society in Lombardy where the fats used for cooking were butter, and *lardo*, which is the fragrant and delicate-tasting, snow white pig's fat that is cured with herbs and spices, most famously in marble tubs in Colonnata in northern Tuscany. In the kitchen of my uncle's hotel and restaurant, olive oil was rarely used, so I was already a chef myself and looking for new flavours and developing dishes before I started to taste and compare different oils, and it was a great adventure. When I eventually discovered the best olive oils of Sicily, made with the three most typical olives, Biancolilla, Nocellara and Cerasuola, they seemed to suit my cooking.

In Sicily butter doesn't really count for much; as always, the terrain decides the produce, and in summer there is not masses of grass to feed the cows to make milk and then butter. One day, though, when I was at our friend Vittorio's restaurant in Porto Palo, and there were some wonderful oysters in the kitchen, I said to them, 'Let me make you some *tagliolini*.' So I made the *tagliolini* with oysters in butter sauce and some cream, the way we do it at Locanda, and they loved it; they thought I was a genius, but also the combination of butter and cream was something quite strange and very different for their palates.

The typical Sicilian oil is very full and fruity, but more gentle than the oils of central Italy, and particularly Tuscany, where they are characteristically more harsh and green. If I had to try to describe the best Sicilian oil, I would say it was full of flavours of artichokes and tomatoes.

Sicily really expanded its production of olives in the late eighties when the European Community offered grants to farmers who planted olive groves. However, wild olive trees are thought to have grown in Sicily from around 10,000 BC, since olive stones have been found in archaeological sites. It was most likely the Greeks who began cultivating them and introducing irrigation systems. In order to produce plump, fatty olives full of oil, the trees need water, but also you need maximum exposure to the sun, so not all of the island is good for growing olives, and in some mountainous areas you see that only one side of the mountain has olive trees.

When the terrain gets very dry, you have a problem, as the olives don't mature to the same level of fat inside, and so the oil production is compromised. So usually the groves are around water, by lakes, or rivers, so that water can be pumped from the source. In the production area of Castelvetrano, each of the trees has a water system going round it, which helps to keep a high yield every year.

**Olives in the mountains**

I first met Alessio Planeta when I was cooking at Olivo in London, and he came there to show us his wine. He always tells everyone I was this crazy man with hair everywhere, who came out of the kitchen all dishevelled and smelling of fish, and seemed to be going at everything at a hundred miles an hour. He thought: 'if he carries on this way, this guy is going to be dead in a couple of years!' But we got on straightaway; he is such an intelligent guy with a brilliant, dry humour. He makes me laugh so much. In some ways I think the Sicilian humour is very close to the English one: very sharp, a little cruel, but very funny.

When Alessio first showed me his olive oil project at Capparrina, outside Menfi, I was so impressed. His groves are right in front of the sea, so there is a high exposure to the sun and a high salinity: you feel you can almost taste the flavour of the sea in the oil. Over the last ten to twenty years there have been huge advances in the understanding of olive oil, and the way that picking at the right moment, and then squeezing the fruit within three hours of harvesting, will maximise the polyphenol count and therefore the health properties and quality of the oil. You can take each season's oil to a laboratory and have the content of polyphenols measured, so that you can compare the quality season on season.

Over the years I learnt more and more about oil from Alessio, and also from Armando Manni, who makes some of the most expensive oil in the world on Mount Amiata in Tuscany, and was the one who showed me just how important it is to store the oil in dark bottles, keeping out light, heat and air, in order to keep it at its organoleptic best.

I thought it would be great to make our own oil for Locanda, on a small scale. Alessio suggested that we do something with him at Planeta: no risk. But you know sometimes I like to take a bit of a risk. And so, almost by accident, we found Antonio Alfano – a third generation importer of Italian produce into England, whose parents used to have an alimentary store in Soho, near the famous Italian shop I Camisa, which has been there since the 1920s. Antonio and his cousin had inherited a piece of land in Cammarata, high up in the mountains, right in the middle of the island, close to Enna, with 11,000 trees, a mixture of very old ones and some younger, in two groves: both Nocellara and Biancolilla. And so we decided to go into business with them, and make our own oil.

The reason for growing the two varieties of olives is that the Biancolilla trees cannot inseminate each other, they need another variety to help, so for every few trees of Biancolilla that you plant, you also have to have one or two of Nocellara. Of the two, the Biancolilla is a little smaller, but produces more oil than the Nocellara, which is fatter and more buttery, and so can also be cured and eaten as a table olive.

The groves are very atmospheric. You can climb to the top of the mountain and look down over them, but because the top trees are high up, they are also vulnerable, and can be damaged by storm clouds that come in low and deposit their rain straight on to the trees. If that happens at the wrong time, the olives can be turned black.

My first experience of harvesting in November was incredible. The olive harvest follows the grape harvest, which makes for a great autumn festival season in the countryside. One of the things that really shocked me was the abundance of olives on each tree, and the thought that we had to pick them all. Very quickly.

The older trees must be harvested by hand, using a rake that lets the fruit drop into a tarpaulin, but for the younger trees that are less delicate we can use a little tractor that goes underneath and shakes the trees, so that the olives fall into a kind of upside-down umbrella. Then all the olives have to be loaded very, very carefully into a little truck, so that the ones underneath don't suffer too much pressure and start to sweat out oil.

By the time I sat down to dinner at night, my arms were aching so much that I could hardly lift them on to the table to eat, but by comparison I had it easy, because later in the day, when the pickers were still hard at work, I went down to the *frantoio* (the olive press) to see the production of the oil.

## Liquid gold

It is very rare in Sicily for people to have their own *frantoio*; instead they take their olives to the local 'oil factory' where the guys press the olives for lots of different local people and farmers, who sometimes come together under a consortium, putting their olives under one name.

These guys who press the oil are very proud of their skills and they become totally absorbed in what they are doing. The kids, wife, family … everyone gets ignored until the olives are pressed. During the harvest, you see cars pulling up two or three times a day, and often an old guy will get out and bring in two or three boxes of olives from the back of the car. Families might have one or two trees, and so they will get together with another family, pool the olives and then take them to the *frantoio* to be pressed. When they come back in the evening, they might each have sixty or seventy litres of oil, which will be put into a dark place in a cellar or under the stairs, and should be enough to last a family for a year. If you go into the small supermarket in Menfi, you will see very little oil, maybe just two or three generic brands, because most people know someone who makes oil locally. And when you go to people's houses, it is a matter of great pride if they have their own oil, and of course sometimes it is fantastic, sometimes less fantastic.

One of the things we have invested in is reserving a day at the local *frantoio*, when only our oil is made, because it seemed easy for olives from different groves to occasionally get mixed up.

When you take away the twigs and leaves and press the olives into paste you have to separate the olive oil and water, which is done in a centrifuge which pulls the oil to the top. And that is it. This first, cold pressing is what gives you Virgin Olive Oil, and provided it has an oleic acidity of less than 1 per cent, it can be labelled Extra Virgin Olive Oil, the very best quality. If an oil is just labelled Olive Oil, it will be a blend of Virgin Oil and inferior oil that has been refined in some way, or the oil will have been extracted using a faster process which involves heating. There is no doubt that this way you get more oil, but you don't have the quality.

Some people still leave stalks and leaves among the olives when they are pressed in the way that used to happen, when the olives were ground between stones, the top one being pulled by a donkey which walked round and round in a circle as the olives were crushed. Leaves and stalks give the oil a high colour, but I don't think they do any good to the flavour. I believe that you should do nothing to the oil but cold press it, that is it.

Some people play with flavoured oils, which I am not keen on. The exception is the guys in Castelvetrano who have both lemon groves and olive groves, and what they do is take the skin of the lemons and add them to the olives when they press them, and the result is brilliant.

The first time I tasted the oil we had made, I thought it was extraordinary. All the artichoke, tomato flavours were there, with no bitterness or sharpness, just a wonderful rounded feeling in the mouth. It is hard to describe what a very special thing it is to think that you can be in the olive groves picking the fruit in the morning, and literally that evening you have your oil. Of course it is not the finished oil at this point, you have to let it rest for four or five weeks, so that the sediment settles and it can be filtered until it is clear and shining, but it is *your* oil.

### Sicilian Samurais

Olive trees grow very aggressively; even the one we started off in a pot at home in London. When it got too big for the pot I dug a massive hole and planted it out in the garden, and when next I looked there were about twenty new shoots already. Because the trees produce shoots in such abundance, once the harvest is over the olive farmers have to do the *scalzatura*, literally the 'scaling down'. They go round like Samurais, with a sharp implement that is something between a shovel and a hoe, slicing away the new growth with clean, deadly accuracy. You watch and think, 'They are going to hit the tree,' but they never do. Even so, you inspect the trunk, expecting to see little cuts, but there is nothing.

Along the road from Porto Palo towards Castelvetrano, there are olive trees everywhere, all trimmed, and suddenly you see one that has been let go, and you can't believe how enormous it is. That is when you really understand the purpose of the *scalzatura*.

### Olives for the table

When you travel around Sicily, sometimes in an old village between the bakery and the shop selling relics of the saints you can find someone selling the typical produce of the area. I found the green Nocellara table olives from Castelvetrano that we serve in Locanda in this way. I tasted the olives, and

thought they were so fruity and rich and beautiful that I looked up the name of the producer and found it on the map. Sometimes when you approach growers they can be very secretive, and wary, but the farmer was happy to talk to me and now we import his olives. A journalist who wrote a review of Locanda wrote that you could tell our seriousness straight away by the type of olives that were served. He said that he had eaten a lot of olives in his time, but these were something new.

The point is that even though olives have been grown in Sicily for thousands of years, they have rarely been seen outside the island. Apart from the Nocellara, varieties like the big, green Verdello, Cerasuola, which is produced near Sciacca, Tonda Iblea, from Ragusa, and Moresca, grown around Catania, Siracusa and Ragusa, are all eaten as table olives, sometimes served as *cunzate*, with pieces of garlic, onion, carrot and celery. Or you have *pane e cunzate*: you take the bread, crush a tomato into it with some extra virgin olive oil, salt, pepper and oregano, and eat it with the olives.

There is also a Slow Food Presidium that brings together small producers of the Minuta olive, a very old variety from the hills of Nebrodi, where the old trees grow in the forests where the rare black pigs roam. As well as being pressed for oil, the olives are traditionally cured in a *tinello*, a brine of water and sea salt flavoured with local herbs: wild fennel, garlic, bay and rosemary.

# Cuscus e zuppa
# Couscous and soup

Make couscous not war


– Motto of the Couscous Festival of 'cultural
integration', held at San Vito lo Capo, Trapani

One March, we spent a long weekend in the little coastal town of San Vito lo Capo, above Trapani, a very beautiful place with brightly painted fishing boats, a long sandy beach and spectacular mountains behind. It was off-season, and everywhere was half closed, but the town's two or three restaurants that specialise only in couscous (or *cuscus*, as it is often written) were open. On Saturday night the place began to come alive, and on Sunday people from Palermo and the villages in the mountains all seemed to come down to the town for their Sunday lunch of couscous.

It was the Arabs who brought the idea of these little balls of semolina to Sicily during their rule of over 150 years between the ninth and eleventh centuries. Often we talk about couscous grains, but in fact although they look like grains, they are made by combining coarse and fine semolina flour with a little water to form balls. Traditionally, women used to make the couscous by hand, working the semolina with damp fingers and the lightest of touches – a technique known as *'ncocciatura*. Then the couscous would be graded into different sizes and allowed to dry so that it could be stored. As well as giving an alternative to rice or pasta, this must also have been a useful way of prolonging the life of the flour, because the dried couscous would keep better. In the province of Trapani, which stretches around the west coast of the island, facing Tunisia, from Erice down to Agrigento, the couscous tradition has remained strong. All around this coast you see tiny houses, with little windows and thick walls to keep the heat out, and you think, 'This could be North Africa.'

In June each year there is a big competition in San Vito lo Capo among chefs to see who will represent Italy at the massive couscous festival later in the year, in September, when he or she will compete against chefs from countries like Morocco, Egypt, Algeria, Tunisia, Israel and France for the title of best couscous chef of the Mediterranean. Then you see all kinds of crazy things, but that is not what most people come for throughout the year. They come to eat couscous in the traditional way it has been eaten here for centuries, and to enjoy the conviviality that comes with sharing big bowls of food.

When you talk about couscous to people around Trapani it is clear that it is something very special to them. In a way it reminds them of who they are. I feel the Sicilian pride in the fact that they have inherited this tradition, and they are the only people in Italy who make this dish – almost, they are the only people on the island who do it, because it is a very localised thing.

You do find semolina elsewhere in Italy, such as *fregola*, but the balls of semolina dough are much larger, and tend to be added to soup, whereas in Trapani the couscous is served separately in a bowl in the same way as in North Africa, but with one big difference: in the North African tradition a full-blown couscous involves many different meats and sausages, with vegetables in a soupy sauce, whereas the true Trapanese couscous is done with fish. You are given a big bowl of couscous, and then the fish stew or soup is served separately and you mix the two together. Of course, you can find meat couscous too, but it is the fish one that people come especially to eat.

Sometimes the fish stew (or soup – the words are really interchangeable) is done with tomatoes, sometimes not, sometimes with lots of little fishes. Once this would have been the poor fisherman's version, born, like the French bouillabaisse, out of the need not to waste the fish that were too small to be sold at market; the irony being that these little fish are usually full of fantastic, gelatinous flavour, because the ratio of bone to flesh is very high.

In the time we were in San Vito lo Capo, I ate couscous every day. There were some made with tuna, clams and mussels, Plaxy fell in love with a beautiful one made with the local brown lobster, and you could even have couscous for breakfast – with vegetables and a few prawns, capers, onions and diced cucumber.

So much variety, and all so good. You never understand, until you have eaten a really good couscous, what it should feel like: the sheer velvetiness in your mouth. In London we have got used to couscous being almost a fast food. Now in Sicily most people buy good-quality, ready-prepared couscous that needs only a single steaming, but for a couscous to be really special it must be double-cooked, so that it swells up and becomes really plump and can properly absorb the fish soup that it is served with.

Watching the people doing this, in the way they have done it for decades, is a privilege. First they wet the grains, then they put them into a *couscoussiera*, which is like a colander with a lid that sits over a deep pot of boiling water, so that the steam envelops the grain. They mix some flour and water into a paste, dip a cloth into it, and tie this around the point where the 'colander' meets the pot, to seal it so that no steam can escape and inside the temperature is at its maximum. Then they let it steam for about twenty to thirty minutes, depending on the size of the grains. Next, and this is the most important stage, they turn out the couscous, spray it with cold water and you can literally see the grains swell up in front of you. The problem is now that some of them will start to stick together, so you must work it with your hands to break it up. Then you are ready to go. About ten to fifteen minutes before you want to serve the couscous you put it back into the *couscoussiera*, and when you take it out, it will have the perfect, soft silky texture to take up the flavours of the sauce that you are going to serve it with.

When you travel south from San Vito lo Capo to Marsala and Mazara del Vallo, there is a big Tunisian population; many Tunisians work on the fishing boats and on the land, and some of the restaurants are entirely Tunisian. We ate at one, in Mazara del Vallo, and the meal blew me away. The restaurant was run by a family. The mother and daughter were both beautiful and the father was a wonderful character but the worst waiter you could imagine. Every time he came to our table he forgot something, but when the food arrived it was extraordinary: flat unleavened bread with bowls of spicy vegetable dips, made with aubergines, and artichokes, and there was a kind of *caponata*, but with no vinegar, and to follow, an incredible couscous. It was as if, in this one meal, you could actually taste the two cultures of North Africa and Sicily merging.

**Cuscus con zuppa di pesce**
Couscous with fish soup

Serves 4

olive oil
1 tablespoon garlic oil (see page 60)
1 small onion, chopped
2 celery stalks, chopped
2 garlic cloves, finely chopped
1 fresh red chilli, chopped
a pinch of ground cinnamon
2 bay leaves
150g tomato purée
1kg mixed fish (such as grouper, gurnard, cod, monkfish), cut into large
pieces
400g medium couscous
1 tablespoon parsley and garlic (see page 60)

Heat a little olive oil in a large pan and add the garlic oil. Put in the chopped
onion, celery, garlic and chilli, together with the cinnamon and bay leaves,
and cook, stirring, for a few minutes until the vegetables are just tender, but
not coloured. Add the tomato purée and cook for a few more minutes, then
add the fish, together with 4 litres of water, and bring to the boil. Turn down
the heat and simmer for 15 minutes.

Lift out the big pieces of fish (leaving all the little pieces in the pan), transfer
them to a warm plate and cover them with foil, then carry on simmering the
soup slowly for 1 hour.

Meanwhile, steam the couscous for about 20 minutes in a *couscoussiera* (if
you don't have one, put a fine-meshed colander over a pan of water, and
cover with foil so that no steam can escape), then fluff up with a fork. About
10 minutes before you're ready to serve steam the couscous again.

Take out any bones from the bigger pieces of fish, put the pieces into a
pan with enough of the fish soup just to cover, and put on the hob for long
enough to heat the fish through. Transfer to a shallow bowl, and scatter with
half the parsley and garlic.

Put the couscous and the fish soup into separate bowls and scatter the soup
with the rest of the parsley and garlic. Serve with the pieces of fish, and let
people help themselves to some of each.

**Zuppa di pesce**
Fish soup

This is a more elaborate fish soup, which is best served on its own, rather than with couscous. Of course, if I was making this in Sicily it wouldn't seem elaborate at all, because I would just go to the fish market at Sciacca, and have my pick of every kind of fish and shellfish. By marinating the fish for the stock overnight, you infuse it with as much flavour as possible.

Serves 4–6

4 plum tomatoes
300g red mullet fillets
200g swordfish
200g grouper or other firm-fleshed fish
100g monkfish
1 small squid, cleaned
200g clams
200g mussels
140ml dry white wine
1 teaspoon garlic oil (see page 60)
1 fresh green chilli, finely chopped
1 bay leaf
100g medium langoustines
100g shelled prawns
2 rounds of crusty white bread per person
1 garlic clove, peeled
sea salt and freshly ground pepper
1 teaspoon parsley and garlic (see page 60)
a little extra virgin olive oil for finishing

For the stock:
1kg gurnard, cleaned
1 x 400g tin of chopped tomatoes
3 garlic cloves, crushed
2 bay leaves
a small bunch of fresh basil
a small bunch of fresh flat-leaf parsley

For the stock, cut the gurnard into small pieces and put into a bowl with the tinned tomatoes, crushed garlic, bay leaves, basil and parsley. Mix everything together and put into the fridge overnight.

The next day, put the fish mixture into a large pan, add 2 litres of water, bring to the boil, then turn down the heat and simmer for 20 minutes. Pass through a fine sieve and set aside.

Put the plum tomatoes into a pan of boiling water for 10 seconds, then drain under cold water and you should be able to peel them easily. Cut them in half, scoop out the seeds with a teaspoon, and cut each half into quarters.

Cut the red mullet, swordfish, grouper and monkfish into pieces of about 2cm, and cut the squid into rings.

Scrub the clams and mussels separately (pulling any beards from the mussels) under running water and discard any that are open. Put them into a large pan with half the white wine over a high heat, cover, and cook, shaking the pan from time to time, until all the shells have opened. Remove from the heat, then strain off the cooking liquid and reserve it. Discard any mussels or clams whose shells haven't opened. Take about 80 per cent of the mussels and clams out of their shells (discard the shells), and leave the rest in their shells. Keep on one side.

Heat the garlic oil in a large pan, put in the chilli, bay leaf, chopped fish, squid, langoustines and prawns, and stir until all are coloured. Add the rest of the white wine and bubble up until the alcohol evaporates. Add the quartered tomatoes, then the reserved cooking liquor from the mussels and clams and the fish stock. Cook for 5 minutes, then put in the reserved mussels and clams (both shelled and unshelled).

Meanwhile, toast the bread, and rub each slice with the clove of garlic. Season the soup to taste and pour into bowls, making sure each bowl has some of the clams and mussels that are in their shells. Put 2 slices of toast into each bowl, sprinkle with the parsley and garlic and drizzle with a little extra virgin olive oil.

## Zuppa di fave e finocchio
Broad bean and fennel soup

Soup made with dried broad beans is something many of the older generation
in Sicily prefer not to make any more, as it reminds them of the times when
many people were so poor that they often had little else but dried beans
to live on. However, for a younger generation of cooks it is a traditional
dish that should be celebrated, and adding some fresh broad beans gives a
contrast in textures.

Serves 4

600g dried broad beans
1 teaspoon chopped wild fennel (or 1 teaspoon of fennel seeds, soaked
in a little water)
200g fresh broad beans
olive oil
1 small onion, finely diced
1 medium carrot, finely diced
1 celery stalk, finely diced
sea salt and freshly ground black pepper
extra virgin olive oil for finishing

Soak the dried broad beans in cold water overnight, then drain.

The next day, put the soaked beans and the wild fennel (or the soaked fennel
seeds) into a pan, add enough water to cover, and bring to the boil. Put a
lid on the pan, then turn down the heat and cook slowly for about 2 hours,
or until the beans are completely soft, adding water as necessary. Blend by
hand or machine until smooth and set aside.

While the dried beans are cooking, blanch the fresh beans in boiling unsalted
water for a couple of minutes, then drain and peel off the skins.

In a separate pan, heat a little olive oil, then add the diced onion, carrot and
celery and cook until soft but not coloured. Add the fresh broad beans and
the blended beans and cook for 15 minutes, then season and serve drizzled
with a little extra virgin olive oil.

## Zuppa di ceci e calamari
Chickpea soup with squid

Serves 4

500g dried chickpeas
a sprig of rosemary
a small bunch of sage leaves
2 bay leaves
olive oil
1 onion, finely chopped
2 carrots, finely chopped
4 celery stalks, finely chopped
1.5 litres vegetable stock
sea salt and freshly ground black pepper
1 teaspoon garlic oil (see page 60)
200g squid, cut into rings
1 dessertspoon parsley and garlic (see page 60)
a little extra virgin olive oil for finishing

Soak the chickpeas in cold water overnight, then drain.

Tie the rosemary, sage and bay leaves together with some kitchen string to make a bouquet garni.

Heat a little olive oil in a pan and add the chopped onion, carrots and celery. Cook until the vegetables are soft but not coloured. Add the chickpeas and the bouquet garni. Cook for 5 minutes, stirring until everything is well mixed. Add 1 litre of the stock, bring to the boil, then turn down the heat and simmer for 45 minutes or until the chickpeas are soft, adding more stock as necessary.

Put the contents of the pan into a food processor. Blitz until smooth and then pass through a sieve. Taste and season. The soup should be quite thick and creamy, but if it is too thick, add a little more stock.

Heat a little more olive oil in a pan and add the garlic oil. Add the squid and cook for no more than a minute, otherwise it will be tough. Add the parsley and garlic.

Pour the soup into bowls, with some squid in the middle of each one. Drizzle with a little extra virgin olive oil and grind some fresh black pepper over the top.

### Ganeffe alle zafferano
Cheese and saffron rice balls in beef broth

This a soup that is typical in Enna, and there are all kinds of small variations. The most usual of these is a 'white' version of the soup, which is made with chicken stock instead of beef stock, and no saffron.

Serves 4

500g arborio rice
1 teaspoon sea salt
a pinch of good-quality saffron threads (about 15)
4 large eggs
60g pecorino or caciocavallo cheese, grated, plus another 80g for serving
plain flour, for dredging
vegetable oil for deep-frying
240ml good beef stock

Bring 1.6 litres of water to the boil in a pan. Add the rice, salt and saffron, bring back to the boil and cook for about 15 minutes, until the rice is tender and the liquid has been absorbed. Remove from the heat, leave to cool, then beat in 3 of the eggs and 60g of the cheese. Form the mixture into little balls, the size of hazelnuts.

Beat the remaining egg. Have the flour ready in a shallow bowl, and the beaten egg in another, and dip the rice balls first into the flour, and then into the egg.

Heat around 2.5cm of vegetable oil in a large pan, making sure the oil doesn't come any higher than a third of the way up the pan. The oil must be hot, but not smoking, before you add the rice balls (if you have a thermometer it should be around 170°C, otherwise test it by putting in a few breadcrumbs – if they sizzle gently the oil is ready). Working in batches (being careful not to crowd the pan or you will lower the temperature of the oil), fry the rice balls for a few minutes, moving them around until they are golden all over. Drain well on kitchen paper.

Meanwhile, bring the stock to the boil in a pan. Divide the rice balls between bowls, pour the beef stock over the top and scatter with the rest of the grated cheese.

**Sciusceddu**
Meatballs with cheese soufflé in broth

This is a typical Easter soup in Messina. Traditionally, *sciusceddu* is made in a similar way to *stracciatella*, with breadcrumbs, ricotta and egg poured into hot beef broth and the egg broken up in strands with a fork.

This is a slightly different take on it, in that the ricotta and egg are made into a little soufflé instead. The soufflé is made with both grated and chopped cheese – the chopped cheese will melt inside as the soufflé cooks.

Serves 4

80g bread, soaked in a little milk
400g minced beef or veal
150g pecorino cheese, grated
2 eggs, beaten
1 small onion, chopped
1 tablespoon parsley and garlic (see page 60)
1 litre good beef stock

For the soufflé:
4 large eggs, plus 4 large egg whites
450g good sheep's milk ricotta
4 tablespoons grated aged pecorino or caciocavallo cheese
2 tablespoons young pecorino or caciocavallo cheese (or you could use Emmenthal), chopped
sea salt and freshly ground black pepper
a little melted unsalted butter for greasing the ramekins
about 2 tablespoons fine breadcrumbs (see page 45) for dusting the ramekins

Preheat the oven to 180°C/350°F/gas 4.

To make the meatballs, squeeze the bread and put into a bowl with the minced meat, cheese, beaten eggs, onion and the parsley and garlic. Form into balls about 1.5cm in diameter.

Bring the stock to the boil in a large pan, ready to cook the meatballs.

Meanwhile, separate the 4 whole eggs.

Put the ricotta through a sieve so that it is smooth and combine it with the egg yolks, cheeses, salt and pepper. Beat the remaining 4 egg whites with the extra egg whites until stiff peaks form, and gently fold into the ricotta mixture.

Paint 4 soufflé dishes with melted butter. Spoon in some breadcrumbs, shake the ramekins so that the butter is well covered in crumbs, then tip out the excess. Divide the ricotta mixture between the ramekins. It should come about three-quarters of the way up the dishes.

Put into the preheated oven and bake for 8–10 minutes, until puffed up and golden.

Don't open the door while the soufflés are baking, or you will let cool air in and they will deflate.

While the soufflés are in the oven, put the meatballs into the boiling stock, turn the heat down to a simmer and cook for about 5 minutes, until the meat is cooked through.

To serve, turn out the soufflés, put one in the centre of each bowl and spoon the stock and meatballs around.

# Pasta

To celebrate his feast day, to confirm his status, and to satisfy his soul, what the Sicilian really craved was a nice big plate of pasta!

– Mary Taylor Simeti, *Sicilian Food: Recipes from Italy's Abundant Isle*

There is a story, dating back to the first part of the thirteenth century, about a kind of pasta miracle that happened when a hermit from Ragusa called Brother William was invited to eat at the house of a local man. This man played a joke on the hermit by filling the macaroni with some kind of mud, but when Brother William arrived, he blessed the food, and when the people started to eat, the mud had turned into ricotta (apparently this story was presented as evidence for William's beatification, centuries later). So we know that by the thirteenth century the Sicilians had pasta, and not only that, they had tubular pasta; and they also had ricotta. So they were way ahead of everyone else in Italy. Already they had understood how to transform and shape pasta dough into something that worked ergonomically and could be filled with ricotta.

According to ancient frescoes found near Rome, some kind of pasta had been made in Italy since Etruscan times, and the Romans who followed the Etruscans made *lugane*, a kind of lasagne, by mixing flour and water, which was most likely baked on the fire, but later may have been cooked in water.

The Romans in Sicily turned the island into their own granary, planting the plains with durum wheat, but it was the Arabs who propelled the growing of wheat and the production of pasta into something that could be done on a commercial basis, building underground irrigation systems which took water through pillars of cement, to nourish the wheat, and producing a kind of dried vermicelli on a large scale.

By the twelfth century, when the Normans, who followed the Arabs, had conquered the island, the making of an early form of pasta was already established. In 1154 the Norman King Roger II commissioned an Arabian geographer, Al-Idrisi, to publish a survey of the island, which became known as 'The Book of Roger'. In it Al-Idrisi talks about this food made from semolina, shaped into long strands – he called it by the Arab name of *itriya* – which was manufactured in Trabia near Palermo, 'in such great quantity as to supply both the towns of Calabria and those of the Muslim and Christian territories as well, to which large shipments are sent'.

So it is clear that centuries before pasta became the favourite food of all Italy, and Naples, with its southern heat and warm dry sea winds, became known as the epicentre of dried pasta (*pasta secca*), Sicily, just across the water and sharing a similar microclimate, was already becoming known as an island of *mangiamaccheroni* (macaroni-eaters). Even now there is such a love of pasta in Sicily that many people think nothing of eating it twice a day.

In my native northern Italy, we specialise in fresh and filled pasta, made with eggs. If you were to go into a *pasteria* in Turin, in front of you would be trays full of ravioli, ravioli, ravioli in all shapes and sizes. But in Sicily, as in Naples, most of the pasta is dried. Even when it is freshly made at home, it is without eggs and it is allowed to dry out. It is simply that the Sicilian climate, which allows the people to dry pasta very successfully, makes it difficult to work with fresh pasta, which is quite delicate, so you always have

to work at keeping it at the right temperature and humidity, in order that it stays soft. In a hot Sicilian kitchen, the moment you laid it out to fill it and cut it into shapes, it would start to dry out and crack. One of the few times I had ravioli was with ricotta and pork at Easter time in Modica.

While straight pasta, such as spaghetti or vermicelli, would mostly be bought in the shops, at home mothers and grandmothers would make their own pasta and cut and twist it into all sorts of different shapes, and in most Sicilian homes you see little iron implements that would have been used for the shaping. But what I see is a more relaxed attitude to what shape goes with what sauce, compared to other regions of Italy, where there are always very specific and strict local rules concerning the ergonomics of a pasta dish.

In a way, the use of pasta is like a barometer of Sicily's social history. From having been the food of the poor for so many years, suddenly you reach a point around the fourteenth and fifteenth centuries when pasta became the food of the barons and the upper classes, and great ceremonial timballi would be prepared with spices, truffles and ingredients such as chicken livers mixed with macaroni, and encased in pastry. The most famous description of one of these baroque dishes is in *Il Gattopardo (The Leopard)*, Giuseppe Tomasi di Lampedusa's beautiful but mournful story of Don Fabrizio, Prince of Salina, railing against the forces of revolution and change that would mean the end of his aristocratic way of life, as Garibaldi's men landed in Sicily.

Having retreated to his country residence, Donnafugata, the Prince entertains the local dignitaries, stalwartly refusing to follow the new French fashion for beginning the meal with soup. Instead, 'three lackeys in green, gold and powder entered, each holding a great silver dish containing a towering macaroni pie ... the aspect of those monumental dishes of macaroni was worthy of the quivers of admiration they evoked. The burnished gold of the crusts, the fragrance of sugar and cinnamon they exuded, were but preludes to the delights released from the interior when the knife broke the crust; first came a spice-laden haze, then chicken livers, hard-boiled eggs, sliced ham, chicken and truffles in masses of piping hot, glistening macaroni, to which the meat juice gave an exquisite hue of suede.'

Sometimes you still find these incredible kinds of dishes. At carnival time I have seen *pasta al forno* (baked pasta), made with layers of lasagne, and in between the layers is short pasta, with salami, cheese, tomato sauce and béchamel. At Easter time there may be eggs inside, or *polpette*, meatballs (see page 237).

In one restaurant I even came across a layered baked pasta made with *cipperones* (small calamari – the name comes from the Spanish *chipirones*), almonds and cheese. Such an unlikely combination – again that shellfish and cheese mixture, the idea of which horrifies northern Italians – but in Sicily you just have to forget about these beliefs, because the way they make the flavours work is incredible.

*Timballo di maccheroni* (page 245)

One of the big traditions around the coast is to take a *pasta al forno* to the beach for Sunday lunch. It is 40 degrees in summer, and the families arrive with this big tray of pasta straight from the oven. You see the little kids with their paper plates being given big slices of it, and then the mothers don't let them swim for three hours because they have eaten so much. I suppose, though, that this is less of a tribute to baronial cooking than a throwback to the tradition of the mothers and grandmothers taking a baked pasta out to the workers in the fields. The workers, known as the *bracciante* (*braccio* is the word for arm), would live in the village, but at times of harvest they would move out into the fields, sometimes staying in the little houses that were dotted around the farmland, going from one to the other, but still the food had to be brought out to them by the women of the village. So, you can imagine, a hot, filling dish of *pasta al forno*, taken from the oven, would stay warm as the women walked out with the food.

As well as seasonal pastas, and pastas for every religious feast day, each of the nine provinces of the island, Agrigento, Caltanissetta, Catania, Enna, Messina, Palermo, Ragusa, Siracusa and Trapani, has its own special pasta dish that represents the local traditions and ingredients of the area, though of course they will be made slightly differently in every village. In the kitchen at Locanda we have five Sicilian chefs, some from Sciacca in the west of the island, and some from Catania in the east, and if one of them mentions a recipe from the west side, the boys from the east will say: 'I don't know that one.'

In Agrigento in the south, which is the province I know best, the typical pasta is *maccaruneddi* (short tubular pasta) *con salsa rossa e melanzane*: small macaroni with aubergines, and a 'pink' sauce made with tomatoes. In inland Caltanissetta, the characteristic pasta is *cavatieddi al sugo di maiale* (with a ragù of pork), and in Catania it is the famous *pasta alla Norma*, with aubergine, tomato and ricotta (see page 186). In Enna, the only Sicilian province not to have a seashore, instead of pasta you have *frascatula di polenta di grano e verdure*, which is maize, cooked like polenta and mixed with vegetables. Messina is known for *pasta ai quadrucci di pesce spada* (see page 232): short pasta with a sauce made with squares of swordfish, because the swordfish that come through the straits of Messina are the best in the world, they say.

Palermo is famous for one of the most well-known Sicilian pastas, the sweet and sour *pasta con le sarde*, with fresh sardines, salted anchovies, sultanas, pine kernels, and the wild fennel that grows everywhere (see page 215). Ragusa, known for the production of *fave* (broad beans), has a pasta dish with puréed dried beans, *rigatoncini* (a smaller version of the short, ridged tubular *rigatoni*) *con maccu di fave*. *Pasta fritta* is the typical dish from Siracusa, made with *capellini*, fried so that it is crispy, in fresh orange juice, with breadcrumbs and *miele di timo* (thyme honey). And finally, in Trapani, *spaghetti alla trapanese* is the signature recipe, made with *pesto trapanese*: tomatoes, pounded with almonds, garlic and basil, and sometimes with pecorino over the top, not grated, but cut roughly so you can bite into it (see page 199). What is interesting is that of the nine provinces, only one of them includes meat in its representative dish.

## A note about cooking pasta

The way to keep pasta separate when it is cooking, so the strands or shapes don't stick to each other, is not to add oil to the cooking water, but to make sure there is plenty of water. The ratio I use is 1 litre of water to every 100g of pasta.

You need to salt it well, otherwise the pasta will taste bland – to every litre of water I add 5g of sea salt. I used to say 10g but I'm getting older and more health-conscious! Put it in as soon as the water starts to boil, so that it disperses evenly.

A typical Sicilian way of cooking pasta with vegetables such as broccoli is to blanch the vegetable first in a big pan of salted water, take it out ready to sauté and toss with olive oil, and then re-use the vegetable water to boil the pasta.

The way they tend to prepare the pasta in Sicilian homes is just to put the sauce and pasta in a big bowl and toss it all together; however, in the recipes in this chapter, I have suggested you do as we do at Locanda, and toss the pasta through the sauce in the pan in which you have made it, adding some of the cooking water from the pasta. This allows the starch in the cooking water to thicken the sauce and helps it to cling to the pasta.

## Reginette alla Norma
Reginette with aubergine, tomato and salted ricotta

My first real job in a kitchen was at Il Passatore in Varese, about half an hour's drive north of Corgeno, where I grew up. Although everyone was upset with me that I didn't want to go and work in La Cinzianella, my uncle's hotel and restaurant, it was through someone who had worked with my uncle that I got the job. Il Passatore was quite a famous restaurant, and it was there that I worked with the legendary Corrado Sironi, the 'Risotto King'. Sironi was a wonderful, crazy character and the kitchen at Il Passatore was an exciting place to be.

After I had been there a while a guy called Antonio arrived who was from Catania. At seventeen I had never really come across a Sicilian before, so it was fascinating to hear him talk about the island and the food; he always gave such a positive impression of Sicilian cuisine. He was much older than most of us, very small, but such a sweet guy. He was in charge of the pasta, and he used to stutter: I remember him trying to call away the pappardelle … pa, pa, pa … it was very funny.

One day someone said, 'Cook us a Sicilian dish,' and so he made *pasta alla Norma*, the famous dish with fried aubergines, tomato and basil, with short pasta, which is named in honour of the opera *Norma* by Vincenzo Bellini, who was born in Catania. The story is that the name was created when Nino Martoglio, a Sicilian writer, poet and theatre director who was a contemporary of Bellini, tasted the dish in Catania, and loved it so much that he compared it to Bellini's operatic masterpiece.

I could understand this because I, too, was completely blown away that a pasta could taste so good. It was one of the most vibrant dishes I ever had in my life, and I still remember the flavours. I had never had fried aubergine before, let alone with pasta. In our house aubergine went into ratatouille, that's all. It wasn't a vegetable that was well known or really used much in the north before the sixties and seventies. It was also the first time I tasted salted ricotta, which is a very special thing in Sicily (see page 190). Everyone thought the pasta was brilliant – mind you, they never let Antonio put the dish on the menu. It may have been good, but it was, after all, a *southern* dish!

After a year, he went back to Sicily, and whenever I go there, I think it would be good to look him up, but you can't just roll up in Catania and say, 'Anyone know a guy called Antonio?'

In Sicily, around Siracusa and Noto, this is often made with *taccuna di mulinu*, which is homemade durum wheat lasagne, rolled up, then cut into strips and left to dry for a couple of hours before cooking, or a wavy-edged pasta, such as *reginette* or *malfadine*, as in this recipe. Or you might see it done with *sedanini*, which is short ridged tubular pasta, similar to *penne*, but thinner and slightly curved. If you can't find it, use *penne* instead.

Serves 4

3 aubergines (preferably the round, pale violet ones)
sea salt and freshly ground black pepper
3 garlic cloves
a sprig of rosemary
5 plum tomatoes
500ml vegetable oil
2 tablespoons olive oil
2 tablespoons tomato purée
400g *reginette* or *mafaldine*
a bunch of fresh basil
3 tablespoons salted ricotta, chopped
extra virgin olive oil, to serve

Preheat the oven to 220°C/425°F/gas 7.

Cut 2 of the aubergines into dice of about 3cm, sprinkle with salt and leave
to drain in a colander for at least 2 hours.

Cut the remaining aubergine in half lengthways, then put the halves, skin
side down, on a clean work surface and with a sharp knife score the flesh
diagonally one way, quite deeply, and then the other way, to give a diamond
pattern.

Slice one of the garlic cloves finely, and push the slices into the aubergine
halves at the points where the scoring crosses. Push some small sprigs of
rosemary into the remaining slots.

Put the halves of the aubergine back together, wrap in foil and put into the
oven for about 20–25 minutes, until soft. Take out the garlic and rosemary
and discard them, then scoop out the aubergine flesh and put it into a
colander. Leave to drain and cool, then chop it finely.

Put the tomatoes into a pan of boiling water for 10 seconds, then drain
under cold water and you should be able to peel them easily. Cut them in
half, scoop out the seeds with a teaspoon, and then cut each half in half
again.

Heat the vegetable oil in a deep pan, making sure it comes no higher than
a third of the way up the pan. It should be 180°C. If you don't have a
thermometer, put in a few breadcrumbs, and if they sizzle straight away
the oil is ready. Gently squeeze the diced aubergines to get rid of the excess
liquid, put them into the oil and fry them until golden, a handful at a time.
Drain on kitchen paper, and pat dry.

Finely chop the remaining 2 cloves of garlic. Heat the olive oil in a pan large
enough to take the cooked pasta later, then add the chopped garlic and cook

gently without colouring it. Add the chopped aubergine flesh, cook gently for a couple of minutes, then add the tomato purée, stir, cook for another minute or so, and season.

Meanwhile, bring a pan of water to the boil, add salt, and put in the pasta. Cook for about a minute less than the time given on the packet, so that it is al dente. Drain, reserving some of the cooking water, and add to the aubergine sauce, along with the fresh tomatoes. Toss all together for a minute or so, then add the fried aubergine and the basil. Toss again with a small amount of the salted ricotta, adding a little of the reserved cooking water if necessary to loosen the sauce. Serve scattered with the rest of the salted ricotta, and drizzle with some extra virgin olive oil.

### 'Everybody eats it. Everybody understands it'

In some old stables in Modica I watched ricotta being made in an enormous cauldron over a fire of olive branches. I promise you the ricotta pot was about five feet tall. The cheesemaker had just made some fresh *tuma*, pushing the just-coagulated curds into the bamboo baskets that give the rind of the cheese its rough-edged pattern. And now he was reheating the whey that was left over, to make ricotta.

*Ricotta*

Ricotta literally means 're-cooked', and this is what it is: the whey from cheesemaking is brought up to a high temperature, which causes the proteins to come to the surface in little lumps, which are skimmed off and drained in rush baskets, ready to be sold as *ricotta fresca* (fresh ricotta).

Sicily is possibly the best place in the world to eat ricotta. Everybody eats it, everybody understands it, everybody knows everything about how it tastes. So the quality is very, very high.

When I tasted that ricotta in the stables in Modica, I thought, 'I am never going to eat ricotta like this again.' It was hot and creamy and incredible. Unusually for Sicily it was made with cow's milk. The more usual ricotta is done with sheep's milk, since the island's heat and terrain are much more suited to sheep than cows, and most of the cheeses are made with sheep's milk.

But the cheesemaker had decided that his sheep's ricotta would be too strong for my taste. It would certainly be too strong for the taste of the rest of my family. My son Jack still remembers the rustic sheep's cheese ricotta we tasted many years ago near Sambuca, inland from Sciacca.

A shepherd was cooking up some ricotta for his lunch, and he invited us to taste some. I thought it was amazing, but Jack still says the flavour of the animal was so strong, it was like kissing a sheep!

Because *ricotta fresca* is such a delicate thing it cannot be kept for long, so it is also preserved by dry-salting, pressing and maturing, so that it becomes semi-hard. Then it is known as *ricotta salata*, and when it is made with sheep's cheese it has a punchy, salty, slightly farmyardy bite, that is brilliant grated, sliced or crumbled over dishes, most famously *pasta alla Norma* (see page 186).

*Ricotta salata*

## Pasta alla carrettiera
Truck drivers' pasta

This gets its name because it is the kind of typical, simple, quick pasta that drivers could get at a truck stop – some say it goes back to a time when carters pulled up by the side of the road and boiled pasta over a fire. The raw sauce would be ready-made, and only had to be tossed through the pasta. One thing about spaghetti in Sicily: I rarely saw anything other than big spaghetti – spaghettoni really – from no. 14 upwards. You could substitute linguine or bucatini.

Serves 4

450g chopped ripe tomatoes
2 tablespoons extra virgin olive oil
2 garlic cloves, finely chopped
10 basil leaves, finely chopped
5 mint leaves, finely chopped
sea salt and freshly ground black pepper
400g spaghetti, linguine or *bucatini*
80g pecorino cheese, grated

Put the chopped tomatoes into a bowl with the extra virgin olive oil, chopped garlic and herbs, season and leave to infuse for 1 hour.

Bring a pan of water to the boil, add salt, then put in the pasta and use a fork to curl it around the pan, so that it is all submerged under the water quickly.

Cook for about a minute less than the time given on the packet, so that the pasta is al dente. Drain, reserving some of the cooking water, and add to the tomatoes, with most of the pecorino. Toss well, adding some of the cooking water from the pasta if necessary. Finish with the rest of the pecorino.

**Reginette ricce con ricotta e cavolfiore fritto**
Wavy pasta ribbons with ricotta and sautéed cauliflower

When you look at a recipe that just has cauliflower, ricotta and pasta as its main ingredients, I have to admit it doesn't sound very exciting, but in Sicily the cauliflowers are bright green and bursting with flavour – sometimes, to be confusing, they are also called *broccolo*. When you see box upon box of them piled up in the back of the little Ape Piaggos that the growers drive around, they look amazingly colourful. When they are tossed through the pasta with the best fresh ricotta, this is a really beautiful, simple dish, one that people make all the time at home. The key is to buy really good ricotta. If you want to add a few different flavours and textures, you could try the Sicilian favourites of toasted pine nuts and sultanas.

Serves 4

350g cauliflower
sea salt
2 tablespoons olive oil
1 tablespoon garlic oil (see page 60)
400g *reginette* or *malfadine* (wavy-edged pasta ribbons), or *fettuccine*
200g good fresh sheep's ricotta
100g pecorino cheese, grated

Optional:
1 tablespoon toasted pine nuts
1 tablespoon sultanas

Break the cauliflower into florets and cook in plenty of lightly salted boiling water until just tender; drain well, reserving the cooking water, allow to cool and then chop into smaller pieces.

Heat the olive oil and garlic oil in a pan and sauté the cauliflower until it begins to turn golden. Remove and drain on kitchen paper.

Bring the cauliflower cooking water back to the boil, then put in the pasta and cook for about a minute less than the time given on the packet, so that it is al dente. Drain, reserving a few tablespoons of the cooking water, then transfer to a warmed bowl and add the ricotta, sautéed cauliflower, the pine nuts and sultanas, if using, and most of the grated pecorino. Toss everything together, adding a little of the reserved pasta cooking water if needed, to loosen. Finish with the rest of the grated pecorino.

## 'Emerald green and tender, soft and creamy'

Pistachios are a big story in Sicily. They are famous all over the island, but the finest production is in Bronte, where the producers have their own Slow Food Presidium, and the nuts have been awarded a *Denominazione di Origine Protetta* (DOP) that acknowledges the special microclimate, the characteristics of the volcanic soil, which is rich in mineral salts, and the particular way the farmers tend the trees which only grow every two years. Also they only survive by being planted on the roots of another tree. The intervention of Slow Food has helped to protect these very special nuts, and put them on a pedestal, in the face of cheaper competition from around the world.

The fabulous thing about these pistachios is that they are a bright emerald green and tender and soft and creamy, with the texture more of a pine kernel, whereas the ones that are grown elsewhere in the world, particularly in the Middle East, might be bigger, but they are quite hard and nutty in comparison and have a more yellowy-coloured kernel. There is a distinctive warmth to the flavour of the Bronte nuts, which opens up when you add them to dishes, sweet or savoury. The difference between an ice cream made with run-of-the-mill pistachios or pistachio flavouring, and the nuts from Bronte, is incredible: taste it and you experience a huge, creamy, intense sensation in your mouth.

Bronte is a very beautiful area. If you take a cable car from Catania, up to the highest point of Mount Etna that it will reach, you can see Bronte on the other side. It was often part of the Grand Tour of Europe that the sons of the English gentry used to take in the seventeenth and eighteenth centuries. They would travel to Messina, Taormina and Bronte, and down to the baroque tip of the island around Siracusa and Modica.

It also has another particular connection with England. In 1798 Admiral Nelson stopped at Naples after being at sea for six months. He had already lost an eye, and had been wounded in the arm. He stayed for a year, looked after by his mistress, Emma Hamilton, and while he was there he fought off the uprising of the Francophile Republic of Naples and saved the throne for Ferdinand, the King of Spain. Ferdinand made him Duke of Bronte, and, as a present, gave him a piece of land there, in the same territory that was once the home of the mythical Cyclops, who also only had one eye. The pistachios that grew in Bronte were already famous, and were used in the cuisine of all the European courts.

Originally introduced by the Arabs, the trees grow almost miraculously in the steep, rough ground among the lava rocks below Mount Etna. They are not even irrigated, but like the ancient olive trees, they seem to symbolise

*Il pistacchio verde di Bronte*
The green pistachio of Bronte

the fortitude and strength of the Sicilian people, overcoming their harsh circumstances to produce a wonderful crop every other year. With that special understanding that seems to unite the people and produce of Sicily, in the alternate years when the trees are resting, the farmers help them out by cutting them back, so that the trees can use all their energy to produce nuts the next year.

The terrain is too rough for machinery, so the local people turn out to help pick the pistachios by hand. The nuts are then removed from their tough outer husks and laid out to dry in the sun, before being shelled and, finally, their purple skins are peeled away to reveal the bright green kernel inside. This is the way they are usually sold, and because of their fabulous quality, they are able to command high prices.

Pistachios are traditionally used to decorate *cassata*, the famous Sicilian cake (see page 358), and to give a vivid green colour to the almond paste that the people of the island love so much, for decorating, and for forming into elaborate figures and tableaux for saints' days and at Easter time. But I love the fact that the pistachios are also used in savoury things, for studding through salami, or crushing into a pesto for tossing through a pasta with prawns (see page 219). Often they are used almost as a condiment, crushed quite finely and sprinkled over grilled fish – and they give an unbelievable flavour to carpaccio of raw swordfish, along with olive oil and lemon juice.

The only thing to remember is that if you are pounding or crushing pistachios, you should use them straight away, because if you leave them, once the crushing has released their oils, they can turn rancid very quickly.

### Casarecce con pesto di pistacchio
Casarecce with pistachio pesto

*Casarecce* is a short, twisted pasta, similar to *strozzapreti*. You can substitute this, or use *penne* if you can't find it.

Serves 4

70g shelled pistachio nuts (preferably *pistacchio di Bronte*, see page 194)
2 garlic cloves
40g fresh basil
200ml extra virgin olive oil
30g pecorino cheese, grated, plus a little extra for finishing
sea salt and freshly ground black pepper
400g *casarecce*

Preheat the oven to 180°C/350°F/gas 4. Lay the pistachios in a single layer on a baking tray and put them into the oven for about 8 minutes. As long as they are in a single layer you don't need to turn them. Keep an eye on them to make sure they don't burn. Take them out and chop them.

Using a pestle and mortar, pound three-quarters of the pistachios to a paste with the garlic, then add the basil, pound again, and gradually add the extra virgin olive oil (alternatively, if you want a smoother sauce, do this in a blender). Add the rest of the pistachios and the pecorino and pound or blend very briefly (about 15 seconds), in order to keep some bigger pieces of pistachio. Season to taste.

Bring a pan of water to the boil, add salt, then put in the pasta and cook for about a minute less than the time given on the packet, so that it is al dente. Drain, reserving some of the cooking water, and put the pasta back into the pan. Toss with the pesto, adding some of the cooking water if necessary to loosen. Serve with a little extra grated pecorino.

**Busiate al pesto trapanese**
Busiate with pesto trapanese

*Pasta al pesto trapanese* is one of the most famous recipes around Trapani, made with the pesto sauce that is named after the city. At a restaurant in Trapani, I watched one of the women making fresh *busiate* – long twists of durum wheat pasta – by hand, with the lightest, quickest touch I have seen in my life. And yet her hands must also have been so strong to have worked this pasta in the same way for years, the way her mother and grandmother had most likely done before her, rolling the lengths of pasta around a special needle, then sliding them off into spirals that stayed perfectly in shape when she laid them on trays to dry. Like people who make gnocchi, she had wonderful dexterity, and watching her was like watching a little slice of Sicilian history.

In Trapani you can buy artisan *busiate* in small *pastiere*, made either by hand, or with little extruders that twist the pasta. It is also sold dried in packets. If you don't want to make your own *busiate*, or can't find any dried, you can use any long twisted pasta or *bucatini*, broken in half, instead. Sometimes I like to add some olives and capers at the very end.

Serves 4

1 quantity of *pesto trapanese* (see page 73)

For the pasta:
175g semolina flour
75g '00' flour plus extra for dusting
1 egg yolk
1 teaspoon olive oil
1 teaspoon sea salt

Put all the pasta ingredients into a food mixer with a paddle and whiz until everything comes together in a dough, then leave it to rest for 20 minutes.

Have ready a baking sheet, dusted with flour. To form the *busiate*, roll the dough out into a rectangle about 2mm thick. Cut it lengthways into strips 1cm wide. Take each strip and coil it tightly along the length of a large skewer or clean knitting needle. Roll the skewer or needle gently over your work surface, so that you flatten the pasta slightly and help the coil of pasta to stick to itself, then push it gently off the skewer or needle and lay it on the floured baking sheet. Repeat with all the strips of pasta, laying them on the sheet in a single layer to dry for about an hour, until they hold their shape.

Bring a large pan of water to the boil and add salt. Put in the *busiate* and cook for about 5 minutes, or if using packet pasta, for 1 minute less than directed. Drain lightly, put back in the pan, add the pesto, and toss all together.

## Tagliatelle con fiori di zucchine
Tagliatelle with courgette flowers

Serves 4

2 tablespoons olive oil
1 medium onion, finely chopped
110ml chicken stock
a pinch of saffron threads (about 15)
3–4 baby courgettes
15 courgette flowers
sea salt and freshly ground black pepper
400g tagliatelle
2 large egg yolks, beaten
60g pecorino cheese, grated

Heat 1 tablespoon of olive oil in a pan, add the onion and cook gently until soft but not coloured. Add the stock and bring to the boil, then put in the saffron. Take off the heat, cover with a lid and leave for 5 minutes to let the saffron infuse the stock.

Cut the courgettes into thin strips. Clean and chop the courgette flowers. Heat the rest of the oil in a large pan (big enough to take the pasta later) and sauté the courgette strips and the chopped courgette flowers until golden. Add the saffron stock and season to taste.

Bring a pan of water to the boil, add salt, then put in the pasta and cook for about a minute less than the time given on the packet, so that it is al dente. Drain, reserving some of the cooking water. Add to the pan of courgette flowers and toss through, adding a little of the reserved cooking water if necessary to loosen. Add the beaten egg yolks and toss again. Finish with the grated pecorino.

## Pasta con broccoli

Like the cauliflower, the Sicilian broccoli is a very intensely flavoured vegetable that the islanders love to serve with pasta. What is slightly confusing is that, in and around Palermo, cauliflower is known as *broccolo*, whereas broccoli is called *sparaceddi*.

Pasta and broccoli might seem an odd unpromising mix, but when you add various combinations of anchovies, pine nuts, raisins, cherry tomatoes, pecorino, chilli, toasted breadcrumbs and parsley and garlic, it is really delicious. I have seen pasta made with broccoli, anchovies and olives described as 'Pasta for Hard Times' in old books, but with ingredients like these I would say it was a pasta for good times.

Here are four slightly different recipes made with various pasta shapes and including one that is baked in the oven.

### Pasta con i broccoli soffritti
Pasta with sautéed broccoli

This is one of the simplest pasta and broccoli dishes. As usual, the vegetable is first cooked in plenty of water, so that it can also be used to cook the pasta, then the broccoli is simply sautéed with some garlic and tomato and mixed with the pasta.

You have to remember that in Sicily the intensely flavoured broccoli and the sun-drenched tomatoes produce an explosion of taste, so to come close, try to use local broccoli that has been freshly picked, and the best tomatoes you can find.

Serves 4

sea salt and freshly ground black pepper
450g broccoli, broken into florets
60ml olive oil
1 garlic clove, chopped
100g Pachino or cherry tomatoes
400g spaghetti
extra virgin olive oil for finishing
80g pecorino cheese, grated

Bring a large pan of salted water to the boil (big enough to take the pasta later), then put in the broccoli and cook until just tender. Lift out (retaining the cooking water for the pasta), and put into some iced water to stop the cooking and keep the bright green colour. Drain and pat dry, then cut into smaller pieces.

Heat the olive oil in a pan and sauté the broccoli, garlic and tomatoes for 4–5 minutes, then season and turn off the heat.

Bring the broccoli cooking water back to the boil, put in the spaghetti and use a fork to curl the pasta around the pan, so that it is all submerged under the water quickly.

Cook for about a minute less than the time given on the packet, so that it is al dente. Drain, reserving some of the cooking water, and combine with the broccoli and tomatoes, adding some of the cooking water if necessary to loosen. Drizzle with extra virgin olive oil and serve with grated pecorino.

**Casarecce con broccoli, acciughe e pinoli**
Casarecce with broccoli, anchovies and pine nuts

Serves 4

40g breadcrumbs (see page 45)
3 salted anchovies or 6 anchovies in oil
sea salt and freshly ground black pepper
450g broccoli, broken into florets
1 tablespoon garlic oil (see page 60)
4 tablespoons olive oil
1 garlic clove, chopped
1 fresh red chilli, finely chopped
30g pine nuts
20g sultanas
400g *casarecce* (a short, twisted pasta) or penne
60g fresh caciocavallo or pecorino cheese, grated
60g aged caciocavallo or pecorino cheese, grated

Toast the breadcrumbs in a dry pan over a medium heat, until they are quite a dark golden brown. Take care not to burn them.

If using salted anchovies, rinse and dry them. Run your thumb gently along the backbone to release it, and you should be able to easily pull it out. If using anchovies in oil, drain them.

Bring a large pan of salted water to the boil (big enough to take the pasta later), then put in the broccoli and cook until just tender. Lift out (retaining the cooking water for the pasta), and put into some iced water to stop the cooking and keep the bright green colour. Drain the broccoli from its iced water and pat dry.

Heat the garlic oil in a pan, add the anchovies and stir with a wooden spoon to 'melt' them, taking care not to let them burn. Add the toasted breadcrumbs and set aside.

Heat the olive oil in a large pan and put in the garlic and chilli, then add the broccoli and stir until the broccoli is heated through, then season, add the pine nuts and sultanas, and cook for a few more minutes.

Meanwhile, bring the broccoli cooking water back to the boil, put in the pasta, and cook for about a minute less than the time given on the packet, so that it is al dente. Drain, reserving some of the cooking water, and add to the pan of broccoli, tossing everything together well for another minute and adding a little of the cooking water if necessary to loosen. Mix the two cheeses and scatter over the top, with the reserved anchovies and breadcrumbs.

# Rigatoni con broccoli in tegame
Rigatoni pasta with broccoli, anchovies, pine nuts and sultanas

Serves 4

50g butter for greasing the baking dish
2 salted anchovies or 4 anchovy fillets in oil
sea salt and freshly ground black pepper
1 head of broccoli, separated into florets
4 tablespoons olive oil
1 medium onion, finely chopped
30g tomato purée
400–450g chopped tinned tomatoes
400g *rigatoni*
2 tablespoons pine nuts
2 tablespoons sultanas
150g pecorino cheese, grated

Preheat the oven to 180°C/350°F/gas 4 and butter a baking dish.

If using salted anchovies, rinse and dry them. Run your thumb gently along the backbone to release it, and you should be able to easily pull it out. If using anchovies in oil, drain them.

Bring a large pan of salted water to the boil (big enough to take the pasta later), then put in the broccoli and blanch for a few minutes. Lift out (retaining the cooking water) and put into some iced water, to stop the cooking and keep the bright green colour.

Heat the oil in another large pan, add the onion and cook gently until soft but not coloured. Add the anchovies, stirring and crushing with a wooden spoon so that they 'melt' into the oil – but take care not to let them burn. Add the purée and tomatoes, cook for a few more minutes, then season.

Drain the broccoli florets from the iced water and add to the pan, then cover with a lid and simmer until the florets begin to come apart.

Bring the broccoli cooking water back to the boil, put in the rigatoni, and cook for about 3 minutes less than the time given on the packet, so it is al dente. Drain, reserving some of the cooking water, and add to the pan of broccoli sauce, along with the pine nuts and sultanas, tossing together well, and adding a little of the pasta cooking water to loosen if necessary.

Transfer to the greased baking dish and cover with the grated cheese. Bake for about 15–20 minutes, until the cheese melts and is golden brown.

### Ditalini con broccoli, acciughe, olive e pangrattato
Ditalini with broccoli, anchovies, olives and breadcrumbs

Serves 4

2 tablespoons olive oil
40g breadcrumbs (see page 45)
12 good whole black olives in brine
6 salted anchovies or 12 fillets in oil
sea salt and freshly ground black pepper
1 head of broccoli, cut into florets
1 tablespoon garlic oil (see page 60)
2 tablespoons dry white wine
1 teaspoon dried chilli flakes
400g *ditalini rigate* (a short tubular pasta)
1 tablespoon parsley and garlic (see page 60)

Heat 1 tablespoon of olive oil, put in the breadcrumbs and toast over a medium heat until dark golden brown. Take care not to burn them.

Drain the olives and pat dry. With a sharp knife, make three or four cuts in each olive from end to end, then cut each segment away from the stone as carefully as you can.

If using salted anchovies, rinse and dry them. Run your thumb gently along the backbone to release it, and you should be able to easily pull it out. If using anchovies in oil, drain them.

Bring a large pan of salted water to the boil (big enough to take the pasta later), then put in the broccoli and blanch for a few minutes. Lift out (retaining the cooking water), and put into some iced water to stop the cooking and keep the bright green colour.

Warm the rest of the olive oil and the garlic oil in a large pan and when the garlic in the oil begins to turn golden add the anchovies, stirring and crushing with a wooden spoon so that they 'melt' into the oil – but take care not to let them burn. Add the wine and bubble up until the alcohol has evaporated. Add the broccoli and mix in very gently so that it doesn't fall apart. Season and sprinkle with chilli flakes to taste.

Meanwhile bring the broccoli cooking water to the boil, put in the pasta and cook for around 1 minute less than the time given on the packet, so that it is al dente. Drain, reserving a little of the cooking water, and add to the sauce. Add the parsley and garlic and the olives, and toss everything together, adding a ladleful of the cooking water from the pasta if necessary to loosen. Serve scattered with the breadcrumbs.

### Ditalini rigati con acciughe e pomodori secchi
Ditalini with anchovies and sun-dried tomatoes

Serves 4

6 anchovies in oil
120g breadcrumbs (see page 45)
4 tablespoons olive oil
1 teaspoon garlic oil (see page 60)
12 sun-dried tomatoes in oil, drained and chopped
120ml white wine
a pinch of dried chilli flakes
sea salt
400g *ditalini rigate*
1 tablespoon parsley and garlic (see page 60)
60g pecorino cheese, grated

Drain the anchovies, and cut 3 of the fillets into strips.

Toast the breadcrumbs in a dry pan over a medium heat, until they are quite a dark golden brown. Take care not to burn them.

Heat the olive oil and garlic oil in a large pan over a medium heat, add the 3 whole anchovy fillets and cook very gently, stirring, just for a minute, to break them up and 'melt' them a little. Stir in the sun-dried tomatoes, then add the wine and bubble up to let it evaporate. Add the chilli flakes.

Bring a pan of water to the boil, add salt, and put in the pasta. Cook for about a minute less than the time given on the packet, so that it is al dente. Drain, reserving some of the cooking water, add to the anchovy and tomato sauce and toss together, adding a spoonful of the cooking water from the pasta if necessary to loosen. Add the parsley and garlic and toss again. Serve sprinkled with the toasted breadcrumbs, the grated pecorino, and the strips of anchovy.

## 'A flavour out of this world'

If you have a tomato in a Sicilian salad, you are never disappointed, ever. Whenever I go back to Sicily, I forget just how intense, explosive, sweet and juicy is the flavour of even the most misshapen fruit. Nobody cares about what a tomato looks like, it is all about the taste. Even though tomatoes weren't introduced to Italy until the sixteenth century (from Spain, via South America), and the cultivation of them didn't really happen until a few centuries later, the use of them is so ingrained in Sicilian culture that if you look in old recipe books, there is no real recipe for a tomato sauce, because everyone assumes that the people know what to do with tomatoes. Mostly this is to treat them as simply as possible, cooking them with some olive oil, salt, garlic and herbs. I have eaten pasta just tossed with chunks of fresh tomato, only flashed in a pan, with lots of extra virgin olive oil, salt and basil, and the flavour was out of this world.

*Pomodori*
Tomatoes

All over the island different varieties are grown, and over hundreds of years of working things out in a natural way, the Sicilians have understood what grows best where, but the ones that have become the most famous are the vine tomatoes of Pachino, which are grown under glass in the volcanic soil of Mount Etna, and are so good that once you start eating them, you can't stop yourself.

The power of the volcano to change the soil and produce such richness is in stark contrast to the fear and destruction it has caused in previous centuries. In 1669 molten lava destroyed the old city of Catania, killing 17,000 people and flowing all the way to the sea, burning boats and carving a new coastline, where the new city was built.

The volcano has been controlled for a long time now – these days there is a big American base in Catania, and whenever the lava starts to come down the wrong way, they are able to use explosives to divert it. But I remember as a young man, watching pictures on TV of the volcano erupting, and seeing the people desperately getting out of their houses, with the lava coming down towards them. It was such a moving thing to see, and it is incredible to go to the top of this moon-surface environment and experience the power and heat that comes from the centre of the world.

It is the ash from the volcano that gives the soil its special characteristics, which, added to some of the most intense sunshine in Europe, especially suits tomatoes.

When I visited the producer of the tomatoes we buy and saw the way they are grown, in such a particular way, it was incredible. Each of the 2,000-metre greenhouses is planted at a slightly different time, and one person looks after each one, which has about twenty plants. When you walk into the greenhouses the smell is so intense, it is like breathing in a gazpacho; tasting it almost.

Each plant is trained in a circle, round and round and upwards, held up by stakes which have hooks and strings, so the plant is constantly travelling and spiralling for about sixty to eighty metres. It is watered very little – with ground water that is salty from the sea – which it doesn't like, so the plant is always pushing itself to survive, and forcing all its strength into the fruit. In April, the guys start to pick the tomatoes from the bottom, and when the first ones are already ripe and picked, the ones higher up are unripe, but starting to get red, and at the top the fruit is completely green. From the base of the plant to the tip is about three months of production, so the last of the tomatoes will be harvested around July/August.

It sounds a harsh way of twisting nature to man's advantage, but it is done in such a respectful way. The producer is the son of the farmer who started the whole production in Pachino around fifty years ago, using a kind of tomato that was grown in another part of the island, but developing this unique way of growing. He has his own bees, which cross-pollinate only the plants inside the greenhouse, and he talks about the tomatoes in a beautiful way, saying that the greenhouses are not to make the plants grow better, but to protect them, in the same way you would build a house to protect your wife and kids. The glass prevents the temperature changing strongly from night to day, and the salt in the water produces a higher salinity in the fruit itself. If you take a Pachino tomato and slice it, and do the same with another variety of tomato, you will notice the difference.

With other varieties of tomato, when there is an overproduction, the typical thing to do is to sun-dry them. In the case of the small cherry ones, they are traditionally hung up in bunches to dry in the sun. You can buy the dried tomatoes in the grocers' shops, take them home and rehydrate them. In London there was a big fashion for sun-dried tomatoes, and over-use of them, a few decades ago, but in Sicily they have almost been the poor man's food, a way of making tomatoes go a long way out of season.

Most families also make their own tomato passata to keep them going throughout the winter. If they don't grow their own tomatoes, they will buy about ten boxes of them, then boil up the tomatoes with salt and bottle it. Or, sometimes, still, they make *'strattu*.

Such a Sicilian thing, the making of the *'strattu* was often communal. Wooden trestle tables would be put out in the village square, and the people from all the surrounding houses would put boxes and boxes of tomatoes through a mincing machine, push them through sieves to remove the skin and seeds, then spread out this purée very, very thinly – really just smearing it – on the tables to dry in the sun and wind for a day. Gradually the tomatoes would lose their moisture, and the purée would become dark and dense and intensely flavoured. Then it would be scraped up, put into jars and divided up between everybody.

My head chef, Rino, remembers his grandfather making *'strattu* in the garden, leaving it out on the wooden table over the hot days, guarded by a home-made bamboo scarecrow that made a noise to keep away the birds.

Even if most people don't make their own any more, in the small shops you can buy locally made *'strattu* in big bowls, which is weighed out for you into containers; or sometimes it is packed into little tins or jars, and then when you make pasta you can add a spoonful. It has a very special flavour, less intense than tomato purée which is concentrated by boiling. I first used *'strattu* when I was making a *pasta con le sarde* and it made a big, big difference to the flavour.

### Pasta con le sarde
Pasta with sardines, anchovies, fennel, raisins and pine nuts

I remember one night a famous American art critic came into Locanda to eat. This guy looked at the menu and then said, 'You know, I have just come back from Sicily and I loved the pasta they made with the *sarde*.' I went back into the kitchen and said to Rino, my head chef, who is from Sciacca, on the south coast of Sicily, 'We have to cook this pasta for him.' We had some perfect sardines, beautiful sultanas, and I had just come back from Sicily myself, so I had brought some of the wild fennel that grows so freely. We cooked the pasta for him, and every single year since he has sent me a card at Christmas, saying, 'That pasta with the *sarde* was the best I ever had.'

This is a dish that sums up Sicily for me: the Arabic combination of sultanas, nuts and saffron (I think it needs lots) shows the history of the island, yet the ingredients themselves have been indigenous there since classical times. In Palermo, they make the dish in the same way but pile the pasta into an ovenproof dish, with the breadcrumbs on top, and bake it in the oven for ten to fifteen minutes at around 170°C/325°F/gas 3.

There is another version of the dish that is typical of the other aspect of Sicilian cooking, which is all about making do with what you have … it is known as *pasta con le sarde a mare*, which means 'pasta with sardines that are in the sea' – in other words, they had the pine nuts and the sultanas and the breadcrumbs and all the other ingredients to make the dish, but they didn't have any sardines, so they made it anyway, just without the fish!

If you can't find any wild fennel, use a teaspoon of fennel seeds instead. Soak them, whole, in just a little water – only enough to cover them – for a couple of hours, and add them instead of the wild fennel.

Serves 4

3 salted anchovies or 6 anchovy fillets in oil
100g breadcrumbs (see page 45)
120ml extra virgin olive oil
1 medium onion, chopped
50ml white wine
2 tablespoons *'strattu* or 1½ tablespoons tomato purée (see page 211)
8 fresh sardine fillets
30g sultanas
30g pine nuts
a good pinch of saffron (about 20 threads)
3 sprigs of wild fennel, finely chopped, or 1 teaspoon of fennel seeds, soaked in a little water (see above)
sea salt and freshly ground black pepper
200g pasta, such as *bucatini*

If using salted anchovies, rinse and dry them. Run your thumb gently along the backbone to release it, and you should be able to pull it out easily. If using anchovies in oil, drain them.

Toast the breadcrumbs in a dry pan over a medium heat, until they are quite a dark golden brown. Take care not to burn them.

Heat half the extra virgin olive oil in a pan and add the onion. Sauté until softened but not coloured, then add the anchovy fillets, stirring them until they 'melt'. Add the wine and bubble up to let it evaporate, then add the *'strattu* or purée and bring back to the boil, adding just enough water to give a sauce consistency. Add the sardine fillets, sultanas, pine nuts, saffron and chopped fennel or soaked seeds. Taste and season if necessary, stir gently, and cook for 10 minutes.

Bring a pan of water to the boil, add salt, then put in the pasta and cook for about a minute less than the time given on the packet, so that it is al dente. Drain, reserving some of the cooking water.

Toss the pasta with the sardine sauce, adding a little of the pasta cooking water if necessary to loosen the sauce, and sprinkle with the toasted bread-crumbs.

**Pasta con la mollica**
Pasta with breadcrumbs and anchovies

This is so simple it hardly needs a recipe, but it really shows that no matter what the poverty and suffering of the Sicilian people at various points in their history, they have always been really clever at using whatever they had. Let's not forget we are talking about a land that the ancient Greeks could not believe when they landed: such a paradise of luscious food, but because of the massive inequality of rich and poor, there were times when many people had very little to eat.

So you baked bread and used the breadcrumbs instead of cheese, and if you were lucky you had a few anchovies, preserved in salt, to add to your pasta.

Serves 4

10 salted anchovies
240g breadcrumbs (see page 45)
sea salt
400g spaghetti
60ml extra virgin olive oil

Rinse and dry the anchovies. Run your thumb gently along the backbone to release it, and you should be able to easily pull it out.

Toast the breadcrumbs in a dry pan over a medium heat until they are quite a dark golden brown. Take care not to burn them.

Bring a pan of water to the boil, add salt, then put in the spaghetti and use a fork to curl the pasta around the pan, so that it is all submerged under the water quickly.

Cook for about a minute less than the time given on the packet, so that it is al dente. Drain, reserving some of the cooking water.

Meanwhile, heat the olive oil in a pan and add the anchovies, stirring and crushing them with a wooden spoon so that they 'melt' into the oil and make a little sauce – but take care not to let them burn. Drain the pasta and toss with the anchovy sauce, adding a little of the cooking water from the pasta if necessary to loosen it. Serve sprinkled with the breadcrumbs.

## Spaghetti con gamberi e pistacchio
Spaghetti with prawns and pistachio

Serves 4

40g shelled pistachios (preferably *pistacchio di Bronte*, see page 194)
sea salt and freshly ground black pepper
400g spaghetti
2 tablespoons olive oil
1 teaspoon garlic oil (see page 60)
1 teaspoon chopped fresh red chilli
200g shelled prawns (keep the shells for the stock)
70ml white wine
1 teaspoon parsley and garlic (see page 60)
1 tablespoon extra virgin olive oil

For the stock:
1 tablespoon extra virgin olive oil
½ carrot, cut into chunks
½ onion, cut into chunks
1 celery stalk, cut into chunks
1 garlic clove, crushed
2 black peppercorns
2 parsley stalks
heads and shells from the prawns (see above)
½ tablespoon tomato purée

Preheat the oven to 180°C/350°F/gas 4. Lay the pistachios in a single layer on a baking tray and put into the oven for about 8 minutes. As long as they are in a single layer you don't need to turn them. Keep an eye on them to make sure they don't burn. Take them out and chop them roughly.

To make the stock, heat the extra virgin olive oil in a large pan and add the vegetables, garlic, peppercorns and parsley stalks. Cook for a couple of minutes until softened but not coloured.

Add the prawn heads and shells and crush them. Once the heads turn bright red, add the tomato purée and carry on cooking over a low heat for a couple of minutes. Add 2.5 litres of cold water, bring to the boil, skim the surface of froth, then turn down the heat and simmer for 15 minutes. You will end up with about 2 litres of stock. Strain through a fine sieve into a bowl.

Wash out the pan, and pour all but 200ml of the strained stock back in. Keep this 200ml to one side. Add a litre of water to the stock in the pan and bring to the boil. Add salt, then put in the spaghetti and use a fork to curl the pasta around the pan, so that it is all submerged under the water quickly.

Cook for about a minute less than the time given on the packet, so that it is al dente. Drain, reserving some of the cooking water.

While the spaghetti is cooking, heat the olive oil and garlic oil in a clean pan large enough to take the pasta later. Add the chilli and stir for a minute. Add the prawns and cook for half a minute, moving them around the pan, then add the white wine and bubble up until the alcohol evaporates. Add the reserved 200ml of stock, then season and turn off the heat.

Drain the pasta, reserving some of the cooking water, and add to the sauce. Toss together for a minute, add the parsley and garlic and the extra virgin olive oil, toss again and serve with the toasted pistachios sprinkled on top.

## Spaghetti marinara alla Vittorio
Vittorio's seafood spaghetti

In Sicily, traditionally, they just toss the pasta and the sauce together in a bowl. It is the northern Italians who toss the sauce with the pasta in the pan. Vittorio is from northern Italy originally and at his restaurant da Vittorio in Porto Palo, he takes the idea even further, really cooking the spaghetti in the sauce, so that it dries around it and he has become famous for it.

Serves 4

100g clams
100g mussels
100ml dry white wine
1 tablespoon garlic oil (see page 60)
1 fresh red chilli, chopped
80g swordfish, diced
80g cleaned squid, cut into rings
100g peeled prawns
sea salt and freshly ground black pepper
250g tinned chopped tomatoes
400g spaghetti or linguine
2 tablespoons parsley and garlic (see page 60)
2 tablespoons olive oil

Scrub the clams and mussels separately (pulling any beards from the mussels) under running water and discard any that are open. Put the clams and mussels into a large pan with half the white wine over a high heat, cover, and cook, shaking the pan from time to time, until all the shells have opened. Remove from the heat, strain off the cooking liquid and reserve this. Discard any clams or mussels whose shells haven't opened. Take the rest out of their shells and throw the shells away.

In a pan large enough to take the pasta later, heat the garlic oil and chilli, then add the swordfish, squid and prawns. Season, sauté for 1 minute, then add the rest of the wine and bubble up to let the alcohol evaporate. Add the tinned tomatoes and the reserved liquor from cooking the shellfish and simmer for 5 minutes.

Meanwhile, bring a pan of water to the boil, add salt, then put in the spaghetti and use a fork to curl the pasta around the pan, so that it is all submerged under the water quickly. Cook for at least 2 to 3 minutes less than the time given on the packet, so that it is very al dente. Drain, then add to the pan of seafood and sauce, along with the parsley and garlic and the olive oil. The secret is to keep tossing the pasta and sauce in the pan for about 5 to 6 minutes, until the sauce dries and caramelises around the spaghetti.

### Spaghetti tagliuzzati con zuppa di aragosta
Spaghetti and lobster

You need to buy very fresh lobsters for this, from a fishmonger that you trust; or, preferably, buy live ones and despatch them yourself. I know this is an emotive issue, but we have done a lot of research into killing lobsters painlessly, and in the kitchen we have a special machine that knocks the lobster unconscious. At home the best way is to put the lobster into the freezer for about fifteen minutes, so that the creature goes into a torpor, then, holding the claws still, insert a sharp knife into the head behind the eyes and cut straight down, so that the head is cut completely in half. It is agreed that this is much more humane than plunging a live lobster into a pan of boiling water.

As the name of the dish suggests, this is quite a soupy sauce, which Italians call a broth, and the spaghetti is broken up into shorter lengths before being cooked and added to it.

Serves 4

1 medium fresh or live lobster (about 1kg)
4–5 plum tomatoes
2 tablespoons olive oil
2 onions, diced
1 large carrot, diced
1 celery stalk, diced
2 tablespoons chopped flat-leaf parsley
1 bay leaf
1 tablespoon tomato purée
1 tablespoon garlic oil (see page 60)
1 teaspoon chopped fresh red chilli
40ml dry white wine
sea salt
400g spaghetti, broken into pieces
1 teaspoon parsley and garlic (see page 60)
1 tablespoon extra virgin olive oil

If using live lobsters, despatch them as described above. If using fresh ones, split the heads in half between the eyes. Separate the heads from the tails.

Put the tomatoes into a pan of boiling water for 10 seconds, then drain under cold water and you should be able to peel them easily. Cut them in half, scoop out the seeds with a teaspoon, and then chop the flesh.

To make a little stock, heat the olive oil over a low heat, add the vegetables, parsley and bay leaf and cook gently until the vegetables are golden. Add the

lobster heads and the tomato purée, cook for 3 minutes, then add enough water to cover and bring to the boil. Turn down the heat and simmer for 20 minutes, then pass the stock through a fine sieve and set aside.

Bring a pan of water to the boil. Put in the lobster tail and blanch for 20 seconds, then remove and cut lengthways through the shell so that you have two halves. Remove the shell and cut each half lobster into slices of about 1.5cm.

In a pan large enough to take the pasta later, heat the garlic oil. Put in the chilli, stir for a minute, then add the lobster meat and cook for a couple more minutes. Add the white wine, bubble up and stir until the alcohol evaporates, then add the chopped tomatoes and finally the reserved lobster stock.

Bring a pan of water to the boil, add salt, then put in the broken spaghetti and cook for about a minute less than the time given on the packet, so that it is al dente. Drain, reserving some of the cooking water, and toss with the lobster sauce for about a minute, adding a little of the cooking water if necessary to loosen. Add the parsley and garlic and the tablespoon of extra virgin olive oil, then toss together again and serve.

## Pasta al nero di seppia
Spaghetti with cuttlefish ink

If you ask your fishmonger to prepare the cuttlefish for you, make sure he gives you the ink separately. The sweet-tasting ink is stored inside the body of the cuttlefish (which looks similar to a squid, but is bigger), ready to squirt at enemy fish. Sometimes the sac can get punctured when the cuttlefish is caught, but most fishmongers sell the ink in jars or sachets, so even if you are unlucky and there is none inside the cuttlefish, you will be able to buy some.

Serves 4

450g cuttlefish, cleaned and with its ink
4 tablespoons olive oil
1 tablespoon garlic oil (see page 60)
1 x 400g tin of chopped tomatoes
sea salt and freshly ground black pepper
400g spaghetti

Cut about two-thirds of the cuttlefish into pieces, then cut the remainder into thin strips.

Heat half the olive oil with the garlic oil until the garlic in the oil turns golden. Add the pieces of cuttlefish, reserving the strips, then add the tomatoes, season and add the ink. Cook for another 15 minutes.

Meanwhile, bring a pan of water to the boil, add salt, then put in the spaghetti and use a fork to curl the pasta around the pan, so that it is all submerged under the water quickly. Cook for about a minute less than the time given on the packet, so that it is al dente. Drain, reserving the cooking water.

While the pasta is cooking, heat the rest of the olive oil in a frying pan, put in the strips of cuttlefish, and move them around the pan. The moment the strips turn opaque, take the pan off the heat and drain them on kitchen paper.

Toss the drained pasta with the cuttlefish sauce, adding a little of the cooking water if needed to loosen. Serve with the strips of cuttlefish on top.

## Spaghetti al polpo
Spaghetti with octopus

Serves 4

1 octopus, cleaned (fresh, or frozen and defrosted)
2 fresh red chillies
6 tablespoons extra virgin olive oil, plus a little extra for finishing
a large handful of flat-leaf parsley, with stalks
3 garlic cloves
sea salt and freshly ground black pepper
400g spaghetti
2 plum tomatoes, halved
2 tablespoons parsley and garlic (see page 60)

If the octopus is fresh, beat it with a meat hammer to tenderise it and rinse it very well under cold running water, with the help of a clean sponge, to remove any excess saltiness. If it has been frozen, you don't need to do this, as freezing has the effect of tenderising it.

Split one of the chillies in half lengthways.

Put half the extra virgin olive oil into a large pan with the split chilli, the parsley and the garlic cloves. Add the octopus (don't season it, as it will be salty enough), cover with a lid, put on the heat and let it simmer, over a low heat for about 1 hour, stirring occasionally. The octopus will cook in its own juices, and as it does so, make sure the tentacles are under the liquid. Towards the end of the cooking time, taste the cooking liquid, and if it is too salty add some plain water.

Bring a pan of water to the boil, add salt, then put in the spaghetti and use a fork to curl the pasta around the pan so that it is all submerged under the water quickly. Cook for about a minute less than the time given on the packet, so that it is al dente. Drain, reserving some of the cooking water.

While the spaghetti is cooking, finely chop the remaining chilli. Heat the rest of the oil in a pan that is large enough to hold the pasta later, then add the tomatoes and crush them. Add the chopped chilli and the reserved octopus. Taste the reserved octopus cooking liquid, and if it isn't too salty, add about 4 tablespoons of this reserved liquid to the pan. If it is too salty, add some plain water to the pan instead. Let the octopus heat through, taste, and season with black pepper – you probably won't need any salt.

Add the pasta to the pan of octopus and sauce. Toss in the pan for about a minute, adding a little of the cooking water, if necessary, to loosen. Add the parsley and garlic and extra virgin olive oil, toss quickly again and serve.

**Cavatelli con ragù di tonno**
Ricotta pasta with tuna, anchovy and tomato sauce

*Cavatelli* are like gnocchi, but instead of the dough being made with potatoes (combined with flour and egg), it is done with ricotta.

Serves 4

1 lemon
sea salt and freshly ground black pepper
1 x 500g piece of fresh tuna, preferably yellow fin or bonito
1 garlic clove, sliced
about 8 mint leaves, cut into strips
about 30 whole black olives in brine
2 tablespoons olive oil
1 medium onion, chopped
4 anchovy fillets in oil
2 tablespoons tomato purée
200g tomato sauce (see page 75)
40ml red wine
½ tablespoon sugar

For the *cavatelli*:
200g plain flour, plus extra for dusting
1 teaspoon salt
190g ricotta cheese
1 egg

To make the *cavatelli*, put the flour and salt into a bowl, make a well in the middle and put in the ricotta and the egg.

With a circular motion, slowly incorporate the flour into the eggs and cheese. Once it is all combined, knead until you have a soft dough. It shouldn't be sticky, so if necessary, add a little extra flour. Shape the dough into a rough square, wrap in clingfilm, and set aside to rest for at least 30 minutes.

Lightly flour your work surface. Cut the dough in half and roll into a rectangle about 3mm thick, then cut it lengthways into strips, about 1.5cm wide. Now cut each strip crossways into strips about 1cm deep – so that you end up with lots of pieces, roughly 1.5 x 1cm.

Have a floured tray ready. With a spatula or the flat blade of a large blunt knife, press down on each piece of dough and slide the spatula or knife blade towards you, so that the piece of dough curls. Put into the floured tray until ready to use.

Squeeze some lemon juice into a bowl of cold, salted water and put in the tuna. Put a plate over the top, and leave until some of the blood is drawn out of the fish and it turns a lighter pink colour. Lift the fish out and dry. With a sharp knife, make slits in the flesh of the tuna and push in the garlic slices and about three-quarters of the mint.

Drain the olives and pat dry. With a sharp knife, make three or four cuts in each olive from end to end, then cut each segment away from the stone as carefully as you can.

Heat the olive oil in a large pan and sear the tuna on all sides, then remove and set aside. Add the onion to the pan and cook gently until soft but not coloured, then add the anchovies, stirring and crushing them with a wooden spoon so that they 'melt' into the oil – but take care not to let them burn. Add the olives, tomato purée and sauce and bring to a simmer. Put the reserved tuna back in with the rest of the mint, the red wine and sugar and break up the tuna with a fork, stirring it into the mixture.

Bring a pan of water to the boil, add salt, then put in the *cavatelli* – the moment they float to the top they are ready. Drain and add to the pan containing the tuna, toss everything together and serve.

### Fusilli con tonno, melanzane e mandorle
Fusilli with tuna, aubergine and almonds

Serves 4

1 medium aubergine
sea salt and freshly ground black pepper
100g almonds
4 plum tomatoes
4 tablespoons olive oil
250g fresh tuna, preferably yellow fin or bonito
1 teaspoon garlic oil (see page 60)
125ml white wine
400g *fusilli*
extra virgin olive oil
1 teaspoon parsley and garlic (see page 60)

Cut the aubergine into 1.5cm cubes, sprinkle with salt and leave to drain in a colander for 1 hour.

Heat the oven to 180°C/350°F/gas 4. Lay the almonds in a single layer on a baking tray and put into the oven for about 8 minutes. As long as they are in a single layer you don't need to turn them. Keep an eye on them to make sure they don't burn, and when they are golden, take them out and chop them finely.

Put the tomatoes into a pan of boiling water for 10 seconds, then drain under cold water and you should be able to peel them easily. Cut them in half, scoop out the seeds with a teaspoon, and chop the flesh.

Squeeze the aubergines lightly to get rid of the excess liquid. Heat the olive oil in a pan and gently sauté the aubergines until golden. Lift out and drain on kitchen paper.

Cut the tuna into 1cm cubes. Heat the garlic oil in a large pan big enough to take the pasta later. Add the tuna, season, cook for about 2 minutes, then add the wine and bubble up to let the alcohol evaporate. Add the chopped tomatoes, cook for another minute, check the seasoning and set aside.

Meanwhile, bring a pan of water to the boil, add salt, then put in the *fusilli* and cook for about a minute less than the time given on the packet, so that it is al dente. Drain, reserving some of the cooking water, then toss with the tuna and tomato sauce, together with the aubergine, adding a little of the cooking water from the pasta if necessary to loosen the sauce. Add a good drizzle of extra virgin olive oil and the parsley and garlic, toss again and serve sprinkled with the finely chopped toasted almonds.

**Pasta ai quadrucci di pesce spada, capperi e pistacchio**
Pasta with cubed swordfish, capers and pistachio

Serves 4

2 tablespoons shelled pistachio nuts (preferably *pistacchio di Bronte*,
see page 194)
1 tablespoon olive oil
1 tablespoon garlic oil (see page 60)
1 fresh red chilli, chopped
200g swordfish steaks, cut into cubes
sea salt and freshly ground black pepper
2 tablespoons dry white wine
15 cherry tomatoes, chopped
1 tablespoon salted capers, rinsed and well drained
400g short pasta, such as *ditalini*
1 tablespoon parsley and garlic (see page 60)
1 tablespoon extra virgin olive oil

Preheat the oven to 180°C/350°F/gas 4. Lay the pistachios in a single layer
on a baking tray and put into the oven for about 8 minutes. As long as they
are in a single layer you don't need to turn them. Keep an eye on them to
make sure they don't burn. Take them out and chop them roughly.

In a pan large enough to take the pasta later, heat the olive oil with the garlic
oil. Add the chilli and stir for a minute, then add the cubes of swordfish,
season and cook for another minute, stirring them around the pan. Pour in
the wine and bubble up to let the alcohol evaporate, then add the tomatoes
and capers and simmer for 5 more minutes.

Meanwhile, bring a pan of water to the boil, add salt, then put in the pasta
and cook for about a minute less than the time given on the packet, so that
it is al dente. Drain, reserving some of the cooking water, and toss with the
swordfish and sauce for about a minute. Add the parsley and garlic and the
extra virgin olive oil and toss quickly again. Serve sprinkled with the toasted
pistachios.

### Pasta con la bottarga
Pasta with bottarga

*Bottarga* is the salted, pressed and sun-dried roe of either the tuna or the grey mullet. In Sardinia they prefer the grey mullet roe, but of course in Sicily tuna is the favourite fish, and since every part of it is used, it is natural that they make tuna *bottarga* as well. However, because the local blue fin tuna is in such trouble from overfishing, I would say try to buy *bottarga* made from grey mullet instead.

Whereas in Cagliari in Sardinia, if they are serving *bottarga* with pasta, they just shave it like a truffle, with a knob of butter, in Sicily they like to combine it with olive oil, parsley and garlic, and a little chilli.

You can substitute *bucatini* for the spaghetti, if you prefer a chunkier pasta.

Serves 4

100g tuna or grey mullet *bottarga*, plus a little extra for finishing
2 tablespoons garlic oil (see page 60)
1 tablespoon finely chopped flat-leaf parsley
1 fresh red chilli, finely chopped (optional)
4 tablespoons extra virgin olive oil
400g spaghetti

Grate the *bottarga* into a bowl and add the garlic oil, parsley and chilli. Add the extra virgin olive oil and with a fork work the mixture into a paste.

Bring a pan of water to the boil (but don't salt it, as the *bottarga* is very salty), then put in the spaghetti and use a fork to curl the pasta around the pan, so that it is all submerged under the water quickly. Cook for about a minute less than the time given on the packet, so that it is al dente. Drain, reserving some of the cooking water.

Put the pasta back into the pan, add the *bottarga* paste and toss well, so that the pasta 'melts' the bottarga. Serve with a little more freshly grated *bottarga* on top.

**Spaghetti con ricci mare**
Spaghetti with sea urchin

Sea urchin roe with pasta is a very popular thing at the seaside in Sicily; the people seem to really love it.

Serves 4

sea salt and freshly ground black pepper
400g spaghetti
2 tablespoons olive oil
1 tablespoon garlic oil (see page 60)
1 fresh red chilli, chopped
1 tablespoon parsley and garlic (see page 60)
250g sea urchin roe

Bring a pan of water to the boil, add salt, then put in the spaghetti and use a fork to curl the pasta around the pan, so that it is all submerged under the water quickly. Cook for about a minute less than the time given on the packet, so that it is al dente. Drain, reserving some of the cooking water.

While the pasta is cooking, heat the olive oil and garlic oil in a separate pan, large enough to take the pasta later. Add the chilli and cook for a minute, then add a ladleful of cooking water from the spaghetti, stir in and set aside until the pasta is cooked.

Add the drained pasta to the pan containing the oil and chilli. Toss for a minute, adding a little more of the pasta cooking water if necessary to loosen. Add the parsley and garlic, together with the sea urchin roe, then toss well – the heat of the pasta will be enough to cook the sea urchin – and serve.

**Spaghetti con uova di San Pietro**
Spaghetti with John Dory roe

Serves 4

1 tablespoon olive oil
1 tablespoon garlic oil (see page 60)
1 fresh red chilli, chopped
200g John Dory roe
2 tablespoons dry white wine
10 cherry tomatoes, chopped
sea salt
400g spaghetti
extra virgin olive oil
1 tablespoon parsley and garlic (see page 60)

To make the sauce, heat the olive oil with the garlic oil in a pan large enough to take the pasta later, then add the chilli and the John Dory roe and sauté for 1 minute. Pour in the wine and bubble up to let the alcohol evaporate, then add the tomatoes, turn down the heat and simmer for 5 minutes.

Bring a pan of water to the boil, add salt, then put in the spaghetti and use a fork to curl the pasta around the pan, so that it is all submerged under the water quickly. Cook for about a minute less than the time given on the packet, so that it is al dente.

Drain the pasta, reserving some of the cooking water, and add to the pan of sauce, together with a little extra virgin olive oil. Add the parsley and garlic and toss, adding a little of the pasta cooking water, if necessary, to loosen the sauce.

### Timballo di riso con pasta
Rice and pasta baked with meatballs

Serves 10

unsalted butter for greasing
3 tablespoons breadcrumbs (see page 45)
500g macaroni
5 large hard-boiled eggs
300g fresh caciocavallo, *tuma* or young pecorino cheese, cut into pieces

For the rice:
1.3 litres chicken stock
500g arborio rice
200g caciocavallo or pecorino cheese, grated
3 eggs

For the *besciamella* (béchamel sauce):
60g unsalted butter
60g plain flour
1 litre milk
sea salt and freshly ground black pepper

For the meat balls:
200g minced beef
1 onion, finely chopped
1 egg
1 tablespoon breadcrumbs (see page 45)
1 tablespoon garlic oil (see page 60)
1 tablespoon parsley and garlic (see page 60)
1 tablespoon pecorino cheese, grated
a little olive oil
1 litre tomato sauce (see page 75)

For finishing:
2 tablespoons breadcrumbs (see page 45)
2 tablespoons unsalted butter, cut into cubes

Preheat the oven to 180°C/350°F/gas 4. Grease a deep round baking dish (about 25cm diameter and 4–5cm deep) with the butter, then tip in the breadcrumbs and shake the dish so that they coat the butter all over the base and sides.

Bring the stock to the boil in a pan, add the rice, bring back to the boil and cook for about 15 minutes, until the rice is tender and the liquid has been

absorbed. Remove from the heat, leave to rest for a minute, then quickly beat in the grated cheese and the eggs and set aside.

To make the *besciamella*, pour the milk into a pan, and bring to just under the boil, then take off the heat. Melt the butter in a separate pan, then add the flour and cook, stirring for a couple of minutes, until all the flour is absorbed. Slowly add the milk a little at a time, stirring continuously, until it is all mixed in. Add the nutmeg, bring to the boil, then reduce the heat and simmer for 3–4 minutes until the sauce thickens. Season and set aside.

In a bowl, mix the minced beef with the onion, egg, breadcrumbs, garlic oil, parsley and garlic and grated cheese, and form into balls a little bigger than hazelnuts. Heat some olive oil in a pan, put in the meatballs and sauté them until they start to take some colour.

Bring the tomato sauce to the boil in a separate pan, then add the meatballs, turn down the heat and simmer for 10 minutes.

Bring a pan of water to the boil, add salt, then put in the macaroni and cook for about 3 minutes less than the time given on the packet, so that it is al dente. Drain and toss with the béchamel and the meatballs with their sauce.

Cut the hard-boiled eggs in half, lengthways.

Using two-thirds of the rice, spread a layer about 1cm thick around the sides and over the base of the dish. Spoon in the pasta mixture, then put in a layer of hard-boiled eggs followed by the fresh caciacovallo, tuma or young pecorino. Spread the rest of the rice over the top, scatter with breadcrumbs and dot with the cubes of butter.

Bake for about 1 hour, until golden. Remove from the oven, carefully place a plate over the top of the dish, then turn them both over together so that the *timballo* turns out on to the plate. Serve immediately.

## Pasta al forno invernale
Baked winter pasta with sausage

An elaborate baked pasta was traditional for Carnival (Shrove Tuesday) and other celebrations – including Easter. During Lent, eggs were not eaten, so you used up what eggs you had at Carnival, and then any that the hens laid during Lent were kept for Easter. On Good Friday, not only were eggs still not allowed to be eaten, but also meat, milk, butter, or cheese: anything that came from the animal world. So you can imagine a dish like this, which combined all those things that had been forbidden for forty days, would be quite special. *Mezze penne rigate* is a shorter version of the regular *penne*, but you could also use *sedanini* which is a little thinner and slightly curved.

Serves 8

120g unsalted butter
150g breadcrumbs (see page 45)
3 tablespoons olive oil
2 medium onions, chopped
900g lean minced beef
190g fresh pork sausage, chopped
110ml dry white wine
2 tablespoons tomato purée
200ml good chicken stock
sea salt and freshly ground black pepper
900g *mezze penne rigate*
200g pecorino cheese, grated
200g cooked ham
2 hard-boiled eggs, sliced
150g caciocavallo or pecorino cheese, grated

For the *besciamella* (bechamel sauce):
1 litre milk
60g unsalted butter
65g plain flour
a pinch of grated nutmeg

Preheat the oven to 190°C/375°F/gas 5. Grease a baking dish with 20–30g of the butter, then put in the breadcrumbs and shake and turn the dish so that the breadcrumbs cling to the butter and line the dish.

Heat the olive oil in a pan and put in the onions. Cook until soft but not coloured, then add the beef, sausage, and wine. Bubble up to let the alcohol evaporate, then add the tomato purée, stir and cook for a minute. Add the stock and continue cooking for about 45 minutes, until the meat is cooked, and the sauce is reduced.

To make the *besciamella*, pour the milk into a pan, and bring to just under the boil, then take off the heat. Melt the butter in a separate pan, then add the flour and cook, stirring for a couple of minutes, until all the flour is absorbed. Slowly add the milk a little at a time, stirring continuously, until it is all mixed in. Add the nutmeg, bring to the boil, then reduce the heat and simmer for 3–4 minutes until the sauce thickens.

Bring a pan of water to the boil, add salt, then put in the pasta and cook for about 3 minutes less than the time given on the packet, so that it is al dente. Drain and toss with the meat sauce, add the *besciamella* and the 200g of grated pecorino, and mix all together. Spoon half the pasta mixture into the greased dish, then layer the ham on top, followed by the eggs and the rest of the pasta. Finish with the 150g grated caciocavallo or pecorino and dot with hazelnut-sized pieces of the remaining butter. Bake for 20 minutes, until the cheese has turned golden.

### 'Cheese on horseback'

In Sicily you frequently see recipes which use caciocavallo, but it isn't easy to find outside the island, as unusually it is made with cow's milk, and since cow herds are quite a rarity, the production is naturally small. The name 'caciocavallo' means 'cheese on horseback'. The cheeses come from the *pasta filata* (stretched curd) family of cheeses, which includes mozzarella, and are shaped like dumpy pouches with a yellowish-coloured rind, tied around their necks with string. The name apparently comes from the old way of hanging them in pairs over a beam in the ageing cellars, so that they looked like saddlebags slung over a horse.

The flavour is a little like provolone, and when it is first made it is quite light and creamy, but as it ages (for up to two years) it becomes quite hard and tangy and salty, and can be grated.

Outside Sicily, most recipes suggest using pecorino, made from sheep's milk, instead. What I have discovered is that in Sicily there is basically one hard sheep's milk cheese that is made in the shape of a drum, but the curds are pressed into a wicker basket. At this point the fresh, young cheese is unsalted and known as *tuma*. Traditionally it is flavoured with peppercorns, though these days you often also find it made with chilli, or rocket. When it receives its first light salting and is aged for a few weeks, it becomes *primosale*. Then if it is salted again and aged until its rind turns brown, it is known as *pecorino*. Sicilian pecorino is very strong and salty, quite unlike pecorino from other parts of Italy. Sometimes it is also called *canestrato*, from the word *canestro*, or wicker basket, because the basket forms a beautiful pattern in the rind, or *tumazzu di piecura* – *tumazzu* is a generic description of aged cheese, whether it is made with sheep's or cow's milk. So one cheese, three different stages, and five different names.

**Caciocavallo cheese**

242

Caciocavallo cheese

## Timballo di maccheroni
Baked pasta with aubergine

Serves 4–6

3 aubergines, preferably the round, pale violet ones
sea salt
2 tablespoons unsalted butter for greasing
5 tablespoons breadcrumbs (see page 45)
olive oil
1 medium onion, thinly sliced
1 garlic clove, crushed
1 x 400g tin of chopped tomatoes
400g *rigatoni* or *penne rigate*
60g caciocavallo or pecorino cheese, sliced

Cut the aubergines into thin slices, sprinkle with salt and leave to drain in a colander for at least 2 hours. Squeeze lightly to get rid of the excess liquid.

Preheat the oven to 180°C/350°F/gas 4. Grease a round cake tin or tart tin, about 3–4cm deep, then put in 2 tablespoons of breadcrumbs and shake and turn the dish so that the breadcrumbs cling to the butter and line the dish.

Heat about 6mm of olive oil in a deep frying pan, and sauté the aubergine slices in batches until lightly coloured. Lift out and drain on kitchen paper, then, using about three-quarters of the aubergines, overlap the slices over the base and around the sides of the greased and breadcrumbed tin.

In a pan, heat a tablespoon of olive oil, put in the onion and garlic and cook until soft but not coloured. Add the chopped tomatoes and season with salt; cover with a lid, and cook over a low heat for 10 minutes.

Bring a pan of water to the boil, add salt, then put in the pasta and cook for about 3 minutes less than the time given on the packet, so that it is al dente. Drain, reserving some of the cooking water.

Spoon a layer of pasta into the aubergine-lined tin, followed by some of the tomato sauce, a layer of the remaining aubergine and a layer of grated cheese. Repeat, finishing with a layer of aubergine, followed by the rest of the breadcrumbs. Bake in the preheated oven for about 25 minutes, until golden.

Leave to stand for about 10 minutes to firm up, then put a plate over the top of the tin, hold both the plate and the tin firmly, and turn both over together, so that the *timballo* turns out on to the plate (see page 183). Serve cut in wedges.

# Pesce
# Fish

... the good fish, with naturally tender, fat flesh,
sprinkle with a little salt only, and baste with oil.
For it contains within itself alone the reward of joy.


– Archestratus of Gela, quoted in Athenaeus

Where we stay near Menfi we are between two ports: Mazara del Vallo to the west and Sciacca to the east. Mazara del Vallo is a beautiful city, very Arabic, and Sicily's biggest, busiest, most important port. Gone are the days when there was such an abundance of fish landed each day that the men used to take whatever was too much to sell in the market around the streets, in wheelbarrows of ice, and stop under the shade of trees, so that the people could just come out of their houses to buy. But it is still amazing to see how many boats come in, how much fish gets landed, and how busy the fish market is where the big refrigerated vans are waiting to take most of the catch to Milan.

Whenever I am there I imagine what it must have been like before the fifties, and the age of refrigeration, when all this fish could only have been enjoyed by the local people rather than the Milanese.

Fishermen have been casting their nets off this part of Sicily for thousands of years, and sometimes these days, as well as fish, the local boats pull up treasures from their complicated past. One of the most spectacular is the ancient Greek bronze statue of a dancing satyr, Il Satiro Danzante, which some fishermen caught in 1998 and which is now in a special museum built in its honour in the town.

In the very deep cold waters off Mazara del Vallo they catch the beautiful, very sweet *gamberi rossi*, the red prawns that have skinnier bodies than warm water prawns, with very strong little legs from swimming against the strong current. Their flavour is incredible. They remind me of the *gamberi di San Remo*, the bright pinky-orange prawns from San Remo Bay in Liguria, which we could sometimes get when the fish man set up his market in Corgeno when I was growing up. Because it takes the fishermen three days to bring the *gamberi rossi* back by boat, they freeze them as soon as they are caught. Normally I use fresh fish, or if it is going to be served raw, I like it to be frozen on board the boat and in this case it is the best and only way to keep the flavour of the prawns.

However, they are becoming more and more scarce, because of fishing quotas, and because the Sicilian fishermen are in competition with the Tunisian boats. You have to remember that Palermo is closer to Tunis than Rome. In terms of airspace it is 418 kilometres to Rome, 321 to Tunis.

Whenever we can get them, though, we bring the *gamberi rossi* in from Sicily to Locanda. I remember once we made a risotto with them, using the heads and shells for the stock, and a Japanese man who was eating in the restaurant said to me after his meal: 'I loved the risotto, but you shouldn't have put sugar into it!' 'Sugar? What are you talking about?' I said. 'We would never put sugar into a risotto.' 'Then why was it so sweet?' So I took him into the kitchen, and gave him one of the prawns to eat, and it was a revelation to him: 'Now I understand.' Risotto is not a Sicilian thing, but I did make that risotto for the people in my friend Vittorio's restaurant one night when we were on holiday there, and they loved it, too.

Sciacca is also very beautiful. This is where my head chef, Rino, comes from, and because we know all his family there, we feel very tied in to the town and with the people, and we feel very at home there. But what we notice is that there is almost a line through the town, between the part that is looking out to sea and the part that is looking inland. In the one side they eat fish, in the other they eat meat, and if you are a fisherman you speak in a dialect that is different to that of the farmers facing inland, so in one town you have people who cannot understand each other!

And in the main piazza in the town, on weekends and feste during the summer, families still follow the old tradition of the *passeggiata*, the afternoon walk. In the old days this had a special significance, because the custom was that during such strolls, young men and women could be casually introduced to each other. The problem was that in Sciacca the sons and daughters of the fishermen would always keep to one side of the square, and those of the farmers to the other, so if you were a daughter of a fisherman, how would you ever get to meet anyone other than a fisherman? Even now, on their Sunday outing, you see the old fishermen walking on the side of the square where they can see the sea, while the farmers keep to the side facing the land.

In Sciacca the port is smaller, but the fish market is bustling, mad and very loud. So much is going on. There are women filleting mounds of sardines and anchovies, already graded by the fishermen on board their boats, ready for salting in special barrels, while all around the fishermen are shouting in their sing-songy way about the catch they have to sell, from swordfish and tuna, prawns and cuttlefish, to the smaller sardines and anchovies that haven't gone for salting; everything is there. You see the people from the restaurants of Palermo buying their fish and you know that if you eat out in the city that night, you are going to have fish so fresh it was landed the evening before and was in the market that afternoon.

This is also the place where local people join in the craziness, squabbling over the best fish. In my kitchen in London I can always start an argument between chefs from different regions over the names of fish, but I swear in Sicily alone there are sometimes thirty different names – if you have four people around a fish stall, they will all come up with different names, and if they aren't sure what a fish is called, it always seems to be *cernia* (grouper) – *addóttu* or *cirenga* in dialect.

The joke on the northern Italian chef from London is that whenever I arrive in Vittorio's kitchen at his fish restaurant in Porto Palo, and the boxes of fish come in, I have to go through my examination, to see what I remembered from last time I was there. Vittorio is originally from northern Italy himself, but after forty-five years he has a head start, whereas when they say to me: 'What is this one, Giorgio?' there is always one I don't know. In particular, there is a gurnard, a really ugly fish that they love, and which they have two main names for: *scorpio* and *gallinella*. If I say 'Scorpio,' they will say, 'No, *gallinella*,' and if I say, 'Gallinella,' they will say, 'No, *scorpio*.'

Bag of mixed fish

Occasionally there are species that you just don't see anywhere else. There is a lobster called *zoccola* (also known as the flat or slipper lobster), which looks like something from prehistoric times; an incredible creature. I don't expect to know everything in life, but to find seafood in Italy that I had never even heard of before was quite a shock. The *zoccola* has the tail you would expect of a lobster, but hardly any head. It is so strange, like a tail with tentacles at the end of it, as if the head has just disappeared – and when it is cooked the meat has a harder, chewier texture than a lobster, but an incredible aroma and flavour.

Something else I have never seen in mainland Italy is the use of *neonata*, baby fish, so tiny the body is still transparent, so you just see the eyes. They take a handful, put them into boiling water to blanch them, turn off the heat, drain them, then sauté them with chilli and garlic, and serve them with pasta, and they are really fantastic, with a taste that is of fish, but also all of its own. Fishing for *neonata* used to be done a lot, when the seas were presumed to be full of an endless supply of fish, but now people are finally realising that if you keep taking baby fish from the sea you are not going to have any big ones, so they can only legally be fished under licence for two weeks of the year. However, you can buy them preserved in oil in cans, throughout the year.

There is also a lovely recipe that truly shows the Sicilian mind at work: nothing must be wasted. When they catch San Pietro (John Dory) in the season when the females are carrying eggs, instead of throwing away the roes they are kept to one side and sold to restaurant kitchens, where they will sauté them with garlic, white wine, chopped tomato, and throw in a little parsley at the end, and, again, serve them with pasta (see page 236). The eggs keep a bit of bite, and are a little like caviar, but not salted. Incidentally, San Pietro is sometimes called *pisci jáddu* in dialect, which means 'looks like a chicken'.

## Pure and simple

On Sunday it is a tradition among many families to go to the seaside and have a fish meal. They just say they would like the fish menu and don't even ask what it consists of, so there will be a selection of fish antipasti, then pasta with fish, and afterwards simply grilled fish for the main course. To eat in a fish restaurant is also a special thing for people living inland, who have more meat in their diet, but still have a reverence for fish that is ingrained in Sicilian tradition.

At the end of the harvest of the olives in our groves in Cammarata, north of Agrigento, I could see that everyone seemed very excited. Because I can't understand the dialect I asked Antonio, who is in charge of the olive oil-making, what the buzz was about, and he said, 'Tonight, to celebrate finishing the harvest, we are going to take everyone to the fish restaurant.' Smack in the middle of Sicily, near Enna, is an amazing fish restaurant, so good that you could almost be beside the sea. So, after days of eating salami and wild boar, we feasted on course after course of fish, which was a real treat for everyone.

Traditionally, all Italians are very purist about serving fish, and I must admit I always respect it when people come into Locanda and ask for their fish to be served separately from any vegetables or sauce, because when the fish is of great quality, you really want to enjoy the flavour without being distracted. At the same time, as a chef, I am torn, because it is interesting to see what other flavours or techniques will enhance the experience.

My experience of Sicily, however, is that if you are serving fish with pasta, then yes, the pieces of fish become part of some kind of simple sauce and there are some traditional recipes that involve cooking the fish with tomatoes. Otherwise you don't mess about with fish, you really don't. The philosophy is that the food should talk, not the chef. The fish must be properly caught, of good quality and cooked well, but beyond that you do the minimum you have to do to allow it to express itself.

In the restaurants they love to use the hot grill plate, the *plancha* – probably this is one of the influences left from the Spanish. For Sicilians this is the way to give maximum expression to a fish that is as fresh and as good as you can get it. So, as a main dish you might have a big, plentiful *grigliata*, a plateful of tiny fishes and shellfish, mixed with slices of bigger fish: some prawns, swordfish, sardines, all grilled and just put in the middle of the table, with some olive oil, sea salt and whole lemons, and nothing else. And when you see it, you think: 'Why bother to decorate and be clever, because this is a work of art; it is what cooking fish is all about, really.' This is what inspires me constantly about the food of Sicily: it takes me back one step from creativity to total simplicity.

It is also a very convivial way to eat, especially if you have bigger fish that must be taken apart and shared out. Something is happening around the table that brings people together in a way individual plates of food cannot do.

I remember one time when we were eating at a restaurant near Menfi, when two very smartly dressed couples arrived, each in a Porsche. They ordered fish and when it arrived, grilled and served with just a lemon, one of the guys, with a big gold Rolex watch and a Milan accent, asked for 'a little *salsetta*'. He was thinking maybe of a little mayonnaise, or a *sauce meunière*, and the waiter just looked at him, very seriously, and said, 'No, we don't do sauce,' and walked away. Of course they had mayonnaise in the kitchen, but this was for serving with the prawns, not with fish. The way they think is that 'you shouldn't have a sauce with the fish, so we are not going to serve it to you', and that is that.

**Fish to go**

In Palermo one of the things I love to see is the guys who chargrill your fish for you on the streets. Often the grills belong to restaurants which set

them up in front at about six o'clock in the evening, so they are cooking for customers and also for people who come along with the fish they have just bought in the market. Sometimes you see queues of people waiting for their fish to be cooked, because in the city most people live in apartments, so they don't have the chance to grill fish outdoors in the way they do in the villages, where most people have a small patch of garden.

I remember one time, with my son Jack, I bought about ten or twelve beautiful red mullet in the Capo market. The fish are smaller than the British ones, more fleshy, and with a stronger flavour. We took them to one of these guys, who was like a machine: he slit the fish, cleaned it with amazing dexterity, took out the liver, then put it back inside, and then he put the whole fish, scales still on, back on the grill, so the livers cooked as a kind of stuffing. It was fantastic. Jack was saying to me: 'They haven't taken the scales off,' because this is something chefs are usually very particular about, but I learned from these guys that it is perfectly acceptable to cook the fish with scales on, because they don't like to eat the skin. So what you do when you get home and bring it to the table is just run your knife underneath the skin and lift the flesh out, leaving the skin behind.

**A miracle in Menfi**

Whenever we are in Sicily and I am getting a bit restless and fidgety and anxious to be in the kitchen, Plaxy says to me, 'Go to Vittorio's, and we'll see you for dinner.' Vittorio has a restaurant at Porto Palo on the coast near Menfi, where we rent the same house each holiday.

Like me, Vittorio is from the north of Italy – a big, larger-than-life character, he comes from Bergamo, and the story of how he ended up in the middle of nowhere in Sicily is a great, romantic one. He was cooking in Switzerland and while he was there he met a Sicilian girl, fell in love with her and they decided to get married. She didn't want to live anywhere but Sicily, so he travelled there for the wedding, and when he arrived with his father, at the station, the way to the village was so long and so rough they had to take a donkey to carry their bags, and the father was saying, 'You want to marry a girl from here? Are you sure? I can't leave you here!'

At first they had nothing, no running water, not even electricity, but they built a little *friggitoria* on the beach, selling snacks to the local people who came out there on a Sunday. Eventually Vittorio bought a piece of land, in a typically complicated Sicilian process. Everyone said, 'This northern guy is an idiot, buying land in the middle of a swamp,' but he has turned the place around and now he has built on to the beautiful restaurant a small hotel, with eight rooms. His wife, Francesca, his two daughters, his son, his son-in-law Ignazio, who is a chef, and Costantino who has worked there for so long he is like another son, help run the business. Just a couple of girls and some guys behind the bar are brought in to help in the summer, when they sometimes serve 100 people out on the terrace alone, and there always seems to be at least one massive family party going on around a big table. He has been there for forty-five years, and they still call him 'Bergamasco', the man from Bergamo. So he is accepted, yet not *completely* accepted.

Everything about Da Vittorio reminds me so much of our family hotel and restaurant back in Corgeno. Perhaps that's one of the reasons that I feel so comfortable there; it all feels familiar, just transported to a very different place. Even the craziness and joking that goes on in the kitchen reminds me of home. As soon as the fishermen come in with something they have just caught, if Vittorio's son Michelangelo is in the kitchen, there is a kind of dance of insults that goes on. Michelangelo looks at me as if to say, 'Now I show you how to do business,' and I know straight away to stay in the background and keep quiet.

It always starts the same way. Michelangelo says the fisherman is asking too much money, and the fisherman will say, 'I've been bringing fish here since you were that high! And now, look at you, you big Yogi Bear, you treat me like this! I should have kicked you when you were little; that's the only thing I regret in my life that I didn't do that. Call your father, I've had

enough of you!' 'My father is in the restaurant. If you want to sell your fish you have to deal with me!' Michelangelo will say. And they go on and on and on, squaring up to each other. You think, surely they are going to fall out forever, and then they sit down together and have a glass of wine. It's so funny. I think that if they didn't go through the ritual both of them would feel insulted!

The restaurant is really just like a big dining room in Vittorio's house, and every afternoon after lunch is finished they set up a long table and all the family who don't work in the restaurant – the children home from school, and the aunties and uncles and grandmothers and grandfathers – all sit down to eat together. I am always invited to join them and it takes me right back to being a kid again, at the big family dinners in Corgeno with my grandfather at the head of the table.

At Vittorio's you don't ask for a menu; as always in Sicily, it is much better to go with whatever they want to give you. You just sit down at the table and always there will be seven or eight things for antipasti, which come with the bread. There might be *sarde a beccafico* (baked, stuffed sardines, see page 264), or *fritto misto* (mixed fried fish, see page 26). All over Italy people love *fritto misto*, but in Sicily, with such a profusion of different small fish, it is always fantastic. When it is brought to you it doesn't come with mayonnaise, or tartare sauce, just olive oil, lemon and salt, as always. As well, there may be the beautiful raw red prawns from Marzara del Vallo, carpaccio of swordfish, with chopped pine nuts or pistachio nuts, some wonderful sweet local melon and ham, or artichokes. While you are eating the antipasti, they will come and tell you what pasta they have, but nobody writes the orders down, they just tell them in the kitchen what you want. On a busy lunchtime they might cook pasta for 190 people – in just two big pasta pots – so the pasta is in and out of the pots all the way through the lunchtime service. Incredible. Finally, after the pasta there will be the main course of fish (or a few meat dishes) – whatever varieties have been caught that day – just grilled and served with a little sea salt, lemon and olive oil: beautiful.

Always as a family our way of eating is dictated by what Margherita can eat, because she has allergies to so many foods, including, sadly, fish. We try to make everything as easy and natural for her as possible, but eating out in restaurants can be nerve-wracking, unless we know and trust the people who are cooking. But because one of Vittorio's granddaughters also has allergies to some foods, he understands, and so, even though he serves very little meat, he will always order whatever Margherita wants and cook it specially for her.

But the best thing is that Vittorio lets me go into the kitchen and cook with him. We go for dinner, and Plaxy and Margherita go in through the front door, and I go in through the kitchen door. Whenever I go in for the first time, I forget how hot a small kitchen can be. I arrive at the kitchen door all fresh and showered and in my holiday clothes, and everyone rushes over and kisses and hugs me and they are all hot and sweaty and unshaven.

What I love is that at Vittorio's it is always the ingredients that decide what you are going to cook. It gives you so much more freedom when you don't have to stick to a menu. And as always there is that Sicilian philosophy of harmony: what grows together goes together, so if the food comes from the same land and sea, it can be put together on a plate, from the fish that is caught less than a mile away, to the melons and artichokes pulled up that morning from local gardens.

And I love their relaxed attitude to life, cooking and running a restaurant. One day when I was in the kitchen, a very elegant, distinguished elderly man came in, a revered lawyer from Palermo. One of Vittorio's daughters took his order and when she came into the kitchen, Vittorio said: '*Che cosa fa l'avvocato vuole mangiare?*' – 'What is the lawyer up to – does he want to eat?' 'He wants sole, the way you cooked it for him last time, because he loved it.' 'But,' Vittorio said, 'I don't have a sole.' 'Well, I'm not going back to tell him. Do something,' said the daughter. So Vittorio took a little turbot that he had in the kitchen – they have beautiful small ones there that would feed two people perfectly – took off a fillet, trimmed it to look like a sole, cooked it, and browned it round the edges so it looked the way a sole would look. He sent it out to the lawyer and watched and waited, and then the waiter sent back a signal to say 'Perfect.'

The lawyer thought it was the best sole he had ever tasted – he must have been so happy to have a sole with no bones! In the kitchen everyone was cheering and laughing, and I was saying: 'This is the first time I saw a miracle. He has transformed a turbot into a sole!' It reminded me that sometimes in our restaurant in London we are so locked into perfection that we lose a little of that sense of fun.

**Sarde a beccafico**
Stuffed sardines

This is one of the dishes from Sicily that has become famous worldwide – the stuffed sardines are called 'beccafico' after the greedy little birds of the same name, who like to gorge themselves and grow fat on figs. You find beccafico done with different stuffings all over the island. Most of the time the sardines are just 'butterflied', i.e. opened out like a book, then re-formed around the stuffing and deep-fried, but you also find them baked, which is the way we usually make them, because it is not as healthy to deep-fry so much – though I must admit, I do like the fried ones!

Sometimes there is orange zest, sometimes lemon zest, anchovies, garlic … I have had beccafico with pistachios, sometimes sultanas, even wrapped in lettuce or radicchio before being baked in the oven.

Sometimes the stuffed sardines are rolled up, with their heads on, or with their tails sticking out, so they really do look like little birds – this is the way we serve them at Locanda, and we make a quite green-looking, more northern Italian herby stuffing with parsley, basil and Parmesan, whereas the ones in this recipe are stuffed with the classic Sicilian combination of sultanas, pine nuts and anchovies.

Serves 4

1kg small sardines, cleaned, scaled and gutted, heads removed
2 lemons
1 orange
24 bay leaves
olive oil
60g breadcrumbs (see page 45), for the topping

For the stuffing:
20g almonds
20g pine nuts
5 salted anchovies
40g whole black olives in brine
100g breadcrumbs (see page 45) (you may need a little more)
20g sultanas, soaked in water for 10 minutes
20g salted capers, rinsed and well drained
zest of 1 lemon
1 tablespoon olive oil
a pinch of sugar

First butterfly the sardines: open each fish out, turn it skin side upwards and press down on the backbone with your hand to release the bone, then turn it

over again and you should be able to easily pull out the bone. Mix the juice of 1 lemon and the orange in a shallow dish, put in the opened out sardines and leave to marinate for an hour.

Heat the oven to 180°C/350°F/gas 4. Lay the almonds and pine nuts in a single layer on a baking tray and put into the oven for about 8 minutes. As long as they are in a single layer you don't need to turn them. Keep an eye on them to make sure they don't burn, and when they are golden, take them out and chop them. Turn the oven up to 240°C/475°F/gas 9.

Rinse the salted anchovies under cold water, then pat them dry. Run your finger down the backbone, then open out the anchovies like a book and take out the backbone. Chop them roughly.

Drain the olives and pat dry. With a sharp knife, make three or four cuts in each olive from end to end, then cut each segment away from the stone as carefully as you can, and chop roughly.

Combine the almonds, pine nuts, anchovies and olives with the rest of the stuffing ingredients – the stuffing should have a firm consistency. If it is too moist, add a few more breadcrumbs.

Remove the sardines from the marinade and pat them dry. Lay each one, skin side down, on your work surface and place some stuffing on one side. Fold the other side over the top, so that the stuffed fish resembles its original shape, then roll up, leaving the tail sticking out. Thread the rolls onto 4 wooden skewers (you should have about 4 or 5 rolls on each), with a bay leaf between each one, and at either end.

Pour a little olive oil over the base of an ovenproof dish and lay in the skewered sardines. Scatter over the breadcrumbs, squeeze over the juice of the remaining lemon and bake in the oven for 20 minutes, until golden.

**Polpette di sarde**
Sardine balls

You could also serve these with pasta.

Serves 4

600g fresh sardines, cleaned, scaled and gutted, heads removed
250g breadcrumbs (see page 45)
50g sultanas
50g pine nuts
2 tablespoons flat-leaf parsley, chopped
olive oil
sea salt and freshly ground black pepper
2 eggs, beaten
50g pecorino cheese, grated
1 litre tomato sauce (see page 75)

Open each fish out, turn it skin side upwards and press down on the backbone with your hand to release the bone. Then turn it over again and you should be able to pull the bone out easily. Chop the fish finely and put into a bowl with the breadcrumbs, sultanas, pine nuts, parsley, and enough olive oil to bind. Mix together and season, then add the beaten eggs and cheese and mix again until all the egg has been incorporated. Form into balls about 3cm in diameter.

Heat the tomato sauce in a large pan, add the sardine balls and cook over a low heat for 10 minutes.

## 'Imagine having a lemon tree outside your back door'

One of the most amazing things in Sicily is eating at the house of friends when they are grilling fish – and they say to one of the kids, 'Run out to the garden and pick two lemons from the tree.' Imagine having a lemon tree outside your back door. I was so in love with the idea I bought a small one in London, but Plaxy and I spent all our time bringing it in and out of the garden in the cold weather, putting it next to the radiator, then worrying that it was too hot. There is no substitute for the sunshine of Sicily, where even in the winter you can often walk around in a T-shirt and eat outside. In the markets you don't see masses of lemons, because everyone has a tree at home, but those that you do see are big, sometimes out of shape and unwaxed. Everything the British supermarkets wouldn't like, but if lemons were meant to be perfectly shaped and shiny, the Almighty would have made them perfectly shaped and shiny!

*Agrumi*
Citrus fruit

In people's back gardens the trees are usually right by the house and are often trimmed and shaped a little, so you have a big umbrella of fruit, ready to use in cooking, squeeze over grilled fish or meat, slice in a salad, or turn into a refreshing granita or lemonade. Strangely, they rarely seem to put slices of lemon into drinks. Even if you are in a bar, you have to ask if you want lemon in your mineral water, or Coke, or gin and tonic. In Sicilian eyes a lemon is much more than a garnish for a drink; it is something savoury to eat.

The variety of lemons that most people have in their gardens is the Lunario, or *lunatici* in dialect – they are called this because apparently every time there is a new moon, the lemon tree makes new flowers. They can be grown all year round, so the lemons are allowed to stay on the tree and are just picked each day as they are needed; that way they manage to have fruit almost all through the year, which is an incredible thing.

One of the things people do, if they have a grill in the garden, is to make some *polpette* (see page 333) – little meatballs made with parsley, garlic and grated pecorino – and flatten them into patties between two big lemon or orange leaves. When they go on to the grill, the essential oils in the leaves come out, so they keep the meat moist and infuse it with a fantastic aroma and flavour. Clearly when you have your own tree you know you haven't sprayed it with any herbicides or pesticides, so the leaves are very natural.

The Arabs did so much to cultivate the citrus fruit by introducing an irrigation system that would allow the fruit to grow, and these days the biggest commercial production is of the Femminello lemon, which is grown mainly around Catania, Siracusa and north-east of Palermo; there is a smaller production of the Lunario and the Monachelli, which look more greeny-coloured and are smaller, more like a cross between a lime and a lemon. There is also an even smaller production of the Interdonato, which is a very special lemon grown on only a few thousand ancient trees on hilly terraces between Messina and Letojanni on the Ionian coast. I only got to know about these lemons, which have been granted Protected Geographical Indication (PGI) status, when we were staying near Taormina, just south of Letojanni, on holiday. I saw the lemons in the market, and the guy selling them told me if I went up into the hills above Letojanni I would find the lemon terraces that have been championed by the Slow Food Presidium, who are campaigning to support the small consortium of growers.

Letojanni is a little strip of a village with the sea in front and mountains behind, and I went up, past the fig and almond trees, until I found the terraces, each like a big garden, bordered by low stone walls. I felt like an explorer who has suddenly come across hidden treasure. The Interdonato is such an individual lemon that even though up until the Second World War it was very popular in England for serving with tea, in Sicily these days they barely know of it on the other side of the island.

The fruit was grown first by one of Garibaldi's colonels, Giovanni Interdonato, who, when he retired from the militia, decided to grow citrus trees in the Nisi Valley. He grafted a *cedro*, or citron, with a variety of lemon called Ariddaru, and the result was this golden yellow lemon with a tight skin and quite a complex structure of flesh inside. In September, when it ripens, they sell it on the streets, and it has a strong scent and flavour. In the morning I always have a cup of water with a couple of slices of lemon in it, but with the Interdonato lemon, I only ever need to use one slice.

The *cedro*, which is grown all over Sicily, is big, sometimes the size of your hand, and knobbly – the skin can be so bumpy it looks a bit like corn on the cob. It is known for its very thick skin and pith, more than for its flesh, and is delicious if you just slice it and eat it with olive oil and salt, or mix it with raw fennel in a salad. When I was in Modica at Easter time, there were people dressed up in folk costume selling *cedro*, which they cut up for you, and they had little pots of salt, olive oil and chilli, so you could choose which to dip the fruit into.

Mostly, though, the skin, which is sweet with only a touch of bitterness, is candied and used to decorate *cassata* and other cakes and desserts.

*

I remember that when we were little, when my brother and I were given an orange we would keep the fine papers they used to come wrapped in, which would have 'Sicily' printed on them, with a logo. Many years later I saw a documentary about the Mafia and recognised the same logo as belonging to a family of *mafiosi*, who were all killed in the 1980s.

Even though bitter oranges had grown in Sicily since Roman times, the sweet orange was brought in relatively late, in the seventeenth century, via

Portugal, but its production was taken up all over the island, with families making their living from generation to generation growing oranges. When you drive along the motorway from Palermo towards Catania and Siracusa there comes a point where you cannot see the end of the orange groves, because they stretch for miles and miles.

In the last ten or fifteen years or so, though, there has been a big crisis in the market for Sicilian oranges, since the Spanish received money from the EU to expand their orange-growing and flooded the market with cheaper oranges, followed by Morocco, Egypt and California. Compared to the Navel or Valencia varieties, which are the ones grown in Spain and beyond, and which taste as if they have had sugar added to them, Sicilian oranges have a higher acidity and a brilliant sweet-sharp flavour that is like no other – but now, even in northern Italy, where we used to get the oranges inside those beautiful Sicilian wrappers, in the fruit shop you see them with labels on that say they come from Spain. Every year the Spanish smash the market price, so the Sicilians are left with so many oranges that they can't sell, and many families have torn up their orange groves and are struggling to make a living, or have used EU money to plant olive groves instead. It is a similar story to that of the traditional English orchards that have been grubbed up to make way for different crops; a whole heritage of apples and pears in different varieties have only been saved by a few individuals determined to keep them going.

So what is encouraging is that after the initial depression, there is now a small but strong move to promote Sicily's most special oranges, the blood oranges that grow around Mount Etna, in the same way that specialist growers in England have championed some of the old varieties of apple in face of the bland varieties that have been taking over the supermarkets. Growers have realised that there is a global market for produce that is special, unusual and with a particular provenance, and so they are managing to turn around the market for their three fantastic varieties of blood oranges, the Tarocco, Moro and Sanguinello, which are grown in the volcanic earth below the mountain and owe their character to the special rich soil and the dramatic changes in temperature between day and night, which alter the composition of the flesh. The Tarocco is very sweet and juicy, with an orangey-red skin and flecks of red in the flesh, whereas the Sanguinello is more streaked with red, and the Moro has a deep orangey-red skin and an amazingly blood-red flesh that can be so dark in some of the oranges that it looks almost black.

What is wonderful is to come down to breakfast in the morning and have the juice freshly squeezed in front of you. The Moro in particular has such an intense flavour, almost like a mandarin, with a smell a little like mango, and when you drink it you know this is a *real* orange, and you can really feel that you are drinking something that is good for you. Because the oranges don't have the sugary sweetness of oranges grown outside Sicily they are also used a lot in salads. If you add a touch of salt and olive oil, they take on a completely different character, somewhere between a fruit and something savoury. Like the tomato, they have that weird ability to cross the line between the two. They are fantastic combined with fennel and sliced onions, then topped with an oily fish, such as sardines, in an *agrodolce* (sweet and sour) dressing. And they make beautiful marmalade.

This fight back on behalf of the blood oranges of Sicily is especially heartening to see, because there is a kind of fatalism sometimes, which I see in the country people in Sicily, that is different to the way people are in the cities. Maybe it is born of centuries of invasion by foreign powers, and is also somehow tied up with the power of the Mafia. It is a kind of resilience but also an acceptance that you can't change who you are or the circumstances in which you live. In London and in America there is this idea that we can all be who we want to be, that you can always make something of yourself, but in the villages of Sicily there seems to be only a small space for you to do something different, otherwise you are the son of the father who has always grown oranges or artichokes or fished for sardines or swordfish.

So it makes me happy to see that what is winning out, once again, is that overriding belief in the produce that the land gives, and the idea that no matter what circumstances history might throw at the island, the land must be respected, and the Sicilians will find a way to keep alive the very particular oranges that have been grown there with pride for hundreds of years.

## Masculini di ognina
Baked anchovies

Serves 4

30g whole black olives in brine
300g breadcrumbs (see page 45)
1 tablespoon parsley and garlic (see page 60)
1 garlic clove, chopped
1 teaspoon salted capers, rinsed, well drained and chopped
a pinch of dried chilli flakes
1 tablespoon chopped fresh basil
sea salt
700g fresh anchovy or sardine fillets
2 tablespoons extra virgin olive oil, plus extra for greasing

Preheat the oven to 150°C/300°F/gas 2. Grease a baking tin.

With a sharp knife, make three or four cuts in each olive from end to end, then cut each segment away from the stone as carefully as you can, and chop them roughly.

In a bowl, combine the breadcrumbs, parsley and garlic, the chopped garlic, capers, olives, chilli and basil with a little salt. Arrange half the fish fillets in rows along the bottom of the baking tin; cover this with a layer of the breadcrumb mixture, then layer the rest of the fillets on top, at a 90-degree angle to the first layer. Finish with the rest of the breadcrumbs. Drizzle a little extra virgin olive oil over the top and bake in the oven for 15 minutes, until the topping is golden.

### 'In the darkness you see the snake of lights from the convoy of boats ...'

Fresh anchovies are something we rarely see here in the UK, but in Sicily, although they are fished almost all year round and then preserved under salt, they are also sold fresh from the day boats. Sometimes they are fished at night, using the *lampara* system of small boats with lamps, which is where the name comes from. You look out to sea and in the darkness you see the snake of lights from the convoy of boats. What happens is that the head boat finds the shoal, and shines the beam of light on to it. When the anchovies see the light, they swim towards it. Then the next boat shines the beam on to the fish, and so on, so that four or five boats fish the same shoal.

*Acciughe*
Anchovies

Sometimes we have been at Vittorio's when the fishermen are out for the *lampara*. You get to the pasta course and the grill is on, waiting, then three or four boxes of anchovies come in. Vittorio throws a massive handful – a fistful really – of sea salt on to the grill first, then the fresh anchovies. If you were to salt the fish, the delicate skin would stick and break, but when you salt the grill, the salt gets hot and the skin attaches to it and doesn't stick. The fresh anchovies taste beautiful, similar to a sardine, but a little less oily.

At other times, when they catch the anchovies in the usual way, the fishermen sort the fish on board, according to size. When they bring them in to the port at Sciacca, they look so beautiful: green and blue. You can almost see them still swimming and shining in the sea. Some get taken straight away to the restaurants, the smaller ones are sold in the market, while the biggest are picked up from the boats by the guys in their little three-wheeler Ape Piaggios and are taken to the women at the 'laboratories' right on the port, to be cleaned, ready for salting. They work right in front of you: maybe ten women sitting around a table, cleaning the anchovies skilfully and layering them in the traditional circular formation in barrels of salt, which will be pressed with a weight, to release the famous 'garum', or anchovy juice, that the Romans used in their cooking. Then the barrels are sealed.

When you buy salted anchovies you have to rinse and dry them, then press down on the backbone, which will release it, so you can just peel it out, and separate the fish into fillets. Always you have to wash off the salt, and dry the fish, but how much salt you take off is up to you. Most people just rinse them well, and then take care with adding salt to whatever dish they are making, but you can soak them in water for a few hours, if you prefer, changing the water regularly.

If you don't want to do all this, of course you can buy anchovies in oil, but try to buy good-quality ones, preferably the ones that lie flat in tins, rather than the jars, in which the fish always seem to be squashed, so they can easily break apart when you try to take them out.

276

### Seppioline ripiene
Small cuttlefish stuffed with breadcrumbs,
capers and anchovies

Serves 4

1kg small cuttlefish, cleaned, without tentacles
1 lemon, cut in half
1 tablespoon olive oil

For the stuffing:
2 salted anchovies or 4 anchovy fillets in oil
60g breadcrumbs (see page 45)
1 tablespoon garlic oil (see page 60)
1 tablespoon chopped flat-leaf parsley
1 tablespoon salted capers, rinsed, well drained and chopped
zest of 1 lemon
2 tablespoons extra virgin olive oil
sea salt and freshly ground black pepper

Preheat the oven to 180°C/350°F/gas 4.

If using salted anchovies, rinse and dry them. Run your thumb gently along the backbone to release it, and you should be able to easily pull it out. If using anchovies in oil, drain them. Chop the anchovies roughly and mix with the rest of the stuffing ingredients.

Stuff the mixture into the cuttlefish, secure with cocktail sticks and arrange them in a baking tray and drizzle with the olive oil. Bake for 30 minutes, and squeeze over some lemon juice just before serving.

## 'The cattle of the sea ...'

It is a tragedy that two of the most beautiful fish in the Sicilian tradition, blue fin tuna and swordfish, are under real threat; because they have been taken so much, they have been treated like the cattle of the sea. Tuna is so important to Sicilians that you still see it in all the markets and restaurants, but I would say, if you are making any dish with tuna, avoid blue fin, and use only yellow fin or bonito (*alalunga*), which are quite plentiful though often sold under the generic name *tonno*.

*Tonno*
Tuna

The cooking and eating of tuna is recorded as far back as the days of Archestratus, a famous gourmet and food writer in the fourth century BC, who travelled in Sicily and believed that the tuna was such a fine fish that it should only be grilled, or 'roasted': 'And have a tail-cut from the she-tunny – the large she-tunny, I repeat, whose mother-city is Byzantium. Slice it and roast it all rightly, sprinkling just a little salt, and buttering it with oil.'

Slices and steaks of fresh tuna are still treated as simply as Archestratus would have liked. *Fette di tonno fresco al forno* is fillets of tuna baked in foil for about twenty minutes at 180°C/350°F/gas 4, with a little olive oil, onion, tomatoes and a sprinkling of salt and oregano – with the foil being opened up towards the end. *Connetto fritto* is simply tuna slices, dusted in flour, then pan-fried and served with lemon slices and chopped parsley; while in *tonna con la cipuddata* the tuna is fried in the same way, after which sliced onions are put into the pan and cooked gently until soft, when some vinegar, salt and pepper and a handful of mint leaves are added, and this is spooned over the fish. However, I have also eaten tuna encrusted with pink peppercorns – that rose-perfumed pepper flavour is very popular in Sicily – and in one restaurant where we ate, the chef made a fantastic dish with a tuna tartare, raw tuna marinated with some spice and tomato, then tossed through pasta, so it just warmed up and cooked very lightly, but stayed quite rare in the middle. At the end he mixed in some pistachio nuts and grated some aged caciocavallo cheese on top. When it arrived with the nuts and cheese, I thought, 'This will never work,' but it was incredible.

The size of a tuna means that not only the prime cuts but also every bit of the fish has been invaluable for feeding whole communities, so from nose to tail it is used, as people inland or in northern Italy would use every part of a pig. Some would be eaten fresh and the rest preserved for the winter months. Up until the turn of the twentieth century tuna was always put under salt to preserve it throughout the year, but then the famous merchant family the Florios of Palermo, who also traded in Marsala wine, came up with a way of putting tuna in oil inside a can. Ironically, the worldwide appetite for canned tuna, compounded these days by the fashion for sushi, has accelerated the demise of this most magnificent of fish.

'Local bonito'

The understanding and knowledge of the tuna in Sicily runs very deep. There are cuts that they prefer to put into a pasta sauce, others for grilling, yet others for tuna with onions and vinegar. Some people go crazy for the cheek and then there is the prized fat belly, the *ventresca*, incredibly rich and oily from the veins of fat that run through it, which can be cut into thick slabs and grilled. Elizabeth David, in *Italian Food*, considered that in order to have 'good tunny fish', it was essential to ask for *ventresca*. Often, when you buy a slice of tuna steak, you are given a little piece of *ventresca*, which you almost 'melt' into a pan and then fry your slice of fish in it. Sometimes you will even find tuna heart, with *ventresca* wrapped around it, preserved in oil in tins, and it is really delicious.

One of the Sicilian specialities that blew me away the first time I tasted it was *mosciame di tonno*, which is tuna loin, cured and then air-dried for fifteen days. Only the loin is used, never the *ventresca*, which is too fatty. It becomes really firm, and traditionally you just slice it thinly like prosciutto and serve it with lemon squeezed over. When I was cooking at Olivo back in 1992 I used to make a kind of Sicilian version of a salade niçoise, using sun-dried tomatoes, pine kernels, and *mosciame*. When Claudio Pulze of the A–Z Group came to eat my food for the first time in Olivo, he loved it so much he said, 'We have to do a restaurant with this guy' – so I swear that *mosciame* is one of the reasons I ended up as chef-proprietor of Zafferano, the restaurant that first made my name in London.

Of the various species of tuna, the blue fin is the most prized, and it used to be that the whole of the north-west coast around Trapani was focused on the fishing of it. In May and June, when the giant fish would naturally be heading towards the coast past Favignana, one of the Egadi islands off the coast between Trapani and Marsala, the local *tonnarotti* (tuna fishermen) would perform the *mattanza*, or massacre. It still happens, but only on a small scale now. The *tonnarotti* make a line of boats for miles out at sea and they bang drums, bong, bong, bong, to create a sound wall which drives the fish through the straits into a series of nets ending in *la camera della morte*, which is inside a kind of corral. The men line up in their boats all around the outside of this trap, ready to haul up the nets as the fish come through, and when the tuna are brought splashing up to the surface, they spear them; some of the men jump into the water to do battle – you have to remember that a blue fin tuna can be over four metres long and around 800 kilos.

Of course, everyone says, 'Oh, the *mattanza* is really, really bad.' Well yes, of course it is savage, bloody, terrible: man against fish; but also, historically, it made sense, because it was only done at a certain time of year, and then only the big tuna would be taken, and the little ones let go. Without doubt these days the blue fin tuna is overfished, but it is its popularity outside Sicily and the modern methods of fishing, especially the enormous Japanese trawlers, which sit out in the sea like transatlantic liners for three or four months solidly, that have meant the tuna is an endangered species. My head chef, Rino, remembers that when he was growing up each town on the coast had its own *tonnara* (canning factory). But most of those local *tonnare* are disused or gone, because there is so little tuna now.

## Tonno con piselli e menta
Tuna with peas and mint

Serves 4

2 tablespoons whole blanched almonds
olive oil
1 shallot, thinly sliced
2 garlic cloves, thinly sliced
1 tablespoon white wine vinegar
1 teaspoon sugar
300g fresh tuna steaks, preferably yellow fin or bonito, cut into 2.5cm cubes
70ml white wine
300g fresh or frozen peas
sea salt and freshly ground black pepper
a sprig of mint

Preheat the oven to 180°C/350°F/gas 4. Lay the almonds in a single layer on a baking tray and put them into the oven for about 8 minutes. As long as they are in a single layer you don't need to turn them. Keep an eye on them to make sure they don't burn, and when they are golden, take them out and chop them.

Heat a little olive oil in a large frying pan, then add the shallots and garlic and cook gently until soft but not coloured. Add the vinegar and sugar and bubble up to burn off the acidity of the vinegar. Take off the heat and set aside.

In a separate pan, heat some more olive oil, put in the tuna and brown it on all sides. Add the white wine and bubble up to evaporate the alcohol. Add a couple of tablespoons of boiling water, just enough to cover the tuna, and add the peas. Season, then chop the mint leaves and add to the pan. Cover and simmer on a low heat for about 5 minutes, until the peas are cooked and the liquid has reduced. Stir in the reserved vinegar and sugar mixture and serve sprinkled with the toasted almonds.

## Baccalà agghiotta
Salt cod with pine nuts, capers, sultanas and olives

It seems strange for an island where all but one of the provinces has a coast
to have so many recipes for different varieties of salted fish, but in the coastal
towns at certain seasons of the year there would be an abundance of fish
which couldn't be wasted. And in the days of only small boats, there would
be days when the weather was so bad it was too risky for the fishermen to
go out. Also, in the salt pans around Trapani some of the best sea salt is
harvested, in the same way that it has been done since Greek and Roman
times – so you have a perfect match of beautiful fish and beautiful salt.

Between Trapani and Marsala the land and seascape are completely changed
by the pyramids of salt piled up, and especially when the sun sets behind
them, it all looks very beautiful. The sea water is channelled through the
*basine*, a series of shallow ponds that look like a network of swimming
pools, and some of the old windmills that were once used to pump the water
through them are still dotted around. During the heat of the summer the sun
and the breeze evaporate the salt into slightly greyish white crystals, which
are harvested by hand and piled up to dry.

Like all sea salt, this is a natural product that is completely different from
harsher industrial salt, which is processed and sometimes has chemicals
added to it to help it flow better. It retains all its trace elements, and is higher
in magnesium and potassium, and lower in sodium chloride. Also, sea salt
has a stronger, more rounded flavour than industrial salt, so when you cook,
you can use less of it.

Serves 4

675g salt-dried cod
1 tablespoon sultanas
10 whole green olives in brine
250g plum tomatoes
60ml extra virgin olive oil
1 medium onion, finely chopped
1 celery stalk, chopped
1 tablespoon pine nuts
1 tablespoon salted capers, rinsed and well drained
2 medium potatoes, peeled and cubed
sea salt and freshly ground black pepper

Soak the salt cod in water overnight (or until it has lost most of its saltiness),
then drain and cut into bite-sized pieces.

Put the sultanas into a bowl and pour over enough cold water to cover. Leave for around 2 hours, until the sultanas soften and plump up, then drain.

Preheat the oven to 165°C/325°F/gas 3. Drain the olives and pat dry. With a sharp knife, make three or four cuts in each olive from end to end, then cut each segment away from the stone as carefully as you can.

Put the tomatoes into a pan of boiling water for 10 seconds, then drain under cold water and you should be able to peel them easily. Cut them in half, scoop out the seeds with a teaspoon, and chop the flesh.

Heat the olive oil in a pan and add the onion and celery. Cook gently until coloured, then add the tomatoes. Continue cooking for a few minutes, then add the salt cod and cook for a few minutes so that the fish can soak up the flavours. Add the sultanas, olives, pine nuts, capers and potatoes and season to taste. When the liquid in the pan begins to boil, turn off the heat and cover the pan or dish. Transfer to the oven and bake for about an hour, until the potatoes are tender.

### 'When they are young, they jump out of the water and play like buffoons'

*Pesce spada*
Swordfish

Ever since Greek and Roman times swordfish has been as treasured in Sicilian culture as tuna. You can understand why a big fish was so valuable if you had a big family to feed. Sardines might be full of flavour, but they are so small, whereas a swordfish can be cut into steaks, grilled and finished with lemon juice, zest and fresh herbs, or with *salmoriglio* (see page 66). They can be sprinkled with oregano and lemon zest, seasoned, then drizzled with olive oil and steamed gently for 10 to 12 minutes, then served with lemon juice squeezed over the top, and a scattering of parsley and garlic. Thinner slices are often rolled up around a filling of parsley, breadcrumbs, capers and onions, skewered and grilled or chargrilled, or simmered in a spicy tomato *ghiotto* sauce. Smaller pieces of swordfish can be made into *polpettine*, little balls of fish, seasoned and flavoured with garlic and lemon zest. In a newer fashion, you also find it served raw as a carpaccio.

In the last few years, the whole world has woken up to sushi and sashimi, and even Sicily is not immune. There, when they serve raw fish, it is known as *pesce crudo*, and instead of the salinity of the soy sauce that the Japanese like so much against the sweetness of the fish, they use citrus juice and zest, with pistachio nuts or almonds, ground very fine, almost like Parmesan, sprinkled over the top, and the lemon juice starts to 'cook' the fish slightly, so it is not completely raw.

In dialect, swordfish have so many names: *pisci-spata, spatu, puddi-cinéddu* – this last one is what they call the smaller ones, because it is also the name for a little kid who is playing and being a bit of a buffoon. When the swordfish are very small, or when they are in their 'love' season, they jump out of the water and do funny things as if they are enjoying themselves, just like *puddicinéddu*.

Like tuna, swordfish is now subject to strict fishing quotas, and can only be fished from May to August, when massive quantities come through the straits from the Sargasso Sea. There is a Slow Food Presidium that supports the traditional methods of harpooning the fish from small, handmade boats, which have oars and a lookout mast. The men stand on a gangway that stretches over the water from the front of the boat, and they throw their harpoons from there, which allows them to take only the bigger fish.

This is a very precise, if less abundant method of fishing swordfish, but of course swordfish are also sometimes caught accidentally, outside the legal season, by fishermen looking for other species, and, as it goes against the Sicilian grain to waste anything, this causes a big dilemma. If you are found fishing swordfish in the wrong season, you can lose your licence, but what is

a fisherman to do, especially if the fish is dead by the time you land it? One time when I was in Sicily one of the local boats accidentally caught an illegal swordfish which had drowned by the time the men got it into the boat. People always think it strange that a fish can drown, but they are creatures that are designed to breathe through their gills as they swim, so when they are pulled sideways, and the water can't go through their gills properly, they drown, and the structure of the flesh is different when you cook it. That is why the best fish are caught on hooks and lines, because they are pulled out alive.

Because it would have broken this fisherman's heart to throw the swordfish away, he quickly cut it up into slices and put it into the freezer, so that even if someone in authority came to check up on him, it would be difficult to know that he hadn't fished it in the correct season and then frozen it.

Note: if you can't find fresh or frozen swordfish you could substitute monkfish in any of the following recipes.

**Pesce spada con peperoni**
Swordfish with peppers

Serves 4

60ml olive oil
1 medium onion, finely sliced
sea salt and freshly ground black pepper
2 sweet yellow peppers, seeded and cut into strips
3 tablespoons tomato sauce (see page 75)
2 medium carrots, peeled
4 x 140g swordfish steaks
1 tablespoon parsley and garlic (see page 60)
extra virgin olive oil
3 large basil leaves, roughly chopped

Heat half the olive oil in a pan, add the onion and cook gently until softened and translucent. Season, add the peppers and cook for a few minutes, then add 1 tablespoon of the tomato sauce and cook for 2 minutes. In a separate pan, cook the carrots in enough boiling water to cover, until just tender, then drain and slice thinly.

Add the carrots to the pan containing the onions and peppers, together with the remaining 2 tablespoons of tomato sauce. Put in the fish and simmer over a low heat for 8–12 minutes, depending on its thickness. Taste and season if necessary, then add the parsley and garlic. Drizzle with some extra virgin olive oil, add the chopped basil and serve hot.

## Pesce spada alla Messinese
Swordfish Messina-style

Serves 4

10 whole black olives in brine
extra virgin olive oil
4 x 140g swordfish steaks
sea salt and freshly ground black pepper
2 spring onions, chopped
2 garlic cloves, chopped
20g salted capers, rinsed and well drained
a pinch of dried chilli flakes
4 anchovy fillets in oil
70ml white wine
1 x 400g tin of chopped tomatoes
100ml tomato passata
1 tablespoon parsley and garlic (see page 60)

Drain the olives and pat dry. With a sharp knife, make three or four cuts in each olive from end to end, then cut each segment away from the stone as carefully as you can.

Heat some extra virgin olive oil in a pan, then put in the swordfish, season and seal on all sides. Lift out and set aside. Add the spring onions, garlic, capers, olives, chilli and anchovy fillets to the pan, and cook gently until the anchovies 'melt' into the oil and the onion is translucent. Add the white wine and bubble up to evaporate the alcohol, then add the tomatoes and passata. Mix well, cover and leave to cook for 30 minutes on a very low heat, adding the swordfish for the last 10–12 minutes. Serve sprinkled with the parsley and garlic.

**Braciolette di pesce spade**
Swordfish steaks with breadcrumbs, capers and cheese

Some of the most beautiful capers you can find are harvested and salted on the hot, windy islands of Salina, to the north of Sicily, and, to the south-west, the volcanic Pantelleria, which was the first stop in the Arab invasion of Sicily, and whose name derives from the Arab *Bint-al Rion*, 'daughter of the wind'. Here the wind can sometimes be so strong you can barely stand up. On these islands there is a massive production of both capers and caperberries, which thrive in the hot, dry climate. Capers are the tight flower buds of the shrub *Capparis spinosa*. If the buds aren't picked they turn into white flowers, and then develop fruits, or caperberries *(cucunci)*. In northern Italy and now increasingly in the UK, caperberries are very popular, and quite expensive, which makes Sicilians laugh, because they have no use for them. 'You crazy northerner,' they say to me, 'you pay even more for the things we have thrown away for hundreds of years.'

Serves 4

6 quite thin slices of swordfish fillet
sea salt and freshly ground black pepper
200g breadcrumbs (see page 45)
1 tablespoon parsley and garlic (see page 60)
50g salted capers, rinsed and well drained
150g caciocavallo or pecorino cheese, grated
35ml extra virgin olive oil
2 medium onions, quartered

Heat a grill to high, or preheat the oven to 180°C/350°F/gas 4.

Flatten the slices of swordfish by tapping them gently with the end of a rolling pin until they are around 5mm thick, then cut each slice in half, so you have 12 pieces, each roughly 10 x 6cm. Season the breadcrumbs and mix with the parsley and garlic.

Take about three-quarters of this breadcrumb mixture, put it into a bowl and mix in the capers, cheese and 2 tablespoons of extra virgin olive oil. Spread some of this mixture over each of the swordfish pieces and roll them up. Thread the rolls of fish on to skewers, three rolls on each one, alternating them with onion quarters.

Have the remaining breadcrumb mixture ready on a plate.

Brush the skewers with olive oil, then roll them in the breadcrumb mixture. Lay the skewers on a baking tray and put under the grill or into the oven for 10 minutes, until the breadcrumbs are golden. Serve hot.

### Mpanata di pesce spada
Swordfish, olive and caper 'pie'

Sometimes when I look at the ingredients for Sicilian recipes, I think, 'That will never work,' and it turns out to be a really delicious dish. These pasty-shaped pies, big enough for six people to share, are very similar in their name and appearance to the Spanish *empanada*, and are a legacy of the Spanish occupation.

Serves 6

400g plum tomatoes
150g whole green olives in brine
olive oil
1 medium onion, finely chopped
1 celery stalk, finely chopped
900g swordfish steaks, cut into large pieces
120g salted capers, rinsed and well drained
200ml tomato sauce (see page 75)
2 courgettes, cut into short batons

For the crust:
600g plain flour
100g caster sugar
230g cold unsalted butter, cut into pieces
6 large egg yolks
sea salt

To make the crust, sift the flour and sugar together, then rub in the butter until the mixture looks like wet sand. Add the egg yolks and a pinch of salt. Knead this mixture briefly, then let it rest in the fridge for 30 minutes.

Preheat the oven to 180°C/350°F/gas 4.

Put the tomatoes into a pan of boiling water for 10 seconds, then drain under cold water and you should be able to peel them easily. Cut them in half, scoop out the seeds with a teaspoon, then cut each half into quarters and set aside.

Drain the olives and pat dry. With a sharp knife, make three or four cuts in each olive from end to end, then cut each segment away from the stone as carefully as you can.

Heat a little olive oil and add the onion and celery. Cook gently until they have coloured lightly, then add the swordfish, capers, olives and tomato sauce. Cook for 15 minutes, then add the fresh tomatoes. Take off the heat and leave to cool. In a separate pan, heat a little more oil, cook the courgette batons until golden, and drain on kitchen paper.

Roll out the dough into a circle about 25–30cm in diameter and about 5mm thick, and lay it on a baking tray. Spoon half the fish mixture on to one half of the circle and scatter with half of the courgettes, then follow with the rest of the fish mixture, and finish with the rest of the courgettes. Fold the other half of the dough over the top to make a half-moon shape and crimp the edges together (like a Cornish pasty).

Bake in the oven for 1 hour, or until golden brown, and serve hot or at room temperature.

### Cernia alla ghiotta
Grouper in caper, olive and chilli sauce

Serves 4

30g whole green olives in brine
2 ripe plum tomatoes
extra virgin olive oil
1 tablespoon garlic oil (see page 60)
½ medium onion, chopped
1 celery stalk, chopped
¼ carrot, chopped
60ml dry white wine
a pinch of dried chilli flakes, or to taste
15g salted capers, rinsed and well drained
sea salt
4 x 170g fillets of grouper or sea bream
2 tablespoons parsley and garlic (see page 60)

Drain the olives and pat dry. With a sharp knife, make three or four cuts in each olive from end to end, then cut each segment away from the stone as carefully as you can.

Put the tomatoes into a pan of boiling water for 10 seconds, then drain them under cold water and you should be able to peel them easily. Cut them in half, scoop out the seeds with a teaspoon, and chop the flesh.

In a pan big enough to hold the fillets of fish, heat a little extra virgin olive oil, then add the garlic oil. Put in the onion, celery and carrot and cook gently until soft, but only lightly coloured. Pour in the white wine, and bubble up to allow the alcohol to evaporate.

Add the chilli flakes, capers and olives, and season with a little salt (be careful, as the capers will be quite salty). Add the fish to the pan, spooning over the sauce to make sure it is covered, then add the tomatoes and, if you like, more chilli.

Place a sheet of foil or greaseproof paper over the top of the pan, and put the lid over it, so the pan is completely sealed. Continue to cook for about 10 minutes, until the fish is opaque. Taste and season with a little more salt if necessary. Scatter with the parsley and garlic.

**Pesce salsito**
Sea bass in olive and caper sauce

This is another variation of the *agrodolce* – sweet and sour – flavours that Sicilians love so much.

Serves 4

10 whole green olives in brine
900g sea bass, filleted
2 celery sticks, chopped
1 large onion, finely chopped
extra virgin olive oil
75g salted capers, rinsed, well drained and chopped
60g tomato purée
2 tablespoons white wine vinegar
2 tablespoons sugar
100ml fish stock
1 tablespoon parsley and garlic (see page 60)

Drain the olives and pat dry. With a sharp knife, make three or four cuts in each olive from end to end, then cut each segment away from the stone as carefully as you can.

Put the sea bass fillets into a steamer (if you don't have one, put them into a colander over a pan of boiling water and cover with a pan lid). Steam for about 10–12 minutes, depending on the thickness of the fish, until firm.

Meanwhile, bring a little water to the boil in a small pan, add the chopped celery and simmer for a minute or two, just to soften. Remove with a slotted spoon and drain on kitchen paper. Add the onion to the same water, and again, blanch for a few minutes to soften, lift out with a slotted spoon and drain on kitchen paper.

Heat a little extra virgin olive oil in a pan. Add the blanched celery and onion and cook gently until they begin to colour, then add the olives and capers. After a few minutes add the tomato purée, vinegar, sugar and fish stock, stir, and bubble up until the liquid reduces and thickens a little.

Put the fish fillets on a serving plate, pour the sauce over them and sprinkle some parsley and garlic on top.

**Orata al forno con patate, caperi e pomodoro**
Baked sea bream with potato, capers and tomato

In the market in Sicily you buy whatever fish looks good on the day, and if there is some gilt-head bream and you have a few people to feed, this way of baking them in the oven is so simple – of course you could substitute pieces of any other sturdy white fish, such as sea bass.

Serves 4

6 medium potatoes, peeled and sliced thinly
24 cherry tomatoes, halved
1 tablespoon salted capers, rinsed and well drained
olive oil
sea salt and freshly ground black pepper
4 sea bream (about 600g each) cleaned, scaled, heads and tails removed
125mls dry white wine
juice of 1 lemon
1 tablespoon parsley and garlic (see page 60)

Preheat the oven to 180°C/350°F/gas 4.

In a bowl, mix together the potatoes, tomatoes, capers, olive oil and seasoning, as if you were tossing a salad.

Put the mixture into a baking dish. Season the fish and place on top. Put into the oven and bake for 4 minutes, then pour the wine over the top and bake for another 15 minutes.

Lift out the fish and remove the bones, then serve with some of the potatoes, tomatoes, herbs and juices spooned over the top. Finish with a squeeze of lemon juice and scatter with the parsley and garlic.

**Orata a scapece**
Escabeche of sea bream

In Sicily this is traditionally made with *palombo*, or tope, a species of shark – but you are more likely to find sea bream. Tope is found in the seas around Britain, but it isn't valued in the way that it is in Sicily. When I went deepwater fishing in Cornwall, if any tope was caught it was thrown back into the sea, which is a shame, because it is delicious: white and meaty. This dish is best if you leave it to cool to room temperature for an hour before serving.

Serves 4

plain flour for dredging
sea salt and freshly ground black pepper
4 x 200g sea bream fillets
olive oil
200ml white wine vinegar
1 medium onion, finely sliced
100g tomato purée
35g pine nuts
35g sultanas
2 tablespoons garlic oil (see page 60)
2 tablespoons parsley and garlic (see page 60)
100ml fish stock

Have the flour ready on a plate, season the fish fillets and dip them into it so that they are coated on both sides. Heat some olive oil in a pan, add the fish and fry until golden on both sides. Remove the fillets from the pan (keep this to one side) and put into a shallow bowl. Sprinkle with the vinegar.

Drain nearly all the oil from the reserved pan and put it back on the heat. Add the onion, and as soon as it becomes translucent, stir in the tomato purée and cook gently for 10 minutes. Add the pine nuts, sultanas, garlic oil and parsley and garlic, then season and stir well. Lift the fish fillets from the bowl and drain well on kitchen paper to remove the excess vinegar. Add to the pan, along with the fish stock, cover the pan, lower the heat, and cook for another 15 minutes.

### Squadro alla matalotta
Monkfish with olives

Ideally this is made with the famous Pachino tomatoes.

Serves 4

12 whole green olives in brine
2 tablespoons olive oil
½ medium red onion, finely sliced
5 Pachino or cherry tomatoes, chopped
1 medium potato, peeled and cut into 5mm slices
1 tablespoon salted capers, rinsed and well drained
a pinch of saffron threads (about 15)
2 tablespoons chopped flat-leaf parsley
a few basil leaves
4 x 200g monkfish tails, cut into approximately 1cm slices
50ml white wine

Drain the olives and pat dry. With a sharp knife, make three or four cuts in each olive from end to end, then cut each segment away from the stone as carefully as you can and roughly chop.

Heat the olive oil in a pan, add the onion and cook until softened. Add the olives, tomatoes, potato slices, capers, saffron, parsley and basil, and cook, stirring, for 5 minutes. Put the fish into the pan, add the white wine, and bubble up until the alcohol has evaporated. Stir, cover and cook for 5 more minutes, or until the potatoes are just soft.

**Risotto alla marinara**
Seafood risotto

Risotto is a rare thing in Sicily, and doesn't really feature in the traditional cooking – whereas in the north of Italy it is a staple dish. In my book *Made in Italy*, I devoted seventy pages to risotto! The only risotto recipe you are likely to come across often in Sicily is made with seafood, and it is done in a slightly different way to the risotto of the north, which owes its creaminess to the *mantecatura* – the beating in of butter at the end (*mantecatura* comes from the Spanish word for butter, *mantequilla*). There is no butter in this recipe – not even to toast the grains of rice at the beginning of making the risotto. Instead, you use oil, and at the end, in place of butter, you beat in some more olive oil and lemon juice. The stock is quite light, but the real flavour comes from adding the seafood in its sauce for the last four minutes of cooking.

Serves 6

450g clams
450g mussels
190ml dry white wine
450g small prawns, shell on
135ml olive oil
1 medium onion, very finely chopped
1 celery stalk, finely chopped
1 carrot, finely chopped
1 fresh red chilli, finely chopped
2 small squid, cleaned and cut into strips
1 tablespoon tomato sauce (see page 75)
sea salt and freshly ground black pepper
450g *vialone nano* rice
juice of 1 lemon
2 tablespoons finely chopped flat-leaf parsley or basil

Scrub the clams and mussels separately (pulling any beards from the mussels) under running water and discard any that are open. Put the clams and mussels into a large pan with 70ml of the white wine over a high heat, cover, and cook, shaking the pan from time to time, until all the shells have opened. Remove from the heat, strain off the cooking liquid and reserve this. Discard any clams or mussels whose shells haven't opened. Take the rest out of their shells and throw the shells away.

Peel the prawns and keep on one side, reserving the heads and shells. Heat 1 tablespoon of olive oil in a large pan, put in the prawn heads and shells and crush them with a wooden spoon to help release the juices. Add 2 litres of water, along with the reserved cooking liquid from the clams and mussels.

Bring to the boil, then turn down the heat and simmer for 15 minutes. Strain into a bowl to remove the prawn heads, then pour back into a clean pan and keep hot on the hob, next to where you are going to make the risotto.

Heat 4 more tablespoons of olive oil in a pan. Put in half the onion, and all the celery, carrot and chilli, and cook until the vegetables are soft but not coloured. Add the squid, and the reserved prawns, mussels and clams. Stir for a minute or so, until the prawns change colour, then pour in 50ml of the remaining white wine and bubble up to let it evaporate. Add the tomato sauce, stir, then add about 100ml of the reserved stock. Taste, season and keep to one side.

Meanwhile, heat another 2 tablespoons of olive oil in a heavy-based pan. Add the rest of the onion and cook very gently, until softened but not coloured, then add the rice and stir around to coat in the oil, and to 'toast' the grains. Make sure all the grains are warm before you add the rest of the wine. Let the wine evaporate completely until the onions and rice are dry.

Start to add the stock, a ladleful at a time, stirring and scraping the pan as you do so. Wait until each addition of stock has almost evaporated before adding the next ladleful. Carry on adding the stock in this way for about 12 minutes, then add the reserved seafood and sauce and cook for another 4 minutes. The grains of rice should be just tender, but still al dente, and the risotto should be quite loose – what we call *all'onda*, i.e. when it is on the plate, if you tilt it, the rice should ripple like waves.

Remove from the heat, beat in the remaining 2 tablespoons of olive oil and the lemon juice, to taste – you don't want it to be too sharp, so start with just a little juice, taste and see what you think, before adding any more – and season as necessary. If you think the risotto is too stiff, add a little more stock. Stir in the parsley or basil, and let the risotto rest for a minute or two before serving.

# Carne
# Meat

So the late afternoon air was filled with the luxuriant, nutty, brown butter smell of meat over flame, and I was wondering where I was going to put one more mouthful, and at six o'clock we started eating again. Or perhaps we had never really stopped. The sausage was good, salty and sweet, and there was more bitter *cicoria* balancing its richness. The *castrato* – both male and female sheep were castrated, explained Franco – was tender and had a marked musky, feral flavour.

– Matthew Fort, *Sweet Honey, Bitter Lemons: Travels in Sicily*

In a restaurant in Ragusa, I ate a plate of very lean beef that had been simply seared in a pan, along with some vegetables, transferred to the oven with wine to cover, and cooked very slowly. Then it was carved, and in between each round of meat was a fresh slice of Sicilian orange. Over the top the chef had scattered some Trapani sea salt, and it was an extraordinary dish. All the more extraordinary because in my experience of Sicily, meat is something that is never worked on much. I completely understand cooking fish very, very simply, but in other regions of Italy the cooking of meat is usually a little more involved: not elaborate, but there is a chance to express your creativity. In Sicily, however, in general people seem to prefer their meat just roasted, baked or grilled with tomatoes, vegetables and potatoes, and maybe some lemon peel and herbs.

A typical family dish is *carne murata*, which is slices of veal, batted out until quite thin, laid in a terracotta dish with a layer of onion, then a layer of potatoes, tomatoes, seasoning and herbs, covered and baked in the oven. But it is more likely that there will be pork or veal chops, or steaks on the bone, simply cooked on the barbecue: perhaps because there have been times in the island's history when to have meat at all was such a luxury that you wanted to enjoy it just for itself, with no adornment. Or perhaps it is because all but one of the nine provinces of Sicily has a coastline, so for most people the ready availability of fresh fish dictates what they eat; and when they don't have fish, they eat vegetables. And pasta, always pasta; again, more often than not, with fish, or vegetables, and only in inland areas are the pasta sauces made with meat.

I must admit that I am also biased towards the coast and the fantastic fish and seafood that can be bought in the markets, because the area between the ports of Sciacca and Mazara del Vallo, up to Trapani and Palermo, is the region that I know best, and where my heart is. But I also have a daughter whose allergies mean that she can't eat fish, so finding good meat as well as vegetables for Dita is always a priority when we are on holiday.

The first time we spent our holidays in Sicily, after I had been into the butcher's shop in Menfi for a few days running, each time with my bags of fish and vegetables and fruit, having been from one little shop to the next, the butcher said, 'You know you can find everything in the supermarket?' Of course, I immediately said: 'I don't want to buy from the supermarket!' but he insisted I went to take a look, because he said, 'We all sell our produce there.' So I went to the outskirts of the village, where there is the one small supermarket, and I couldn't believe it: there was the same guy who had been serving in the butcher's shop previously, along with the local men I had seen selling their artichokes in the square early in the morning. The way it works is that the supermarket is affiliated to a chain, so it sells washing-up liquid and dry goods and everyday stuff, but the fresh meat, along with the fish and the vegetables and fruit, all comes from the local guys in and around the village, who supply them, as well as running their little shops or market stalls. It was such a revelation to see that even though the people have accepted that there is a need for a supermarket, they don't want anyone else selling their meat there.

In the height of the summer season, though, when so many people arrive on the island for holidays, the butcher has to import more meat from mainland Italy, because the local production is only enough to feed the small community. Also in many parts of the island there is no real grass in the dry heat of summer, so the poor animals are quite skinny and bony. It is a terrain more suited to sheep than cattle, and the main breed on the island is the Comisana, which have brown faces, some with a white stripe down their noses, and loppy ears.

In springtime, though, there are baby lambs, and also kid goats jumping around, and this is when Sicilians are tempted to eat the most meat. Lamb has also traditionally been the meat of celebrations, the most obvious being at *la tosatura*, the festival of the shearing of the wool, which Shakespeare used as the setting for a Sicilian scene in *The Winter's Tale*.

Rino, my head chef, remembers a massive party when he was young, held outside the house of someone in the middle of the olive groves. The legs and shoulders of the sheep were baked in the wooden oven with potatoes and tomatoes and olives, and the head and the rest boiled for hours until tender, because the brain and tongue and cartilage were all thought of as delicacies, and the eating went on all day. Rino recalls his mother giving him pieces of the baked lamb that was so strongly flavoured, his father was saying, 'This was the oldest sheep in history.'

And at Easter, of course, everyone celebrates with lamb and makes a big effort to do something special, because traditionally people would not have been eating any meat during Lent. I was in Modica for the famous festival of the Madonna Vasa Vasa, which is an incredible thing to see. The statues of the Virgin Mary and Jesus are carried around the town, and when they find each other, and kiss outside the Piazza San Domenico, doves are released from beneath the Virgin's cloak. Each one has ribbons attached to a leg in the colours of the different quarters of the town and the local people say that according to the way they fly there will be good or bad luck. Everyone is out on the streets, but as soon as the spectacle is over, the people are gone: no need for police to disperse the crowd, they've gone to eat!

Pork was once the meat with which to celebrate Carnevale, the big Shrove Tuesday festival of eating before Lent, and if, out of a family of five or six brothers, one had a piece of land on which to keep a pig, it would be slaughtered just before the festival. Everyone would help on the day of slaughter, and they would divide up the meat between the families. Every-thing would be made use of, and what wasn't eaten fresh would be cured for ham or salami – which, in Sicily, is typically only lightly matured.

These days I see fresh pork used more in sausages (*salsiccia fresca*), which are really dense and meaty, made with pure meat. Very often you go to the butcher's shop and they chop the pork in front of you and season it, maybe adding some fennel seeds. Sometimes the sausages are made with a little wine, or perhaps some pecorino, chopped onion, and other herbs or flecks of chilli. If the sausage is for the cooking pot, it is usually sold in links;

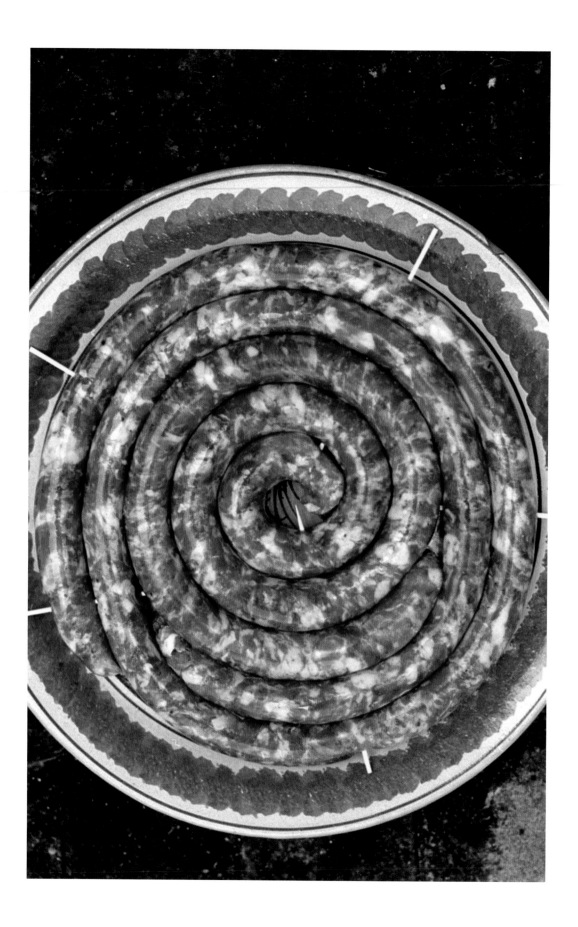

if it is for the coals, it is thinner, and often long lengths are wound into a big coil and skewered in place ready for the barbecue.

Or the pork will be chopped in the same way and made into *polpette* (meatballs) for cooking in tomato sauce (see page 332), or grilling between fresh lemon leaves (see page 333). Thin slices of pork might be bread-crumbed and fried to make a quick lunch of *scallopine*, or rolled up, dusted in breadcrumbs, then sautéed in a pan. A little white wine will be added, and tomatoes, to make a sauce, and after twenty minutes or so, when the meat is cooked through, and the sauce thickened, the meat will be taken out, the sauce tossed through pasta, and the meat eaten as the main course. But I have rarely seen pork cooked any more elaborately than this.

Something else that always strikes me is that you don't really see chickens – yes, they are in the supermarket, brought in from mainland Italy, but not so many running around in back gardens as you might see in other regions. And there is a lack of traditional recipes for chicken, because it has historically been an expensive luxury. The culture of the grain, the grape and the olive took precedence over livestock farming. Only if you had a smallholding inland did you keep a few chickens, mainly for eggs, but when the chicken got a bit old and tough it went into the pot; the meat would be eaten first, and then the stock boiled up to make a soup, with vegetables and pasta, or it would be marinated and braised slowly, to tenderise it, as in the recipe on page 329.

**Braciolette alla Messinese**
Grilled veal Messina-style

In summer these skewered rolls of veal are fantastic cooked on the barbecue.

Serves 4

20g pine nuts
2 tablespoons olive oil, plus a little extra for brushing
1 medium onion, finely chopped
20g sultanas
300g breadcrumbs (see page 45)
2 tablespoons parsley and garlic (see page 60)
150g caciocavallo or pecorino cheese, grated
sea salt and freshly ground black pepper
550g loin of veal or beef
about 20 bay leaves

Heat the oven to 180°C/350°F/gas 4. Lay the pine nuts in a single layer on a baking tray and put them into the oven for about 8 minutes. As long as they are in a single layer you don't need to turn them. Keep an eye on them to make sure they don't burn, and when they are golden, take them out and chop them.

Heat half the olive oil in a pan, then add the onion and cook gently until soft, but not coloured. Add the pine nuts, sultanas and breadcrumbs and cook for a minute, then take off the heat. Stir in the parsley and garlic, the cheese and the rest of the olive oil, and season.

Cut the meat into 6 slices about 5mm thick, then put them between two sheets of clingfilm and bat them with a meat hammer or rolling pin, to tenderise them and make them slightly thinner (about 3–4mm). Heat a grill to medium hot.

Top each slice of meat with a tablespoon of the filling. Roll up tightly, making sure that all the filling is enclosed, and thread on to skewers – 4 rolls on each, with a bay leaf in between each roll and at the end. Brush with a little more olive oil, then grill until the meat has browned and is cooked through (about 5–6 minutes).

**Agglassato**
Onion-glazed beef

Traditionally this is served with roast potatoes and peas. You can use beef stock if you like, but we prefer to use chicken stock as it is a bit lighter.

Serves 6

2 tablespoons olive oil
900g topside or rump joint of beef
sea salt and freshly ground black pepper
about 12 medium onions, roughly chopped
1.5 litres good chicken stock
60ml Marsala

Heat the olive oil in a large pan, add the beef, season well, and brown it on all sides. Remove the meat from the pan, put in the onions and chicken stock, then return the beef to the pan, turn down the heat and let it braise slowly for about 45 minutes to 1 hour, turning the meat on all sides, throughout the cooking time so that the sauce clings to it all over, until the liquid has reduced right down.

Add the Marsala and carry on cooking until almost all the liquid in the pan has evaporated and the onions have become caramelised and jammy and are sticking to the meat (keep moving the meat around to prevent the onions from burning). Slice and serve.

## Agneddu alla Messinese
Messina-style lamb

Serves 4

20 whole black olives in brine
8–12 lamb chops
½ bottle of good red wine
4 garlic cloves
2 medium onions, sliced
4 medium tomatoes, chopped
a sprig of rosemary
2 tablespoons salted capers, rinsed and well drained
2 carrots, chopped
sea salt and freshly ground black pepper

Drain the olives and pat dry. With a sharp knife, make three or four cuts in each olive from end to end, then cut each segment away from the stone as carefully as you can.

Put the lamb chops into a bowl with the rest of the ingredients and the olives and leave to marinate in the fridge for a few hours.

Preheat the oven to 200°C/400°F/gas 6.

Transfer the chops to an oven dish and put, uncovered, into the preheated oven for around 10 minutes, then turn down the heat to 165°C/325°F/gas 3, season, cover with a lid or foil and leave to cook gently for 1½ hours.

**Castrato con fave verdi**
Lamb with broad beans

*Castrato* is neutered lamb. The neutering is done to take away some of the slightly bitter taint that can flavour male lamb meat, so that it stays more delicate. It can be eaten young, but it is also eaten when the sheep is more mature, at about two years old, so it develops a stronger, more gamey flavour, the equivalent of mutton in the UK. Rino, head chef at Locanda, remembers that although in his family it was usually stewed slowly, there were times when older *castrato* ended up on the barbecue, with no marinade to tenderise it first, so 'you needed teeth like a horse to eat it'. It is up to you whether you make this with young lamb, or mutton.

Serves 8

2kg boneless leg of lamb or mutton
juice of 1 lemon or 2 tablespoons of vinegar (if using mutton)
sea salt and freshly ground black pepper
6 tablespoons olive oil
2 tablespoons parsley and garlic (see page 60)
plain flour
1 tablespoon garlic oil (see page 60)
1 medium white onion, chopped
60ml dry white wine
2 litres lamb or chicken stock
500g podded fresh broad beans (or frozen beans)
extra virgin olive oil

If using mutton, put the meat into a bowl with the lemon juice or vinegar, 3 tablespoons of the olive oil and a pinch of salt. Leave overnight in the fridge, then rinse under running water, pat dry, and cut into chunks. This is just to take some of the gamey-ness from the meat.

Make slits in the meat and insert some of the parsley and garlic into each slit. Have the flour ready on a plate. Season the mutton or lamb with salt and dust with flour.

Heat the rest of the olive oil and the garlic oil in a large pan, then put in the meat and brown over a medium heat. When the lamb is well browned, add the onion and cook for a few minutes until translucent. Add the white wine and bubble up until the alcohol has evaporated, then add the stock. As soon as this boils, add the broad beans and cook for about 1–1½ hours, adding a little water (or more stock, if you have any left) from time to time as needed, until the meat is tender and the sauce has thickened. Drizzle with a little extra virgin olive oil.

### 'A meal for a whole family'

On the same day that Jack and I tasted the animal-like ricotta made by a shepherd in a field, we were out in the village with Alessio Planeta when this guy came up and said, 'I've got that goat for you, Mr Alessio.' This man lived in the most extraordinary little house with no roof. I don't know how he managed it, but inside he had an old Fiat from the 1970s, actually parked inside the house. Nobody knows how he could have got it in there; maybe somehow he lowered it in, because the doors were way too small for a car to pass through. And so he had this old car in his 'bedroom' and slept in it under the stars.

*Capretto*
Kid goat

Anyhow, he had a kid goat for Alessio. When the goats that are local to the Agrigento region are fully grown, they are shaggy, with long spiralling horns, and are mainly kept for milk, and cheese, but in the spring, when the baby ones are jumping around, a kid goat makes a meal for a whole family.

Alessio said, 'Why don't you give me the goat, and I'll get Giorgio to cook it?' So there and then, the guy took a knife out of his pocket and slit the throat of the goat, splattering Jack with blood, then skinned it. Jack was only about ten, and his face …! He just stood there in shock, with his mouth open, and when we arrived home and he rushed in, covered in blood, calling, 'Momma …' Plaxy started screaming.

The goat was delicious, by the way. We slow-cooked it so the meat was incredibly tender, with a slightly earthier flavour than lamb, and Jack chomped away on the legs very happily.

## Capretto (o agnello) con acciughe, rosmarino e limone
Roast kid goat (or baby lamb), with anchovies, rosemary and lemon

Serves 4

4 tablespoons plain flour
sea salt and freshly ground black pepper
1kg lamb or kid goat, cut into large chunks (about 6 x 6cm)
150ml vegetable oil
20 cherry tomatoes on the vine
1 fennel, quartered
1 red pepper, quartered and seeded
3 shallots, halved
1 aubergine, cut into thick slices
1 courgette, cut into thick slices
4 large fresh sweet red chillies
olive oil

For the sauce:
6 garlic cloves
8 anchovy fillets in oil, drained
1 bunch of rosemary, leaves picked
200ml dry white wine
200ml white wine vinegar
50ml extra virgin olive oil
zest and juice of 2 lemons

Preheat the oven to 165°C/325°F/gas 3.

For the sauce, using a pestle and mortar, pound the garlic very well and add the anchovies. Pound some more, then add the rosemary and pound to a paste. Add the white wine, vinegar, olive oil, and lemon juice and zest.

Have the flour ready on a plate. Season the meat, then dust with the flour and shake off the excess. Heat the vegetable oil in a roasting pan on the hob. Put in the lamb and sauté on both sides until golden brown. Add the sauce, cover with foil and transfer to the oven. Cook for 20 minutes, then remove the foil for another 25 minutes, or until the meat caramelises. Halfway through this last part of cooking, turn the meat over, being careful that the sauce doesn't burn or it will taste bitter – if it starts to dry out too much, add a little water. At the same time as you remove the foil from the meat, put all the vegetables and the whole chillies on to an oven tray. Season, drizzle with olive oil, and put into the oven to roast for the rest of the cooking time.

When the meat is ready, lift it out of the roasting tin on to a warm plate, add the roasted vegetables and pour the sauce over the top.

**Capretto delle madonie**
Braised goat (or lamb) with mushrooms

You will need to soak the dried mushrooms overnight, so that they plump up.

Serves 4

50g dried porcini
plain flour
sea salt and freshly ground black pepper
1kg lamb or kid goat, cut into large chunks (about 6 x 6cm)
2 tablespoons olive oil
2 medium onions, finely sliced
1 bay leaf
150ml dry red wine
500ml good chicken stock
a sprig of rosemary
2 tablespoons parsley and garlic (see page 60)

Soak the dried porcini in warm water overnight, then drain and chop.

Have the flour ready on a plate. Season the meat and dust in the flour, shaking off the excess. Heat the olive oil in a pan, add the meat, and colour on all sides. As soon as it is golden brown, add the onions and the bay leaf and cook for about 4 minutes, or until the onions start to colour. Add the wine and let it bubble up to evaporate the alcohol, then season.

Pour in enough stock to just cover the meat, add the rosemary and continue cooking for 45 minutes. Add the mushrooms and the parsley and garlic and continue cooking until the meat is cooked through and very tender.

**Coniglio alla cacciatore**
Rabbit 'hunter' style, in red wine and garlic

Hunters out in the woods would usually just stake the rabbits and cook them over an open fire, but if they brought them home, the traditional way would be to cook them in wine, with herbs, olives, almonds, tomatoes, onions, potatoes ... depending on the custom of your village or town.

Serves 4

150g whole blanched almonds
20 whole black olives in brine
1 x 1.1kg rabbit, cut into pieces
1 bottle of red wine
40ml olive oil
1 garlic clove, thinly sliced
a small sprig of oregano
sea salt and freshly ground black pepper
250ml good chicken stock

Heat the oven to 180°C/350°F/gas 4. Lay the almonds in a single layer on a baking tray and put into the oven for about 8 minutes. As long as they are in a single layer you don't need to turn them. Keep an eye on them to make sure they don't burn, and when they are golden, take them out and chop them.

Drain the olives and pat dry. With a sharp knife, make three or four cuts in each olive from end to end, and then cut each segment away from the stone as carefully as you can.

Put the rabbit pieces into a bowl with the wine and leave to marinate for 30 minutes, then lift out, drain and pat dry, reserving the marinade. Heat the olive oil in a heavy pan, put in the rabbit pieces and brown all over. Add the garlic and oregano, season and add 3 tablespoons of the marinade, the chicken stock and the olives.

Turn the heat down to low and continue cooking for about 40 minutes, adding a little water (or more stock, if you have any left) as necessary until the meat is cooked and the sauce reduced. Sprinkle with the chopped toasted almonds.

**Coniglio in agrodolce**
Sweet and sour rabbit

We use the Sicilian Nocellara olives for this – which are plump, fleshy and fruity. As always I suggest you buy them with the stone in so that you keep that little touch of bitterness from the stone right up until you remove it.

Serves 4

25 whole green olives in brine
2 tablespoons plain flour
sea salt and freshly ground black pepper
1 x 1.1kg rabbit, cut into pieces
1 tablespoon olive oil
2 medium onions, sliced
5 tablespoons white wine vinegar
1 tablespoon sugar
250ml good chicken stock
1 bay leaf

Drain the olives and pat dry. With a sharp knife, make three or four cuts in each olive from end to end, and then cut each segment away from the stone as carefully as you can.

Have the flour ready on a plate. Season the rabbit and roll each piece in the flour, shaking off the excess.

Heat the olive oil in a pan, put in the rabbit and sauté on all sides until golden brown. Remove the rabbit, turn down the heat, put the onions into the pan and cook until they turn translucent, then season and add the olives.

Return the rabbit to the pan. Mix the vinegar and sugar together in a cup and pour into the pan. Bring to the boil for about 2 minutes, then add the chicken stock and bay leaf, turn down the heat and simmer for 35 minutes, until the sauce has thickened and the rabbit is cooked (the meat should fall away from the bones).

### Galletto alla calascibettana
Braised chicken

You need a good chicken that has run around a bit for this – a big, free-range one that has been allowed to grow slowly.

Serves 4

1 large free-range, preferably organic chicken, cut into 8 pieces
3 tablespoons white wine vinegar
a sprig of rosemary
1 tablespoon olive oil
2 medium onions, chopped
about 100ml good chicken stock
3 tablespoons white wine
juice of 1 lemon
sea salt and freshly ground black pepper
2 bay leaves

Put the chicken pieces into a bowl with the vinegar and rosemary and leave in the fridge to marinate for a couple of hours. Drain and pat dry.

Heat the olive oil in a large pan, put in the onions and cook until soft but not coloured. Put in the chicken pieces, stock, white wine and lemon juice, season, and crumble in the bay leaves.

Cover the pan with a lid and cook over a low heat for 1 hour, checking from time to time to make sure the chicken isn't burning, and adding a little water (or chicken stock if you have any left), if necessary. When the chicken is done there should be very little liquid left in the pan. Check that the chicken is cooked through – if you insert a skewer into the thickest part of the thighs, the juices should run clear.

### 'Hardy strong little creatures'

The beech and oak forests of the Nebrodi mountains near Enna, Messina and Catania are home to the ancient native black 'swine'. Once wild, they look like miniature wild boar, quite cute and bristly, but they can be just as aggressive. Especially if you come across a mother with little ones – then you don't get out of the car, because if they see you they will run at you.

A bit like the famous Spanish Pata Negra, they are hardy, strong little creatures that run around foraging and eating acorns and berries, and only when the sows are about to have babies, or when the mature pigs are about to be fattened up on beans and cereals for a month before slaughter, are they brought under a traditional *pagghiaru*, a teepee-shaped shelter made with poles and straw and with a base of stones.

The meat, which has a sweet, distinctive flavour, because of the diet of the pigs, and is quite lean, because of their athleticism – is used mostly for prosciutto, pancetta and salami, though some of it goes into fresh sausages.

Because the hams have never been marketed or promoted like the Pata Negra or San Daniele, and the local farmers really only raised them for their families or for the local community, the pigs, which once used to roam the mountains in big herds, were in real danger of extinction until Slow Food came to their rescue and formed a Presidium of a small group of farmers, providing them with the processing facilities that they need to preserve the traditions and promote the Nebrodi pig as something special.

*Suino nero dei Nebrodi*
The black pigs of Nebrodi

Nebrodi pig

**Polpette al sugo**
Meatballs with wild fennel in tomato sauce

You see big bunches of dried oregano and marjoram sold alongside the vegetables in Sicilian shops. Often they are sold in bags, so you snip the corner, hang up the bag, and then, when you want to use some, you squeeze the bag at the corner and some of the crumbled herb comes through.

Serves 4

plain flour
300g pork mince
1 onion, finely chopped
100g pecorino cheese, grated
50g breadcrumbs (see page 45)
1 tablespoon parsley and garlic (see page 60)
1 teaspoon chopped wild fennel, or fennel seeds, soaked in a little water
sea salt and freshly ground black pepper
2 eggs, beaten
2 tablespoons olive oil
2 garlic cloves, chopped
1 x 400g tin of chopped tomatoes
a pinch of dried oregano

Have the flour ready on a plate.

Mix the pork mince with half the onion, the cheese, breadcrumbs, parsley and garlic, and fennel. Season, then mix in the beaten eggs. With your hands, divide the mixture and form into balls (about the size of a golfball). Flatten them slightly, then dust with flour and shake off the excess.

Heat half the olive oil in a pan. Add the chopped garlic and the rest of the chopped onion and cook gently until soft, but not coloured. Add the tomatoes, season and add the oregano. Cover and cook over a high heat until the tomatoes have reduced down to create a sauce (about 10 minutes).

Heat the rest of the olive oil in another pan, put in the meatballs and fry until they are golden brown all over. Add to the pan of sauce, cover, turn down the heat to low, and simmer very gently for a further 10–15 minutes.

**Polpette al limone**
Meatballs cooked with lemon leaves

This recipe is very similar to the previous one, except that instead of flavouring the meat with fennel, you use lemon zest, and then cook the *polpette* between lemon leaves. In Sicily this just means you go into your garden and pick your lemon, with as many leaves as you need. In the UK, you may have to substitute fresh bay leaves. You can also do these on the barbecue, skewering the meatballs with the leaves in between.

Serves 4

300g pork mince
1 onion, finely chopped
100g pecorino cheese, grated
50g breadcrumbs (see page 45)
grated zest of 1 lemon
1 tablespoon parsley and garlic (see page 60)
a pinch of dried oregano
sea salt and freshly ground black pepper
2 eggs, beaten
1 tablespoon olive oil
24 lemon leaves or fresh bay leaves, washed and dried

Preheat the oven to 180°C/350°F/gas 4.

Mix the pork mince with the onion, cheese, breadcrumbs, lemon zest, the parsley and garlic and the oregano. Season, and mix in the beaten eggs. With your hands, divide the mixture and form into balls (about the size of a golfball), then flatten them slightly.

Grease a baking tray with a little olive oil. Lay the meatballs in lines on the tray, with a lemon leaf or bay leaf in between each one. Drizzle with a little more olive oil and bake for about 10 to 15 minutes until cooked through.

### Trippa alla Ragusana
Tripe Ragusa-style

Tripe, spleen, intestines … in Sicily these are all loved, often as morsels of street food, or, in the case of tripe, cooked in so many different ways, from region to region, town to town, house to house. This quite sweet recipe is a very old one that is typical in Ragusa.

Serves 4

2 medium aubergines
sea salt and freshly ground black pepper
1 tablespoon whole blanched almonds
1kg calves' tripe
3 tablespoons olive oil
400ml good chicken stock
3 tablespoons grated caciocavallo or pecorino cheese
1 tablespoon finely chopped hazelnuts
a pinch of ground cinnamon

Cut the aubergines into strips, sprinkle with salt and leave to drain in a colander for at least 2 hours. Squeeze lightly to get rid of the excess liquid.

Preheat the oven to 180°C/350°F/gas 4. Lay the almonds in a single layer on a baking tray and put into the oven for about 8 minutes. As long as they are in a single layer you don't need to turn them. Keep an eye on them to make sure they don't burn, and when they are golden, take them out and chop them.

Wash and dry the tripe and cut it into 1cm strips. Heat 1 tablespoon of the olive oil in a large pan, and when very hot add the tripe and sear very quickly. Season, add three-quarters of the stock and simmer for 1 hour, adding more stock if necessary; however, when the tripe is ready there should only be a little liquid left in the pan. If you taste a little of the tripe it should be meltingly tender.

Heat the rest of the olive oil in another pan. Put in the aubergine, sauté on both sides, then drain on kitchen paper and add to the pan containing the tripe, together with the cheese, chopped toasted almonds, hazelnuts and cinnamon. Taste and check the seasoning, mix everything together very gently, and serve hot.

# Dolci
# Desserts

Scorning the table of drinks, glittering with crystal and silver on the right, he moved left towards that of the sweet-meats … cakes speckled with white almonds and green pistachio nuts, hillocks of chocolate-covered pastry, brown and rich as the top soil of the Catanian plain from which, in fact, through many a twist and turn they had come, pink ices, champagne ices, coffee ices, all *parfaits* and falling apart with a squelch at a knife cleft; a melody in major of crystallised cherries, acid notes of yellow pineapple, and green pistachio paste of those cakes called 'Triumphs of Gluttony', shameless 'Virgins' cakes' shaped like breasts.

– Giuseppe Tomasi di Lampedusa, *The Leopard*

I think the sweetest tooth in the whole of Italy is to be found in Sicily. Whereas in the simplicity of the savoury cooking there is always a sense of harking back to *cucina povera* – literally the cooking of poverty, when whatever ingredients you had needed to be used cleverly – when it comes to the pastry: no! Everyone goes crazy. It is a complete celebration of the baroque, and the harking back is not to poor times, but to the arrival, with the Arabs, of sugar cane, which was planted all over the island and rivalled honey as a sweetener, making possible all kinds of new confections, such as the almond paste that the Sicilians love.

When you cook fish or vegetables or meat in Sicily, you don't really show off, and there is less distinction between home cooking and restaurant cooking: the main thing in the restaurants is that there is more choice. But when you make cakes and pastries and desserts, *then* you show off. Completely. And this is where the pastry chef comes into his or her own.

Everything is very, very highly decorated. In the pastry shops, the mosaic of colours jumps out at you. In the smarter shops there might be more refined, jewel colours; in others, the really loud greens of pistachios, red cherries and the bright yellow and oranges of candied citrus peel mix with icing and chocolate, and colour everything from *cassata* (the famous ricotta cake) and *cannoli* (pastry tubes, again filled with fresh ricotta), to fruit and nut-encrusted biscuits. My daughter Dita, who is allergic to nuts, can't even walk into a pastry shop in Sicily, because the atmosphere is so heavy with the essential oils and aromas of almonds and pistachios.

As is the way throughout Italy, it is no shame to buy your desserts and pastries from a good *pasticceria*, which is what most people do these days. The difference for me as a northern Italian is that at home there is usually a separation between the bar and the *gelateria* or the *pasticceria*. In Sicily they are very much combined. What people do is have their dinner at home, then they all go out to the bar, where the kids might have an ice cream or *granita*, while the parents have a digestif and maybe a pastry. Even in the smallest villages after ten o'clock you often have to stand and wait for a table in the café in the village square. And on Sunday, after Mass, the family might stop off for an apéritif or a coffee on the way home, then buy a tray of little pastries and a tub of everyone's favourite flavoured ice cream and take them home to have after the Sunday lunch.

What is also different is that in the pastry of northern Italy, the historical French and Austrian influence of puff pastry and cream and butter is quite strong, especially as this is a region famous for its dairy produce. But when you work with these ingredients you need cool surroundings. I can see how hard it would be to make perfect millefeuilles in the heat of a small Sicilian bakery, even if there were enough cows to make the butter and cream. So instead of the very fine pastries of the North, you find more robust, nutty, biscuity confections, traditionally made with oil or *strutto*, pure pork fat, rather than butter, and in place of pure cream, you have fresh ricotta (see page 358). Again, there is that Sicilian pattern of hundreds of recipes from the same handful of ingredients – flour, sugar, nuts, candied fruit and fresh ricotta – which range from the *cannoli* in the coffee shop to the *code d'aragosta* (lobster tails) in the bars: fried dough, shaped like the tail of a crustacean and filled with ricotta; to the outrageous *testa di turco*, or Turk's head, a puffed-up pastry, again made of *cannoli* dough, that looks like an Arabian Nights-style sultan's turban filled with ricotta and decorated with bright sugar pastilles.

Of all the desserts and pastries, though, *cannoli* and *cassata* are undoubtedly the two most representative, the flagships, the ones that have travelled all over Italy and beyond. The ingrained Sicilian love of *cannoli* even features in a scene in the final part of *The Godfather*, Mario Puzo's story of the Corleone family, named after the town of Corleone in the heart of Mafia country. The Mafia boss Don Altobello has betrayed Michael Corleone, and in a scene in which the family and Altobello are all at the opera in Palermo, Altobello is given poisoned *cannoli* by his own god-daughter, Michael's sister, Connie. This Mafia boss was so careful about everything, always guarded, but when it came to *cannoli*, he let go, he couldn't resist, and so he died.

In northern Italy, in the pastry shops you will see *crostata di frutta*, fresh fruit tarts; but in my experience it is rare to see these in Sicily. Fruit is fruit and something that is eaten separately. You pick a ripe, luscious black fig from the tree, or buy a slice of cold watermelon from the guys who sell it by the side of the road in the heat of summer. A ripe Sicilian peach is so juicy and so good just eaten as it is, with the juice running down your chin: why would you want to put it into a tart? So instead you put a big bowl of fruit out after dinner: melon, peach, grapes, whatever is in season, with ice underneath. Incidentally, I have also seen plates of raw fennel and celery served at the end of the meal, along with the fruit, to cleanse the palate, after a typically rich and sweet dessert.

Rather than using it in baking, a glut of fruit is candied or made into marmalade and conserves, in the ancient tradition of conserving what you had in season, to eat throughout the year.

Looking at the colourful displays in even the smallest pastry shops, the only way you can remind yourself of *cucina povera* is to remember that at one time such sweetmeats were something special that would appear only on saints' days, Carnevale, Easter, All Saints' Day on 1 November, or the Day of the Dead (All Souls' Day) on 2 November. Only the barons and the rich people could afford to eat such things at other times of the year, so for the poor people these rare, sugary treats must have been something touching paradise. In one way it is wonderful to see pastries like *cannoli* in coffee shops, bars and restaurants all year round; but in another way, it slightly spoils the magic of waiting for a speciality cake, sweet or pastry, just as importing strawberries or asparagus all year round ruins the anticipation of the first home-grown fruit or vegetables in the UK.

Of course, feast days and festivals still give every pastry shop the chance to show off that bit more. In the lead-up to Easter they are full of figurines

made of *pasta reale* (marzipan): little pigs, lambs and donkeys, and these days, motorbikes and cartoon characters, as well as mountains of biscuits, filled pastries and cakes.

And that very Italian conviction that whatever recipe is made in *your* region, *your* town, *your* village is the best and only true rendition is as strong in Sicily as anywhere. Who has the best ricotta? What is the authentic *cassata*? You must have only pistachio. No, you must have pistachio and fruit. But should you also put in chocolate? Everyone has an opinion and an auntie that makes the best. Secrets, too, are very important. Every pastry shop has a secret recipe.

One of the most extraordinary things you see is *frutta martorana*, which was started at the convent of Martorana in Palermo in the eighteenth century. This is *pasta reale*, fashioned into the shapes of fruits and vegetables and skilfully painted with vegetable colouring. The story is that the sisters at the convent were adept at sculpting *pasta reale*, and that one Easter, when the Archbishop was due to visit, the Mother Superior, in a light-hearted gesture of welcome, had the nuns make marzipan fruit to hang on the trees on the cloister gardens.

Later, *frutta martorana* were traditionally made for All Saints' Day on 1 November, but now they are a speciality all over Sicily. You walk past a shop window and you would swear that what you are looking at is displays of lemons and oranges with their leaves, strawberries, cherries, peaches, figs, slices of watermelon, quince, prickly pears, almonds, tomatoes, olives and peppers, but when you come close you can see that everything is made of marzipan. They are so realistic, so beautiful. For presents they are often arranged in beautiful bowls and boxes, wrapped in Cellophane and tied with elaborate ribbons and bows, and you wouldn't know that the fruit wasn't real. Truly the creations are an art … it almost seems terrible to actually eat them.

Until Garibaldi landed in 1860 and the unification of Italy that followed meant that the church's land was confiscated and many convents were forced to close down, they were the powerhouses of pastry and confectionery. In aristocratic families with many daughters, if only one dowry could be afforded, the other daughters would be sent to the convent, and money would be given to the order of nuns to keep them in quiet luxury. But they also needed an occupation, so the tradition of making pastry to give away to the people on saints' days and festivals grew up. There was a great competitiveness between the convents, each of which had their own speciality, such as virgin cakes, made in the shape of breasts. So hot was the competition, that as far back as 1575 it is said that the diocese of Mazara del Vallo had to prohibit the making of *cassata* by the nuns during Holy Week, because they were doing more baking than praying!

Often the nuns would make pastries that were representative of the saint their convent was named after, so there was typically a perfect pastry representation of the part of the human body that the saint was in charge of:

such as St Lucy's eyes. St Lucy is the patron saint of blind people, because her eyes were put out before she was martyred. These things seem quite weird, like nothing I saw anywhere else in Italy, but they were an edible and visual way of connecting and tying people into the church and the stories of the saints. You took home something sugary that symbolised a saint and it was a way of swearing allegiance, so the saint would protect you.

Once the convents began to lose their lands, they struggled to survive, and at some point many began selling their pastries to supplement their charitable gestures. At the Monastero di Santo Spirito in Agrigento they made a celebrated pistachio 'couscous', a version of the *cuccia* on page 374, piled up with pistachios, almonds, cinnamon, chocolate and candied fruits. One of the most famous of these convents is the Monastero delle Vergini in Palermo, which is still there, and is quite a magical place. You go up to the swinging door, and it feels a bit like going to the confessional. You make your request through a grille, and put down your 'gift' of money; then you don't see the nuns, but the door swings round again and there is the cake or pastry that you ordered.

After the convents began to disappear, the first commercial pastry shops and cafés began to spring up in the cities throughout the nineteenth century, and there was an influx of Swiss masters of pastry who set up shop in Palermo, Messina and Catania. Two of the most famous were the family of Caflisch in Palermo, and the Caviezels in Catania. It was much later, at a table at Caffè Caflisch on Viale della Liberta, and also at Caffè Mazzara on Via Magliocco in Palermo, that Giuseppe Tomasi di Lampedusa is said to have written his famous novel *Il Gattopardo (The Leopard)*. As well as bringing new ideas, these commercial cafés and shops also kept alive the traditional pastries and biscuits of the great convents, which still form the basis of pastries you see in cafés, shops and bars today.

## Zeppole di San Giuseppe
St Joseph's Day doughnuts

These are similar to the *sfinci* on page 356.

150g almond flakes
150g plain flour
a pinch of salt
50g ground almonds
1 tablespoon caster sugar
½ teaspoon baking powder
3 eggs, beaten
sunflower oil for deep-frying
250g honey

Preheat the oven to 165°C/325°F/gas 3. Lay the almond flakes in a single layer on a baking tray and put into the oven for about 5 minutes. As long as they are in a single layer you don't need to turn them. Keep an eye on them to make sure they don't burn, and take them out when they are golden.

In a bowl, mix the flour, salt, ground almonds, sugar and baking powder, then add the eggs and mix until everything comes together into a dough. Set aside to rest for 20 minutes in the fridge.

Heat a heavy-based pan with oil at least 3cm deep (make sure the oil comes no higher than a third of the way up the pan). The oil should be 180°C (if you don't have a thermometer, carefully drop a little of the mixture into the oil, and if it starts to sizzle then the oil is hot enough).

Take teaspoons of the mixture and gently drop them into the oil – you will need to do this in batches, so that you don't crowd the pan. Deep-fry the *zeppole*, turning them with a spoon to make sure they are continuously under the oil, and fry evenly on all sides, until they are golden and puffed up. Drain on kitchen paper.

In a frying pan, warm up the honey and add half the toasted almond flakes. Add the *zeppole* and toss for a minute to coat them. Transfer them to a plate and top each one with some of the remaining toasted almond flakes.

**Pignolata**
Sicilian sweets

These are the traditional sweets for Carnevale, the big Shrove Tuesday festival before Lent, and you see them on display in the pastry shops, alongside marzipan pigs. They don't actually contain pine nuts, but they look like them when they are tossed in their shiny honey glaze and piled up to resemble pine cones, the Sicilian word for which is *pigna*. In Messina they are also made at Christmas time, piled up into the pine cone shape, and then one side is glazed with a sweet white lemon icing and the other with chocolate icing.

Before the Arabs brought sugar to Sicily, honey was the only sweetener, and Slow Food has been supporting the nomadic beekeepers of the Iblean mountains who collect wild thyme honey in July and August, then move on through the flowering season: to Nebrodi to collect chestnut honey, and to Siracusa for orange blossom honey. If you like, you can add some finely grated orange zest to the pan when you warm up the honey for the glaze.

Makes enough for 4 'pine cone' clusters

455g plain flour, plus extra for dusting
1 teaspoon baking powder
60g unsalted butter, softened
2 tablespoons caster sugar
2 large eggs
30ml Marsala
sunflower oil for deep-frying

For the icing:
orange blossom honey
ground cinnamon for dusting

Put the flour and baking powder into a bowl and make a well in the centre. Add the butter and work it into the flour. In another bowl, whisk the sugar, eggs and Marsala. Add the mixture to the flour a little at a time, adding a few drops of water if needed to bring the mixture together into a dough, then form into a ball.

Turn the dough out on to a floured work surface. Fold it in on itself and press it with the palm of your hands a few times, until the dough looks homogeneous, then leave to rest for 20–30 minutes.

Divide the dough into 3 pieces, and roll out each piece with a rolling pin into a rectangle about 4.5cm wide. Then cut each piece into 3 strips lengthways (so each strip will be 1.5cm wide).

Take each strip in turn and roll with your fingers, starting at the middle, and then slowly moving outwards as if you were making a breadstick. Each roll should be about 7mm thick. Now cut each roll into 7mm pieces.

Heat at least 3cm of oil in a heavy-based pan (making sure the oil comes no higher than a third of the way up the pan). When the oil reaches 180°C, fry the pieces of *pignolata* until they are golden on all sides, then lift out and drain on kitchen paper (if you don't have a thermometer, drop a little flour into the oil and if it starts to sizzle then the oil is hot enough).

Have a sheet of greaseproof paper ready. In a large pan, warm up some honey. Add the pieces of *pignolata* and, with the help of a spoon, turn them until they are well coated. Pile them up in little mounds on the greaseproof paper, so that they resemble pine cones, then dust with ground cinnamon and leave to cool.

## Cannoli con marmellata d'arance e gelato al pistacchio
Cannoli with orange marmalade and pistachio ice cream

In his very charming book *Sweet Honey, Bitter Lemons*, Matthew Fort wrote of the *cannoli* with orange marmalade that he ate in a restaurant in Licata: 'Creamy, crunchy, soft, sweet, sharp, luxurious, over the top, ludicrously indulgent. Heavens yes.' *Cannoli* are probably the most famous and loved of Sicilian desserts, and traditionally are also the hero of Carnevale. *Cannoli* are tubes of fried dough, stuffed with ricotta cream mixed with various combinations of candied peel, nuts and/or pieces of chocolate. And while there is a big debate about the origins of the name *cassata*, it seems clear that *cannoli* comes from *canna*, which is the Sicilian word for cane, as in sugar cane, and also a gun barrel, which the tubes of pastry resemble. In the best coffee houses and bars, they will fill the *cannoli* for you while you wait, so that they are as fresh as can be. Of course, you can just make the little cones and the filling, without the addition of the sponge, ice cream and orange marmalade, but this is one of the many different ways we serve the dessert at Locanda.

The pistachio sponge recipe will make more than you need, but you can also use it for our pastry chef Ivan Icra Salicru's take on *cassata* on page 360, or just eat the remainder with an espresso, as it is quite delicious.

You need a clean metal tube (1.5cm in diameter) to wrap the *cannoli* dough around – it must be metal, as it has to go into hot oil.

Serves 4

For the orange marmalade (optional):
250g blood orange segments
125g caster sugar

For the pistachio sponge (optional):
50g pistachios
75g plain flour
½ teaspoon baking powder
25g ground almonds
150g caster sugar
200g egg whites (from about 6 or 7 eggs)
150g unsalted butter, melted and cooled

For the vanilla syrup:
100g caster sugar
1 vanilla pod

For the cannoli:
200g plain flour
20g caster sugar
35g *strutto*, duck fat, lard or butter
1 egg, plus a little more beaten egg for sealing the *cannoli*
3 tablespoons Moscato wine
vegetable oil for deep-frying

For the filling:
250g good fresh ricotta
25g candied lemon peel, diced small
25g candied orange peel, diced small
10g dark chocolate (70% cocoa solids), cut into a similar size to the
peel
15g roasted hazelnuts, cut into a similar size to the peel
45g caster sugar
50g whipping cream

To serve:
icing sugar for dusting
pistachio ice cream (optional, see page 397)

To make the orange marmalade, put the orange segments into a pan with
the sugar and cook until the orange breaks down and you have a syrupy
marmalade.

To make the pistachio sponge, first grind the pistachios either using a pestle
and mortar, or in a blender. Mix together the flour, baking powder, ground
almonds, ground pistachios and sugar. Add the egg whites and then the
melted butter and mix together well. Spread in a baking tray and leave to
rest overnight in the fridge.

Heat the oven to 180°C/350°F/gas 4. Remove the baking tray from the
fridge, let the sponge mixture come to room temperature and then bake
in the oven for 10–15 minutes, until a sharp knife inserted into the centre
comes out clean. Turn out and cool on a wire tray.

To make the vanilla syrup, put 100ml of water into a pan with the sugar
and vanilla pod. Bring to the boil, stirring to ensure that all the sugar is
dissolved, then take off the heat.

For the cannoli: put the flour, sugar and fat into a food mixer fitted with
a dough hook and mix for 2 minutes on medium speed until the mixture
resembles breadcrumbs. Add the egg and mix a little more, then add the
Moscato wine and 1 tablespoon of the vanilla syrup and mix until you
have a dough. Wrap in clingfilm and leave to rest for a couple of hours in
the fridge.

When ready to use, roll out the dough to 1mm thick, then cut it into 12 squares, about 7 x 7cm. Wrap one square around the metal tube (see above) and seal in place with a little beaten egg.

Heat some vegetable oil in a deep-fat fryer, or fill a large pan one third of the way up with it. When the oil reaches 180°C, with the help of a fish slice or spider, carefully lower the tube into the hot oil and fry until the *cannolo* turns pale golden. (If you don't have a thermometer drop a little flour into the oil and if it starts to sizzle then the oil is hot enough.) Lift out carefully with the fish slice or spider and drain on kitchen paper. When it has cooled just enough for you to touch it, slide the *cannolo* off the metal cylinder and wrap the next square around it. Deep-fry as before. Repeat until all the *cannoli* are done, then set them aside to cool. They need to be completely cold before you fill them.

Make the filling by mixing all the ingredients together.

Cut 8 small rounds or squares from the pistachio sponge. To serve, spoon some orange marmalade on to one of 4 small deep plates, and put 2 pieces of pistachio sponge on top, to give a base for the *cannoli*. Put the filling into a piping bag, cut the top and use to fill the *cannoli*. Dust each one with icing sugar and arrange on top of the pieces of sponge. Serve with pistachio ice cream.

## Cassateddi fritti o 'nfurnati'
Ricotta cream 'ravioli'

These were traditionally made for Carnevale, especially in the provinces of Trapani and Siracusa. When you are making these, it is a good idea to have some sponge cake or sponge fingers, or biscuit crumbs, to hand, as you may need them to thicken the ricotta filling.

Makes 24

For the filling:
575g good fresh ricotta
115g caster sugar
60g candied fruit, diced
60g dark chocolate (70% cocoa solids), cut into a similar size to the candied fruit
seeds from 1 vanilla pod
a pinch of ground cinnamon
grated zest of 1 orange
a pinch of salt
1 egg, beaten with 1 tablespoon of water, for egg-washing
1 tablespoon honey
icing sugar for dusting

For the dough:
450g semolina flour
65g caster sugar
25ml olive oil
2 large eggs
25ml Marsala
a pinch of salt
zest of 1 lemon

Preheat the oven to 180°C/350°F/gas 4.

In a bowl, mix the ricotta, caster sugar, candied fruit, chocolate pieces, vanilla seeds, cinnamon, orange zest and salt together. The mixture should be thick and creamy, so if it is too watery add some sponge cake or biscuit crumbs.

Mix all the ingredients for the dough together in a bowl and knead for 4–5 minutes, until smooth and quite pliable. Add some water if the dough is too hard to knead. Cover and set aside to rest for 20–30 minutes. Divide the dough into 4 pieces, then divide each piece again into 6 pieces. Shape these into balls, about 2.5cm in diameter.

Have ready a baking tray, lined with baking parchment. Roll each piece of dough with a rolling pin into a circle about 8cm in diameter, and 3mm thick. Put a teaspoon of the filling in the middle of each one, then fold over the dough so that you have a half-moon shape and crimp the edges, making sure they are properly sealed to prevent the filling from leaking. Place them on the baking tray.

Brush with the beaten egg and bake for about 25 minutes, until golden. Then brush with the honey and dust lightly with icing sugar. Serve hot or cold.

**'The grainy texture seems to echo the stone of the city.'**

*Cioccolato*
Chocolate

At L'Antica Dolceria Bonajuto in Modica, the now famous shop that was founded in 1880, the Ruta family make a chocolate that differs from any other serious chocolate I have tasted. Normally a chocolate-maker works very hard at 'conching' (agitating and aerating) the chocolate to make something that is very smooth. But the chocolate of Modica is done in the way of the Aztecs, who ground the cocoa beans with spices to create a pure chocolate mass, which they called *xocoàtl* and often made into a thick drink – a technique that was brought to the city by the Spanish, who saw it almost as a health food, a way of gaining instant energy, and less as something you ate only for pleasure. Often in Modica you would see the *'ciucculattaru'* ('chocolate-man') on the streets, going from door to door with his grinder on a cart, to make this food that the people considered good for them.

When you crack the chocolate bars you can see the graininess of the cocoa and the sugar crystals inside. Somehow the chocolate is right for the place: the texture seems to echo the crumbly texture of the stone from which the new baroque city of Modica was built after the earthquake of 1693, which destroyed the old city. And when you put the chocolate into your mouth, the sugar appears to melt first, so you get the sweetness, and then you start to taste pure cocoa, and it is a really long-lasting flavour. In a blind tasting people might say, 'Something is wrong with this chocolate,' because it feels sandy, but you taste it once, twice, taste it again, and you begin to understand the particularity of it, and the purity. In the view of the writer Leonardo Sciascia, 'whoever tastes it seems to have arrived at the archetype, the absolute, and the chocolate produced elsewhere – even the most famous – seems to be an adulterated or corrupted version …'

The way that the chocolate is made falls somewhere between the ancient way of grinding cocoa beans with a stone tool called a *metate* (a process which must have been back-breaking), and modern chocolate-making. These days the Ruta family no longer grind their own beans, but buy in unprocessed cocoa mass direct from the plantations, and the secret is in the heating of this mass to a very low temperature, between 40 and 50 degrees, so that the sugar crystals don't fully melt. Vanilla or cinnamon is added and that is it. The chocolate is put by hand into bar-shaped containers, which are lined up on a tray, then the tray is picked up and banged repeatedly on to the counter to a special kind of rhythm, which releases all the air bubbles and presses the chocolate into the shape of the tins, then it is allowed to set.

In Modica the chocolate tradition has remained very strong, even in savoury cooking (think of Saint Bernard's Sauce, made with chocolate and anchovies), and the shop also makes *mpanatigghi*, a very old Modica recipe for little sweet and savoury pastries, filled with minced meat, almonds and chocolate, which are really delicious.

**Sfinci di San Giuseppe**
St Joseph's pastries

These are traditional on the feast of St Joseph, 19 March, which is Father's Day in Italy.

Makes about 20

80g butter
a pinch of salt
300g plain flour
6 medium eggs

For the filling:
200g good fresh ricotta
50g caster sugar
grated zest of 1 orange
a pinch of ground cinnamon
seeds from 1 vanilla pod
40g mixed candied fruit, chopped
20g dark chocolate (70% cocoa solids), cut into a similar size to the candied fruit

For frying:
sunflower oil

To decorate:
orange peel, halved glacé cherries and/or crushed pistachios
icing sugar, for dusting

First make the filling: in a large bowl, thoroughly mix the ricotta and sugar until smooth, then mix in the orange zest, cinnamon, vanilla seeds, chopped candied fruits and chocolate.

Put 330ml of water into a large pan with a long handle, add the butter and a pinch of salt, and bring to the boil, stirring occasionally. When it boils, turn down the heat and add the flour all in one go, then turn the heat up again; holding the handle with one hand, and using a wooden spoon with the other hand, stir continuously for about 3–4 minutes, until the mixture forms a ball and makes a hissing sound as if it was frying.

Remove from the heat and transfer into the bowl of a mixer with a paddle. With the motor on a low speed, let the mixture turn gently for a few minutes. Add 1 egg and incorporate it thoroughly into the mixture before adding the rest, one at a time, while the motor is turning. Blend well until you have a smooth, silky dough that is thick enough to stand up in peaks. Cover the dough and leave it to rest for 20–30 minutes.

Heat 3cm of oil in a pan (making sure it comes no higher than a third of the way up the pan) to170°C degrees (if you don't have a thermometer, drop in a little of the mixture, and if it starts to sizzle gently the oil is hot enough). If the oil is too hot the *sfinci* will cook too quickly before they have a chance to expand and become nice and light.

Take teaspoons of the mixture and gently drop them into the oil – you will need to do this in batches, so that you don't crowd the pan. Deep-fry the *sfinci*, turning them with a spoon to make sure they are continuously under the oil, and fry evenly on all sides, until they are golden and puffed up.

Drain on kitchen paper, then leave to cool.

Hold each *sfinci* in your hand and make a hole with your finger. You can either spoon in about a tablespoon of the filling, using a teaspoon – or fill a piping bag, and pipe it in, which can be easier. Smooth the top of the filling, dust with icing sugar, and decorate with orange peel, glacé cherries and/or crushed pistachios.

**Cassata Siciliana**
Ricotta cake

This famous sponge cake (in Sicily the sponge is known as *pan di spagna*) is filled with ricotta, garishly decorated with bright pistachio green almond paste, then sometimes, as here, glazed with a thin layer of icing so that the green colour shines through, and topped with candied fruits. In the pastry shops, the gaudier the better: whole candied fruit and *zuccata*, candied squash, made from strands of the long, thin, pale green *cucuzza* squash, are arranged in dramatic patterns. The cake is traditionally layered up in a mould with sloping sides. According to writer Mary Taylor Simeti, the name *cassata* derives from *qas'ah*, which is the Arab name for the terracotta bowl that was originally used, since it was the Arabs who brought sugar cane to Sicily and made almond paste possible. Others say that an earlier form of *cassata*, made without sugar, derived its name from *caseus*, the Roman for cheese, though this seems less likely.

Allow plenty of time to make this, as the *cassata* needs about 6 hours' chilling time once assembled.

Serves 10–12

900g good fresh ricotta
460g caster sugar
100ml Maraschino (cherry) liqueur (or other sweet liqueur)
150g chopped candied fruit
150g chocolate chips, cut into a similar size to the candied fruit
1 x 24cm round plain sponge cake
2 tablespoons apricot jam, heated until melted

To decorate:
100g pistachios
300g golden marzipan
300g icing sugar, plus extra for dusting
whole candied fruit

Heat the oven to 180°C/350°F/gas 4. Lay the pistachios in a single layer on a baking tray and put into the oven for about 8 minutes. As long as they are in a single layer you don't need to turn them. Keep an eye on them to make sure they don't burn, then take them out and put them into a blender until the nuts release their oil, and you have a paste the density of melted chocolate.

Find a bowl that is about 5cm deep, and preferably has sloping sides, to make your *cassata* in, and line it with clingfilm. Put the marzipan into another bowl and, with your hands, work in the pistachio paste, until the paste is all coloured bright green. Dust your work surface with icing sugar and roll out the paste into a strip that is as deep as the sides of the bowl you are going to make the *cassata* in. Put the strip of paste to one side.

Put the ricotta into a third bowl and work in the sugar, liqueur, candied fruit and chocolate chips.

Slice the sponge cake crossways to form two discs, each about 1cm thick. Put one of the discs of sponge cake in the bottom of the clingfilmed bowl, and brush lightly with some of the melted jam. Line the sides of the bowl with the strip of green marzipan.

Spoon in the ricotta mixture, smooth the top to make it level, and cover with the remaining disc of sponge cake. Refrigerate for at least 4 hours.

Place a plate on top of the bowl and turn the plate and bowl over together, so that you turn out the cake on to the plate. Take off the clingfilm.

Make the glaze by mixing the icing sugar with enough water to make it spreadable. Cover the top and sides with the sugar glaze – very thinly, so that you can see the green of the paste through it. Decorate with candied fruit, and put back into the fridge for at least another hour before serving.

## Ivan's cassata

This is a kind of deconstructed *cassata* that our pastry chef at Locanda, Ivan Icra Salicru, came up with after seeing something similar in Sicily. It keeps all the flavours of the traditional cake, but presents them in a very different way.

This recipe uses the pistachio sponge from the *cannoli* recipe on page 348. You will only need about a third of it, but I am sure you will find plenty of uses for the rest!

Serves 4

400g good fresh ricotta
120g caster sugar
160ml milk
160g candied fruit (orange, lemon, melon etc), chopped
1 x pistachio sponge (see page 348 – you will need about a third of this, about 160g), chopped into pieces
250g pistachio ice cream (see page 397)
a little good chocolate (70% cocoa solids), grated (optional)

For the candied nuts:
165g pistachios
100g caster sugar

Preheat the oven to 180°C/350°F/gas 4. Lay the pistachios in a single layer on a baking tray and put into the oven for about 8 minutes. As long as they are in a single layer you don't need to turn them. Keep an eye on them to make sure they don't burn.

Put the sugar for the nuts into a pan with 45g of water, and heat until it forms a thick syrup but hasn't started to caramelise (if you have a thermometer it will be 117°C). Add the warm nuts, and keep stirring until the syrup sticks to them. Spoon out on to a sheet of greaseproof paper and leave to set.

Put the ricotta, sugar and milk into a bowl and hand-blend until the mixture is smooth and has the texture of double cream.

Sprinkle half the candied fruit, some pieces of pistachio sponge and some of the candied nuts into each of 4 small bowls. Spoon some of the ricotta mixture on top, then add the rest of the candied fruit, caramelised nuts and sponge, arranging some of the pieces of sponge in a rough square shape in the centre to make a base for the ice cream. Spoon two quenelles of ice cream on to the pieces of sponge, and finish, if you like, with a sprinkling of grated chocolate.

**Cannoli di cotognata e mousse alla ricotta**
Quince paste rolls, filled with ricotta

This brings together two typical flavours of Sicily. The quince paste is made with more quince than the recipe on page 411 as it needs to be firmer.

Serves 4–6

600g quinces
1½ lemons
caster sugar, as needed

For the ricotta mousse:
330g whipping cream
120g caster sugar
7 gelatine leaves (21g)
250ml milk
230g good fresh ricotta
2 egg yolks

Make the *cotognata* in the same way as in the recipe on page 411, but instead of pouring the cooked quince purée into a mould or dish, have ready a large sheet of clingfilm and pour it on to that. Place another sheet of clingfilm over the top and, with the help of a rolling pin, flatten to about 2–3 mm thick. Leave to cool, then lift on to a tray and put into the fridge for a day to dry out. When the paste is almost dry to the touch, it is ready.

Whip the cream with 30g of the sugar and set aside. Soak the gelatine in a bowl of cold water and ice for about 10 minutes, then squeeze. (The ice helps retain the properties of the gelatine.)

Warm up the milk with the rest of the sugar to just under a simmer (55°C if you have a thermometer) and take off the heat. Add the gelatine and stir until it dissolves. Allow to cool to 35°C (if you don't have a thermometer, take a little of the mixture and touch it to your bottom lip – it should feel cooler than your body temperature), then add the ricotta and the egg yolks and blend with a hand blender until smooth. Stir in the whipped cream, then put into one or two piping bags and put into the fridge to set for 2–3 hours.

Cut the *cotognata* into squares, about 7 x 7cm, then pipe a strip of ricotta mousse down the centre of each square and roll up. Eat straight away.

**Torta di ricotta**
Ricotta tart

If you want to make a chocolate-flavoured variation of this, you can add 25g of cocoa powder along with the flour when you make the pastry cream.

The quantity of pastry given here is enough for two tarts, because it is much easier to work the pastry if you make it in bigger quantities. You can freeze what you don't need.

Serves 6

450g good fresh ricotta
80g almonds, chopped
80g sultanas
zest of 2 lemons
5 egg whites
75g caster sugar

For the pastry:
seeds from 1 vanilla pod
150g unsalted butter
85g caster sugar
3 egg yolks
250g plain flour
25g ground almonds

For the pastry cream:
300ml milk
4 egg yolks, at room temperature
140g caster sugar, plus extra for sprinkling
30g plain flour

To make the pastry, put the vanilla seeds with the butter and sugar, into a food mixer with a pastry paddle. Whiz for 3 minutes, until pale and creamy. While the motor is running, mix in the egg yolks, one by one, then add the flour and ground almonds. As soon as it is all mixed, turn out the pastry, wrap in clingfilm, and leave in the fridge for about an hour to rest.

Preheat the oven to 180°C/350°/gas 4.

Roll the pastry out into a circle about 5mm thick and use it to line a 20cm tart tin. Line with greaseproof paper, fill with baking beans, and bake for 5–7 minutes, until the pastry has dried out, but not coloured. Take out of the oven, remove the greaseproof paper and beans, and put to one side.

To make the pastry cream, warm the milk in a pan to just below simmering point, then take off the heat. In a bowl, whisk together the egg yolks, sugar and flour, then add to the warm milk, and return to the heat, whisking continuously until the mixture thickens. Take the pan off the heat, leave to cool, then put through a fine sieve to make sure there are no lumps.

Add the ricotta, almonds, sultanas and lemon zest to the pastry cream. In a separate bowl, whip the egg whites with the sugar until they form peaks, then add to the mixture. Pour into the pastry case, sprinkle some sugar on top and put back into the oven for 25–35 minutes, until a sharp knife inserted into the centre comes out clean.

**Riso mantecato**
Rice pudding

In Sicily this is traditionally made with *zuccata* (candied squash), but you can use candied orange and lemon peel instead. In Tindari, home of the Sanctuary of the Black Madonna (the famous statue thought to have been smuggled out of Constantinople in the eighth or ninth centuries and brought ashore during a storm), they make a 'black' version of this for festivals, by adding bitter chocolate as the rice cooks in the milk.

Serves 8

100g blanched almonds
1.5 litres milk
seeds from 1 vanilla pod
80g caster sugar
400g arborio rice
200g chopped candied orange and lemon peel, plus more for decoration
50g chocolate chips, cut into a similar size to the peel, plus more for decoration

Heat the oven to 180°C/350°F/gas 4. Lay the almonds in a single layer on a baking tray and put into the oven for about 8 minutes. As long as they are in a single layer you don't need to turn them. Keep an eye on them to make sure they don't burn, and when they are golden, take them out and chop them coarsely.

Put the milk into a pan over a low heat with the vanilla seeds, sugar and rice. Bring to the boil, stirring constantly, then reduce the heat and simmer until the rice is cooked (the liquid should be completely absorbed). Add half the chopped almonds, candied peel and chocolate chips. Mix well and spoon into serving bowls. Serve cold, decorated with the rest of the almonds, peel and chocolate.

**Torta all'arancia**
Orange cake


Makes 1 x 25cm cake

80g unsalted butter, plus a little extra for greasing
170g flour, plus a little extra for dusting
5 eggs, plus 5 yolks
½ teaspoon baking powder
seeds from 1 vanilla pod
grated zest of 4 oranges, plus juice of 2 of the oranges
230g caster sugar
140ml Triple Sec, or other orange liqueur


Preheat the oven to 180°C/350°F/gas 4.

Prepare a cake tin (25cm in diameter and 5cm deep) by greasing it with butter and then tipping in some flour and shaking it around, so that the base and sides are covered. Tip out the excess.

Separate the whole eggs into yolks and whites. Sieve the flour and baking powder together.

Put the butter into the bowl of a food mixer with a paddle, together with the vanilla seeds and the orange zest. Add half the sugar and mix, then add the 10 egg yolks, one by one. As soon as the yolks are incorporated, add the flour and baking powder and continue to mix.

In a separate bowl, whisk the egg whites with the remaining sugar until they form soft peaks, then fold into the mixture by hand.

Spoon the mixture into the prepared cake tin and bake for 20–25 minutes, until a skewer inserted into the middle of the cake comes out clean. Turn out and leave to cool on a wire rack.

Mix the orange juice with the liqueur and brush over the cake until it has absorbed all the liquid.

**Torta ai pistacchi**
Pistachio tart

This might seem like a lot of pistachios, but they are used to make the paste that lines the tart, and then it is decorated with alternate lines of candied and fresh green pistachios.

Serves 8

For the paste:
700g shelled pistachios, preferably *pistacchio di Bronte* (see page 194), finely chopped
150g caster sugar
seeds from 1 vanilla pod
zest of 2 oranges
ground cinnamon, to taste
2 eggs

For the filling:
800g good fresh ricotta
200g caster sugar
zest of 2 lemons
150g good dark chocolate (70% cocoa solids), grated
3 eggs

To decorate:
150g candied pistachios (see page 360)
100g finely chopped pistachios

Preheat the oven to 170°C/325°F/gas 3.

Mix all the ingredients for the paste together and use it to cover the base and sides of a tart tin (about 5cm deep and 25cm in diameter) with a removable base. Put the tin into the fridge to keep it cool while you make the filling.

Mix all the ingredients for the filling together, then spoon into the lined tart tin. Put into the oven for 30–40 minutes, then remove and allow to cool down in the tart tin before taking it out.

Decorate with alternate lines of candied and finely chopped pistachios.

**Palline di bucce d'arancia**
Orange zest balls

This can be done with any citrus fruit: mandarin, lemon, *cedro*, lime. You can also add a couple of pinches of ginger or cinnamon to the peel and sugar. Soaking the peel for four days really does help to soften it and get rid of all the bitterness before you start.

Makes 25–30

8 large oranges (preferably organic)
caster sugar
250g good dark chocolate (70% cocoa solids) (optional)

Scrub the oranges with a sponge under warm water. Take off the peel in big strips (don't worry about taking off the white pith). Soak the peel in enough water to cover for 4 days, changing the water about 4 times every day. At the end of this time, drain the peel, dry it, then coarsely chop it and blend in a food processor. Now you need to weigh the peel and put it into a pan, adding an equal weight of sugar.

Put the pan containing the orange peel and sugar over a low heat and keep stirring until the sugar has dissolved and the mixture has thickened. Take care not to let it boil and caramelise. Remove from the heat, allow to cool, then form into balls (roughly the diameter of a £1 coin). Put into the fridge for about 1 hour to harden them up.

You can either dust each ball with caster sugar ... or dip them in melted chocolate (the easiest way to melt the chocolate is in a bowl in the microwave on defrost mode, but keep an eye on it, to make sure it doesn't 'seize' – i.e. become dull and grainy, which can happen if you overheat it).

Take the orange zest balls out of the fridge and use a fork to dip each one into a bowl of either sugar or melted chocolate. If using chocolate, let the excess drain off and then lay the balls on a sheet of greaseproof paper and put into the fridge to set. They'll keep for about a week, refrigerated.

## Crispeddi di risu con miele all'arancia
Rice croquettes with orange honey

Makes 15–20

300g carnaroli rice
1 litre milk
½ vanilla pod
zest of 1 orange
zest of 1 lemon
a pinch of ground cinnamon
60g caster sugar
150g plain flour
½ teaspoon baking powder
sunflower oil for deep-frying

For the honey coating:
200g orange blossom honey
zest and juice of 2 oranges
zest and juice of 1 lemon
icing sugar for dusting

Put the rice into a pan with the milk, vanilla pod, orange and lemon zest and ground cinnamon and bring to the boil, then turn down the heat and continue cooking for about 16–18 minutes, until the milk has completely evaporated. Stir in the sugar, then take off the heat and leave the mixture to rest in the fridge until completely cold. Sieve the flour and baking powder and fold into the rice, then put into the fridge for another hour. Form the mixture into balls of 3cm diameter and set aside.

To make the honey coating, warm the honey very gently in a pan with the orange and lemon juice, just to loosen it up. Add the orange and lemon zest.

Heat about 3cm of oil in a pan (making sure it comes no higher than a third of the way up the pan), to180°C (if you don't have a thermometer, drop a little flour into the oil and if it starts to sizzle then the oil is hot enough).

Deep-fry the rice balls until golden, lift out and drain on kitchen paper for a minute, then put them into the pan containing the honey. Shake the pan gently to coat them, then lift them out on to a plate and dust with icing sugar before serving.

**Cuccìa**
Spelt pudding

In the seventeenth century there was a massive famine that gripped the whole of Sicily, so the story is that local people, some say in Palermo, some say in Siracusa, became like pirates and seized some boats full of grain from North Africa on their way to Naples.

When the grain was brought on to land, the people were so hungry that they couldn't wait to dry it in the traditional way and make flour for bread. They just soaked the grains of wheat and boiled them to make a kind of pudding, in the way that the Romans must have done before them. So this is a very old recipe, one that is made very rarely nowadays.

Traditionally, it is also made with *zuccata* (candied pumpkin), but you can substitute candied orange and lemon peel. You can buy ready-cooked farro (spelt), which is labelled '*grano cotto*', in Italian delicatessens, or cook the grain yourself – in which case you will need to soak it overnight first.

Serves 8

200g spelt grains or ready-cooked spelt (see above)
sea salt
400g good fresh ricotta
30ml anise liqueur
60g caster sugar
a pinch of ground cinnamon, plus extra for dusting
40g dark chocolate (70% cocoa solids), chopped into a similar size to
the candied peel
zest of 1 lemon
60g chopped candied orange and lemon peel

If cooking the grains from scratch, soak the spelt overnight in a saucepan with enough cold water to cover. The next day, change the water and cook the spelt in the same pan with a pinch of salt. It will take a couple of hours (it should be completely soft). Drain it and leave to cool.

Pass the ricotta through a sieve into a bowl. Mix in the liqueur, then add the sugar and cinnamon. Stir in the chopped chocolate and the lemon zest, then fold in the candied peel. Add the cooked spelt and mix well. Pour into cups or moulds and refrigerate until cold. Dust with cinnamon before serving.

**Gelo di cocomero**
Watermelon pudding

This has a very specific soft texture that comes from the cornflour and is traditionally Sicilian.

Serves 4–6

60g pistachios
60g blanched almonds
1 watermelon
225g caster sugar
60g cornflour
1 cinnamon stick
100g chocolate chips

Preheat the oven to 180°C/350°F/gas 4. Lay the pistachios and almonds in a single layer on a baking tray and put into the oven for about 8 minutes. As long as they are in a single layer you don't need to turn them. Keep an eye on them to make sure they don't burn, and take them out when the almonds are golden. Crush the nuts and set aside.

Peel the watermelon, cut into chunks and blitz in a blender, then put through a sieve. You need 1.1 litres of juice.

Mix 200ml of the juice with the cornflour. Heat the rest of the juice in a pan with the sugar and the cinnamon stick (to 60°C if you have a thermometer) then add the cornflour mixture and bring to the boil. Turn down the heat and cook gently until the mixture thickens, stirring continuously. Take off the heat and remove the cinnamon stick. Pour it into 4–6 small non-stick moulds. Put into the fridge for about 2 hours, until cold, then garnish with chocolate chips and the crushed nuts.

### Gelatina di arance sang-sang
Blood orange jelly

Serves 4–6

8 leaves of gelatine (24g)
650g blood orange juice
juice of 2 lemons
200g caster sugar
110ml rum

To decorate:
pistachios
orange slices (optional)

Preheat the oven to 180°C/350°F/gas 4. Lay the pistachios you are going to use for decorating in a single layer on a baking tray and put into the oven for about 8 minutes. As long as they are in a single layer you don't need to turn them. Keep an eye on them to make sure they don't burn.

Soak the gelatine in a bowl of cold water and ice for about 10 minutes, then squeeze. (The ice helps retain the properties of the gelatine.) Mix the orange and lemon juice together, then measure 200ml of this and put into a pan with the sugar. Heat (to 80°C if you have a thermometer) until the sugar dissolves and remove from the heat. Then add the squeezed gelatine, stirring until it melts, and mix in the rest of the juice and the rum.

Pour into a mould and put into the fridge until set, then turn out on to a plate and garnish with orange slices, if using, and the toasted pistachios.

### 'Incredible ice-makers for centuries'

I believe there are three great Italian schools of ice cream: the northern Italian one which grew up around Treviso; the southern Italian one, centred around Naples; and the one that is probably the oldest, the school of Sicilian ice cream, sorbets and *granite*.

*Gelati, sorbetti
e granite*
Ice cream, sorbet and granite

There is no one person you can say invented ice cream, and everyone has a different theory, but the Sicilians have been incredible ice-makers for centuries and have a great understanding of *granite*, sorbet and ice cream. The Greeks and Romans used to take the snow and ice from Mount Etna – you have to remember that near the top of the volcano it is cold enough to ski in winter, and snow stays in the caves and crannies, often even in summer. There is a famous cave, the Grotta del Gelo, full of stalagmites and stalactites, that is permanently lined with snow and ice, which is one of the places where the ice could be collected. Until a few decades ago it was known only to shepherds up on the mountain, because it is a long walk over the lava fields to get there. It must have been such tough work to collect the ice, but imagine after a hard day, working in the forty-degree heat, how reviving and refreshing it must have been for the people to have a vessel of ice to put into their wine.

The Arabs are presumed to have introduced the idea of *sarbat* (sherbet) – snow mixed with sugar and fruit pulp – and over the centuries the making of ice became a real industry. Special underground stores on Mount Etna were built, in which snow could be packed tightly and kept frozen by the natural layers of lava surrounding them. According to Mary Taylor Simeti's research, this snow, amazingly, could be packed into sacks, loaded on to mules and then on to small boats for trading as far away as Malta, which, having no ice of its own, 'rented' some of these caverns – but too much trade could mean there wasn't enough precious ice for the Sicilians themselves. Simeti quotes a work by Jean Houel, *Voyage pittoresque en Sicile*, written in 1784. Houel wrote: 'In these climates the lack of snow is feared as much as the lack of grain, wine or oil. I was in Syracuse in 1777; no snow was to be had: it became known that a little ship that was passing was loaded with snow; without a moment's deliberation everyone ran down and demanded that the ship be unloaded, and when the crew refused, the ship was attacked, and taken, and the Syracusans lost several men in the battle.'

Somewhere, somehow, over these centuries the step was made from sherbet to *granita*, and the more refined, churned sorbet. No one can be sure either when 'ices' began to include milk and become 'ice cream', but one of the popular stories is that Francesco Procopio de' Coltelli, a Sicilian from Palermo who emigrated to Paris, had already set up a café, Le Procope, in 1686, serving ice cream to stylish Parisians – though some say it was not

Coffee granita (see page 387)

really ice cream that he made, but sorbet. Certainly by 1775, when Filippo Baldini from Naples, just across the water from Sicily, published a book on frozen confectionery, *De' sorbetti*, there was a chapter on 'milky sorbets'.

What nobody can dispute is the ingrained Sicilian love of all things to do with ice. In the villages the little vans come around every day, sometimes twice a day, with an incredible range of flavours. I am not saying that everywhere ice cream is still made from scratch – a lot is done with pre-prepared mixes, but they use very good-quality pastes of nuts and puréed fruit, and the machines are built with these preparations in mind. Modernity has come through, but still the ice cream is very good. That said, close to us are two ice cream shops: one has around fifty flavours, and the young people go crazy for it, but down the road is a smaller one, where the older people go, and the woman who runs it does only half a dozen flavours, and when you talk to her, she tells you where she buys her milk, and fresh vanilla and almonds, and you can taste the difference. In cafés sometimes you also find *gelato duro*, which is somewhere between churned ice cream and frozen *cassata*, not churned, just put into the freezer, so you order a slab of it.

Of the *granite* you find in the bars and cafés, sometimes these are little more than shards of ice, made with sugared water, or sometimes with a little almond syrup added, and then just lemon juice squeezed over. Because the just-picked lemons are so, so special, the flavour is just extraordinary, so refreshing, and almost impossible to re-create to the same intensity anywhere else. In some places, when you ask for a *granita*, they literally shear off shards of ice from big blocks in front of you, using a special plane.

In one of the local bars near the house where we stay, what they like to do is peel figs in season and put them into a glass, with some sprigs of mint and then a *granatina* (a slushy version of *granita*) over the top. What I especially love are the brilliant coffee *granite* and *granatinas*. Sometimes these are presented like a *caffè latte*, with some frothy, creamy almond milk on top, and they are so good you can't help having two or three of them on a hot evening. Then you are still awake reading your book at five o'clock in the morning.

But they don't have to be sophisticated to hit the spot. In the bar near where we stay outside Menfi, they make up bottles of espresso every morning, some labelled *zuccherato* (with sugar), and some *no zuccherato*. Every so often they give the bottles a shake. So you can go in and order a frozen espresso. The sugar one is so sweet that Plaxy and I order one with sugar, one without, and an extra cup, so we can mix the two: halfway between is perfect.

*Granite*, sorbets and ice cream are all so ingrained in Sicilian life, I have heard local farmers returning home from a trip to Palermo, and what everyone wants to know is, 'What was the ice cream like?' But one of the most simple but touching things I saw was in Noto, watching the little fishing boats come in. While they landed their fish, one of the boys was sent straight away to the ice cream shop to bring back ices for everyone. These tough characters had been out on the seas for a day and a night in the salty heat, and to see them sitting by the port, enjoying the sweet, rich pleasure of the ice cream, seemed like such a contrast to the harshness of their daily lives at sea. It was a beautiful thing to watch, and I felt as if I could savour every mouthful along with them.

## A note about ice cream

Of course you can make ice cream and sorbets by just putting a custard, purée or syrup into a container, putting it into the freezer, then stirring it with a fork every twenty minutes during the first two hours, to break up any crystals; but also most kitchen shops sell ice-cream makers for use at home. Choose a big one with a powerful motor and a small cylinder, if possible, so that you can churn the ice cream as little as possible.

As I said, you can make very simple ice creams, but to make really fantastic, soft, creamy ice cream is a science. At Locanda we are very proud of our ice cream, and over the years, with our very talented and creative pastry chef, Ivan Icra Salicru, we have done a huge amount of research into the ultimate formula, which will allow the ice cream to stay beautifully soft, with no crystallisation.

I am a chef used to working with handfuls of this and that, in the heat of the stoves, rather than the cool of the pastry area; I am far too impatient and spontaneous to be a pastry chef, where everything is about meticulous planning, weighing, measuring and preparing in order for the chemistry to work, and so I understand that it might seem a little pedantic to give all the quantities for the ice cream in weights, to list different sugars and give specific temperatures, but accuracy and science make beautiful ice cream.

We use different sugars because they have different properties. Sugars don't freeze, but they have different levels of resistance to freezing, so by adjusting the ratio of sugars, you can control the freezing point of your mixture, and therefore the texture, as well as the sweetness.

The 'ordinary' sugar that everybody knows is formed of dextrose (glucose) and fructose. If you use it on its own in ice cream, it forms hard crystals, so we also use invert sugar, which is made by heating sucrose and water with an acid and sodium bicarbonate, to produce a sugar that is half dextrose (glucose) and half fructose. This sugar has anti-crystallising properties and helps make ice cream softer, especially when it has a high solid content, for example, chocolate or nuts.

We also use dextrose (glucose), which is pure sugar extracted from maize during a process in which the starch is broken down until only the dextrose (glucose) is left. Because of its low sweetening power, it allows fresh flavours to come through strongly.

Finally we use atomised glucose, which is the name for dextrose (glucose) that still contains some starch. Depending on the level of dextrose (if it is very low, it is known as maltodextrin), this sugar helps either to soften, or harden the ice cream mixture.

In addition to full-fat milk and cream, in some ice creams we also use some milk powder (with 0% fat), which helps to give a more pronounced milk flavour. Some of the recipes include eggs, which contain lecithin, a natural emulsifier; in others, we sometimes use a stabiliser made from natural ingredients (such as plants or seeds) to make sure the ice cream keeps its ultra-softness and smoothness. There is no real need for this at home, but we have listed stabilisers as optional in the recipes, so that you can see how they are used.

The recipes here have all been adapted to work in home ice-cream makers, and, if it is easier, instead of using all the different sugars, you can add up the total amount of sugar each recipe calls for, then make this up using one-third powdered dextrose (glucose) which is easily available, and two-thirds caster sugar. The texture and sweetness will be a little different, but you will still have something very good.

Each recipe follows the same basic method, but the ratio of ingredients varies with each one, in order to achieve the best possible consistency and flavour.

Because precision is important, the quantities for the liquids are given in grams – although 100g and 100ml are equal amounts, if you weigh your milk, cream, etc. it is far more precise than trying to judge the level in a measuring jug.

You also need to use a sugar thermometer, so that you can measure the temperature at the crucial stages of the recipes.

We always use bottled water for making *granita* and sorbet, as there is then no risk of any flavour of chemicals coming through.

**Granita al cocomero**
Watermelon granita


Serves 6

1 watermelon
50g orange juice
250g caster sugar
30g lemon juice


Peel the watermelon, cut into chunks and blitz in a blender, then put through a sieve. You need 800g of juice.

Warm up the orange juice in a pan and add the sugar, stirring until it dissolves. Take the pan from the heat, leave to cool down, then stir in the watermelon and the lemon juice.

Transfer to a freezer container and put into the freezer, bringing it out every 10 minutes and whisking until it forms frozen crystals. Keep it at −8°C until you are ready to serve it, but don't keep it longer than 3 days, otherwise the *granita* will get freezer 'burn' and will lose its fresh flavour and aroma.


**Granita al mandarino**
Mandarin granita


Serves 6

900g mandarin juice (from about 1.5kg mandarins)
250g caster sugar


Heat 100g of the mandarin juice in a pan and add the sugar, stirring until it dissolves. Take the pan from the heat, allow to cool down, then stir in the rest of the mandarin juice.

Transfer to a freezer container and put into the freezer, bringing it out every 10 minutes and whisking it until it forms frozen crystals. Keep it at −8°C until you are ready to serve it, but don't keep it longer than 3 days, otherwise the *granita* will get freezer 'burn' and will lose its fresh flavour and aroma.

### Granita di limone e menta
Lemon and mint granita

Serves 6

1kg (ie 1 litre) bottled still water
30g mint leaves
150g caster sugar
200g freshly squeezed lemon juice

Put 800g of cold bottled water into an airtight container with the mint leaves and leave to infuse for 24 hours (by using cold, rather than boiling water to infuse the mint you will get all the fresh flavour, but not the green colour or the bitterness that the heat brings out; so the finished *granita* will be pale lemon in colour, but will have a wonderful taste of mint).

Put the sugar into a pan with the remaining water and bring to the boil, then take off the heat immediately and leave to cool. Put the mint water through a fine sieve and stir it into the cooled syrup, with the lemon juice.

Transfer to a freezer container and put into the freezer, taking it out every 10 minutes and whisking it until it forms frozen crystals. Keep it at −8°C until you are ready to serve it, but don't keep it longer than 3 days, otherwise the *granita* will get freezer 'burn' and will lose its fresh flavour and aroma.

### Granita al caffè
Coffee granita

Serves 6

900g hot espresso or very strong coffee
250g caster sugar

Pour the hot coffee into a bowl and add the sugar, whisking until it dissolves. Allow to cool down.

Transfer to a freezer container and put into the freezer, bringing it out every 10 minutes and whisking it until it forms frozen crystals. Keep it at −8°C until you are ready to serve it, but don't keep it longer than 3 days, otherwise the *granita* will get freezer 'burn' and will lose its fresh flavour and aroma.

**Sorbetto di (menta e) limone**
Lemon (and mint) sorbet

You can either make a straight lemon sorbet, or add mint, which is a brilliant combination. To make a lemon and mint sorbet, mix the water with 50g of fresh mint leaves and leave in the fridge for 24 hours. By using cold water, you infuse the flavour of the mint, without the colour or any bitterness. Once you have infused the water, follow the rest of the recipe.

Serves 6

155g dextrose
grated zest of 1 lemon
105g caster sugar
4g sorbet stabiliser (optional)
300g lemon juice

Hand-blend the dextrose with 865g of water and the lemon zest until smooth, then put into a pan over a low heat and bring to 40°C. Whisk in the sugar and the stabiliser, if using, and bring up to 85°C. Take off the heat and cool as quickly as you can, so that you don't encourage bacteria.

When cold, add the lemon juice and put into the fridge for 6–12 hours. Put the mixture into an ice-cream maker and churn according to instructions.

**Sorbetto alle arance sang-sang**
Blood orange sorbet

Serves 6

715g blood orange juice
grated zest of 1 orange
150g dextrose
75g caster sugar
5g sorbet stabiliser (optional)

Hand-blend 215g of the blood orange juice with the orange zest and dextrose until smooth, then put into a pan over a low heat and bring to 40°C. Whisk in the sugar and the stabiliser, if using, bring up to 85°C, then take off the heat and cool as quickly as you can, so that you don't encourage bacteria.

When cold, mix in the rest of the orange juice and put into the fridge for 6–12 hours. Put the mixture into an ice-cream maker and churn according to instructions.

### Sorbetto alla fragola
Strawberry sorbet

Serves 6

770g strawberry purée (from around 800g strawberries)
175g dextrose
55g caster sugar
4g sorbet stabiliser (optional)

If making the purée yourself, hull the strawberries and blend to a purée. Hand-blend 220g of the purée with the dextrose until smooth, then put into a pan over a low heat and bring to 40°C. Whisk in the sugars and the stabiliser, if using, bring up to 85°C, then take off the heat and cool as quickly as you can, so that you don't encourage bacteria.

When cold, mix in the rest of the strawberry purée and put into the fridge for 6–12 hours. Put the mixture into an ice-cream maker and churn according to instructions.

### Sorbetto alla pesca
Peach sorbet

You can buy very good white peach purée, which is the best to use for this. Or you can make your own, provided you can find ripe, juicy peaches. In which case, just skin them, cut them in half, remove the stone and blend them to a purée. Otherwise, use the same weight of peach juice.

Serves 6

150g dextrose
75g caster sugar
5g sorbet stabiliser (optional)
500g peach purée

Hand-blend the dextrose with 270g of water until smooth, then put into a pan over a low heat and bring to 40°C. Whisk in the sugar and the stabiliser, if using, bring up to 85°C, then take off the heat and cool as quickly as you can, so that you don't encourage bacteria.

When cold, mix in the peach purée and put into the fridge for 6–12 hours. Put the mixture into an ice-cream maker and churn according to instructions.

**Sorbetto a melone**
Melon sorbet

When wild strawberries are in season, they are fantastic with this sorbet and an orange sauce. To make the sauce you just simmer 250ml of fresh orange juice in a pan with 75g of caster sugar until you have a spooning consistency, then leave it to cool.

Makes 1kg

745g melon juice (whiz pieces of melon in a food processor, or put through a juicer, then strain it through a fine sieve)
180g dextrose
20g caster sugar
5g sorbet stabiliser (optional)
50g lemon juice

Put 200g of the melon juice into a pan, add the dextrose, hand-blend and bring to 40°C. Whisk in the sugar and the stabiliser, if using, bring up to 85°C, then take off the heat and cool as quickly as you can, so that you don't encourage bacteria.

When cold, mix in the rest of the melon juice and the lemon juice and put into the fridge for 6–12 hours. Put the mixture into an ice-cream maker and churn according to instructions.

### Sorbetto al fichi d'India
Prickly pear sorbet

Sicilians love prickly pears, which are the fruit of a cactus that was brought to Sicily from South America and taste a little like watermelon. They are everywhere in the late summer. They grow at the sides of the streets, where you see the bright coloured fruit, either *bianco*, which are in fact golden-yellow, or *rosso*, which are purple or red, clinging to the tips of the enormous green cactus leaves, and it looks like they are just left to their own devices, that they belong to nobody. Then the next time you pass by somebody has picked them, to eat after dinner or make marmalade from. At Pizzo e Pizzo, a very smart, shiny, beautiful Milanese-style *salumeria* and restaurant in Palermo, where they specialise in hams and salami, often from northern Italy, married with Sicilian produce such as cheese, *'strattu* (sun-dried tomato paste) and preserves, I had some Ragusano cheese with a prickly pear mustard. The fruit was cooked down to a syrup with mustard essence, and it was the most amazing thing.

You have to handle prickly pears very carefully, because they really are prickly, so when they are for sale in the markets the stallholders have tongs to help you. If you buy them in supermarkets in the UK, though, the prickles will have already been taken off. To peel them, use a fork to hold them in place, if they still have their prickles, and cut off each end of the pear, then make a vertical cut all the way along the length of the fruit. Now you can easily pull off the peel and discard it. The flesh contains seeds, which are edible, if you just want to eat the fruit as it is; but if you are puréeing it to make this sorbet, you need to discard them.

Serves 6

140g dextrose
85g caster sugar
5g sorbet stabiliser (optional)
around 4 prickly pears

Peel the prickly pears (see above), then hand-blend and put through a sieve to remove the seeds. You need 570g of purée.

Hand-blend the dextrose with 200g of water until smooth, then put into a pan over a low heat and bring to 40°C. Whisk in the sugar and the stabiliser, if using, bring up to 85°C, then take off the heat and cool as quickly as you can, so that you don't encourage bacteria.

When cold, mix in the pear purée and put into the fridge for 6–12 hours. Put the mixture into an ice-cream maker and churn according to instructions.

## Gelato alla vaniglia
Vanilla ice cream

Makes 1kg

545g whole (full-fat) milk
85g whipping cream
50g milk powder
170g dextrose
40g caster sugar
10g invert sugar
100g egg yolks
2 vanilla pods

Hand-blend the milk, cream, milk powder and dextrose until smooth. Put into a pan and bring to 40°C.

Whisk in the sugars and the egg yolks, then scrape in the seeds from the vanilla pods and add the halved pods to the pan as well. Bring up to 85°C, take off the heat, and cool as quickly as you can, so you don't encourage bacteria.

When cold, put into the fridge for 6–12 hours. Remove the vanilla pod, then put the mixture into an ice-cream maker and churn according to instructions.

### Gelato alle mandorle
Almond ice cream

Makes about 1kg

255g whole (full-fat) milk
85g whipping cream
60g milk powder
140g dextrose
10g caster sugar
100g invert sugar
5g ice-cream stabiliser (optional)
20g egg yolks

For the almond paste:
50g blanched almonds
50g caster sugar

First make the almond paste. Preheat the oven to 180°C/350°F/gas 4. Lay the almonds in a single layer on a baking tray and put into the oven for about 8 minutes. As long as they are in a single layer you don't need to turn them. Keep an eye on them to make sure they don't burn, and when they are golden, take them out and chop them. Put them into a blender with the sugar and whiz to a paste. Keep to one side.

Hand-blend the milk, cream, milk powder and dextrose with 300g water until smooth. Put into a pan and bring to 40°C. Whisk in the sugars, the stabiliser, if using, the egg yolks and the almond paste. Bring up to 85°C, take off the heat, then cool as quickly as you can, so you don't encourage bacteria.

When cold, put into the fridge for 6–12 hours. Put the mixture into an ice-cream maker and churn according to instructions.

## Gelato al latte di mandorie
Almond milk ice cream

You can buy almond milk in cartons in health food stores and some super-markets.

Makes about 1kg

565g almond milk
170g whipping cream
40g milk powder
135g dextrose
50g caster sugar
25g invert sugar
6g ice-cream stabiliser (optional)

Hand-blend the almond milk, cream, milk powder and dextrose until smooth. Put into a pan over a low heat and bring to 40°C. Whisk in the sugars and the stabiliser, if using, bring up to 85°C, then take off the heat and cool as quickly as you can.

When cold, put into the fridge for 6–12 hours. Put the mixture into an ice-cream maker and churn according to instructions.

### Gelato al pistacchio
Pistachio ice cream

If you like, when you roast the pistachios to make the paste, you can do some extra, chop them, and sprinkle them over the finished ice cream when you serve it.

Makes 1kg

200g pistachios
320g whole (full-fat) milk
60g milk powder
140g dextrose
60g caster sugar
25g invert sugar
5g ice-cream stabiliser (optional)
40g egg yolks

Preheat the oven to 180°C/350°F/gas 4.

Lay the pistachios in a single layer on a baking tray and put into the oven for about 8 minutes. As long as they are in a single layer you don't need to turn them. Keep an eye on them to make sure they don't burn, then take them out, let them cool and chop them.

Put the nuts into a food processor and whiz until they become oily. Keep this paste to one side.

Hand-blend the milk, milk powder and dextrose with 340g of water until smooth. Put into a pan and bring to 40°C. Whisk in the sugars, the stabiliser, if using, the egg yolks and the pistachio paste. Bring up to 85°C, take off the heat, then cool as quickly as you can, so you don't encourage bacteria.

When cold, put into the fridge for 6–12 hours. Put the mixture into an ice-cream maker and churn according to instructions.

## 'The words baroque and ice cream seem to fit together'

In the old baroque town of Noto, I met Corrado Assenza who is the fourth generation to run the family pastry shop, Caffè Sicilia, in Noto, since it opened in 1892. It is a very beautiful, very complete place. I had one of the best espressos I have ever had in his caffè, such a chocolatey, incredible flavour, and so, you can imagine, his coffee ice cream was also out of this world. It was his ice cream I had wanted to taste. Many people believe it to be the best on the island. Not only is it superb quality, but also it encapsulates the essential flavours of Sicily. One of his specialities is to serve two flavours of this very special ice cream on a soft brioche-style sweet bread.

Back in 1693 an earthquake flattened the town of Noto and it was rebuilt in grand baroque style. Somehow ice cream fits the town perfectly – just the words baroque and ice cream seem to go together: both are a bit overdone, not in the sense of being spoilt, but exaggerated, elaborated. A *granita* is something simple; a fantastic ice cream has to be worked on.

Corrado Assenza is a very serious, very lovely man who has a background in chemistry and biology and is recognised as someone at the cutting edge of food, who brings his understanding of science to what he does. He is a man who can tell, just by listening to you grate a lemon, whether you have strayed from the zest into the pith. He showed me the rhythm of the way he grates a lemon, and it was like a song. And in the next room I could hear the old lady grating the lemons to the same beat.

But I don't see him as a Heston Blumenthal or a Ferran Adrià. He is all soul, very poetic in the way he talks about food, and his heart is rooted in the land, the territory, the ingredients. What blew me away was to meet somebody with such depth of knowledge who uses that understanding to express not his own creativity, but his emblematic belief in, respect for, and attachment to the produce of the land. The only spark for a recipe is a beautiful Sicilian almond – no imported almonds for him – some jasmine flowers, the best blood oranges or the lemons he grows himself. When he mentioned his new recipe to me, and I asked when he had made it, he said, 'Five years ago.' Imagine. That is so Sicilian: so resistant to novelty for novelty's sake, so determined not to make something up to impress or shock; so true to the Sicilian idea that everything should simply be about allowing the flavours to come through and the land to talk.

The way Corrado described his almond *granita* summed it up for me. He told me that when people tasted it, he wanted them to feel the way he does, when he is sitting under an almond tree looking out to sea, breathing in the scent, and feeling the breeze.

Corrado Assenza

**Gelato al cioccolato**
Chocolate ice cream

Makes 1kg

490g whole (full-fat) milk
145g whipping cream
30g milk powder
20g dextrose
30g caster sugar
220g invert sugar
5g stabiliser (optional)
60g good cocoa powder

Hand-blend the milk, cream, milk powder and dextrose until smooth. Put into a pan over a low heat and bring to 40°C. Whisk in the sugars and the stabiliser, if using, and bring to 60°C. Add the cocoa powder and bring to 85°C. Take off the heat and cool as quickly as you can, so you don't encourage bacteria.

When cold, put into the fridge for 6–12 hours. Put the mixture into an ice-cream maker and churn according to instructions.

### Gelato al limoncello
Limoncello ice cream

Limoncello is the brilliant liqueur made with local lemons. At my friend Vittorio's restaurant in Porto Palo, he makes his own.

Makes about 1kg

545g whole (full-fat) milk
95g whipping cream
35g milk powder
70g dextrose
50g caster sugar
20g invert sugar
90g egg yolks
110g limoncello liqueur
20g lemon juice

Hand-blend the milk, cream, milk powder and dextrose until smooth, then put into a pan and bring to 40°C. Whisk in the sugars and the egg yolks. Bring up to 85°C, take off the heat, then cool as quickly as you can and put into the fridge, so you don't encourage bacteria.

When cold, mix in the limoncello and lemon juice. Put into the fridge for 6–12 hours. Put the mixture into an ice-cream maker, and churn according to instructions.

**Torrone**
Nougat

When made with sesame seeds, this is also called *cubaita* in Sicily, after the Arabic *qubhayt*.

Makes 1 slab, enough for about 8 people

120g almonds
120g pistachios
50g sesame seeds
350g honey
350g caster sugar
grated zest of 3 oranges
½ teaspoon ground cinnamon

Heat the oven to 180°C/350°F/gas 4.

Have ready two large sheets of greaseproof paper.

Lay the almonds, pistachios and sesame seeds in a single layer on a baking tray and put into the oven for about 8 minutes. As long as they are in a single layer you don't need to turn them. Keep an eye on them to make sure they don't burn. When the almonds and seeds are golden, remove the tray from the oven.

Put the honey, sugar, orange zest and cinnamon into a pan over a medium heat, stirring continuously, for 5–10 minutes. Add the toasted nuts and seeds and continue to heat until you have a light caramel (if you have a thermometer it will be 158°C). Pour on to one of the sheets of greaseproof paper, and lay the other sheet on top. Using a rolling pin, flatten the mixture to about 5mm (don't worry if the nuts break up). Cool, then break into pieces (if you prefer to cut the nougat into shapes, you need to do this before it gets cold).

This will keep for a week in an airtight container.

### 'In old-fashioned pharmacy cupboards, are trays of exquisite almond biscuits, studded like jewels'

In Erice, down a narrow little street, I came across a little 'laboratory' where they make biscuits and pastries, and beyond, there was a recess with a door, and in the recess, four old-fashioned pharmacy cupboards, glass-fronted. In each were three tiers, and on each tier were two or three different kinds of exquisite biscuits, made of almond paste (*pasta di mandorle*), studded like jewels with different jams like *cedro* (see page 407) and orange, and glazed with cane sugar. They looked amazing, and if you wanted some, as if you had asked to see a diamond ring, or an emerald or a ruby, the woman from the shop would come out to the cupboards with her keys, open the doors, and show you the biscuits.

I imagined that this is what the *dolci di riposto* that became fashionable around the seventeenth century might look like: 'cupboard sweets' – little biscuits, petits fours, almost, made with almond paste, and inside pieces of fig, quince, preserved *cedro*, that you would keep in a cool cupboard in the living room, so that if an unexpected visitor called you could offer them something sweet to eat, along with a drink. My friend Vittorio makes something similar at his restaurant, Da Vittorio, in Porto Palo: almond paste, with a little orange marmalade inside, then candied orange peel and crystals of sugar cane on top, so that you bite into the peel first, and then into the almond biscuit.

The days when Sicily was an island of sugar plantations has long gone, and cheaper beet sugar might be imported from across the world and used in most things, but I have noticed that cane sugar is still used for glazing and finishing, because it is more crystallised and pure. Sometimes the little crystals just encrust a biscuit and they gleam like little diamonds.

How many different biscuits can you find all over the island made with flour, sugar and almonds, candied fruit, or fruit marmalade? Hundreds. From *amaretti* to the little pistachio biscuits you see in bars, wrapped in silver foil, to have with your morning espresso, or the trays of after-dinner biscuits brought out in restaurants after your meal, when you really have had enough to eat, but you can't resist. Rarely will these have been made in the restaurant kitchens. They will have been bought from a favourite pastry shop, and it is a badge of honour to proclaim that your biscuits come from the most expensive *pasticceria* in town.

*Biscotti*
Biscuits

**Pasta reale**
Almond paste

Almond paste is used to make amazingly dramatic creations which fill the pastry shops for festivals and Easter, but it is also formed into simple rounds or shapes, flavoured with everything from coffee to pine nuts, and baked to make little festive biscuits.

Makes enough for 6 people

650g caster sugar
560g ground almonds
zest of 3 lemons
150g egg whites (from about 5 eggs)
a little beaten egg, for brushing

For decorating the plain biscuits:
glacé cherries, candied peel

Put the sugar, ground almonds, lemon zest and egg whites into a bowl and mix by hand until you have a smooth paste. Set aside to rest for 1 hour.

Preheat the oven to 180°C/350°F/gas 4.

Now you can roll out the paste and cut it into shapes – whatever you like: plain rounds, stars, half-moons. Place on a baking tray, brush with beaten egg, and bake in the oven for 8–12 minutes. When cool, decorate the biscuits with glacé cherries or candied peel.

Alternatively, before rolling out the paste, you can mix in whatever flavourings you prefer, by hand:

Coffee: Mix 200g of the almond paste with 1 teaspoon of coffee essence until it is all incorporated, then shape as you like.

Coconut: Mix 200g of almond paste with 50g of desiccated coconut until well incorporated. Shape as you like, and dust with another 30g of desiccated coconut until covered all over.

Pine nuts: Toast 300g of pine nuts in a single layer in the oven at 180°C/350°F/gas 4 for 8 minutes until golden, keeping an eye on them to make sure they don't burn. Crush a third of them and mix with 200g of almond paste. Shape as you like, then encrust with the remaining whole pine nuts.

Chocolate: Mix 200g of almond paste with 20g of good cocoa powder, then shape as you like.

## Biscotti di pasta frolla
Jewelled biscuits

To make a chocolate version of these, just substitute 100g of the flour with cocoa powder and follow the same process.

Makes about 30

180g plain flour
1½ teaspoons baking powder
150g unsalted butter, softened
120g caster sugar
65g egg yolks (from about 4 eggs)
candied orange or lemon peel, or some strawberry jam

Preheat the oven to 170°C/325°F/gas 3.

Sift together the flour and baking powder. In a food mixer, mix the butter and sugar until fluffy. Add the egg yolks and mix for 3 minutes, then add the flour and baking powder and mix until everything comes together into a dough. Turn out the dough and form it into rolls about 3cm in diameter. Set aside to rest in the fridge for 20 minutes to firm up the dough, then slice each roll into discs about 1.5cm thick.

Lay the discs flat on a baking tray and press a piece of candied fruit, or a little bit of strawberry jam into the centre of each one.

Bake for 10 minutes, until golden.

**Rino's mum's cucciddati**

Almond- and fig-filled Christmas cookies

These are the biscuits that our head chef Rino's mum makes for the family at Christmas in Sciacca. She uses *strutto*, which is pure pork fat, and gives a quite particular texture and flavour to baking. It has much more character than the lard you buy in the UK and is traditional in Sicilian pastries and biscuits, but you could also substitute butter.

Makes about 25–30

For the dough:
500g plain flour, plus extra for rolling out
1½ teaspoons baking powder
125g caster sugar
grated zest of 1 lemon
seeds from 1 vanilla pod
125g *strutto*, lard, or butter
1 egg
50ml milk

For the filling:
250g blanched almonds
400g dried figs, finely chopped
50g sultanas
about 100g honey
a pinch of ground cinnamon
1–2 tablespoons cocoa powder
2 egg yolks, beaten

For the filling, preheat the oven to 180°C/350°F/gas 4.

Lay the almonds in a single layer on a baking tray and put into the oven for about 8 minutes. As long as they are in a single layer you don't need to turn them. Keep an eye on them to make sure they don't burn, and when they are golden, take them out and chop them finely.

Put the almonds into a pan with the figs, sultanas, honey and cinnamon and mix well. Stir in the cocoa, then cook on a very low heat, stirring continuously, until the mixture forms a homogeneous paste. Spoon out into a bowl, cool and then put into the fridge for an hour to firm up.

In a bowl, mix the flour, baking powder, sugar, lemon zest and vanilla seeds. Melt the fat and add it to the mix, then add the egg and finally the milk and mix to a soft and firm dough. Rest in the fridge for an hour.

Preheat the oven to 180°C/350°F/gas 4 again and have ready a baking tray lined with baking parchment. Take the fig filling from the fridge, and roll into 2 long cylinders about 2cm in diameter.

Take the dough out of the fridge. Roll it out on a floured surface to 3mm thick, then cut it into 2 rectangular strips the same length as the cylinders of filling and about 8cm wide. Place a cylinder of filling in the centre of each rectangle, roll up and press the edges to seal. Cut each roll into 2cm pieces, place them on the lined baking sheet, seam side downwards, and brush with the beaten egg yolks. Bake for 20 minutes, or until the biscuits are golden brown. Serve either hot or cold.

**Taralli**
Ring biscuits

Makes 20

275g plain flour
100g caster sugar
60g unsalted butter (at room temperature)
2 medium eggs and 1 yolk
a pinch of sea salt
½ teaspoon baking powder
½ teaspoon bicarbonate of soda
zest of 1 lemon

For the icing:
100g icing sugar
juice and zest of 1 lemon

Put the flour into a food mixer with the sugar and butter and mix together. Add the eggs and yolk, salt, baking powder, bicarbonate of soda and lemon zest. Mix until everything comes together, then turn out and knead into a dough with your hands, but don't overwork it. Put into the fridge to rest for 1 hour.

Preheat the oven to 180°C/350°F/gas 4.

Cut the dough into 4 equal pieces. Shape each piece into a rough sausage shape, then roll with your fingers, starting at the middle, and then slowly moving outwards as if you were making a breadstick, until you have a long rope of dough, about 2cm in diameter. Cut each rope of dough into 5 pieces and shape each piece into a ring, twisting the ends together. Place on a baking tray and bake for about 12–15 minutes, until the biscuits are a light golden colour. Leave to cool.

Mix the icing sugar in a heatproof bowl with the lemon juice and zest, and a tablespoon of water. Put the bowl over a pan of simmering water and stir until it becomes creamy. Brush some of the icing over the top of each biscuit.

**Cotognata**
Quince paste

This is traditionally eaten with cheese.


Makes 1 slab, about 700g

450g quinces
1½ lemons
caster sugar, as needed


Put the whole quinces into a pan with half a lemon and enough water to cover and cook for about 30 minutes, or until they are soft enough for a knife to go through them easily. Drain the quinces and leave to stand until the fruits are just cool enough to handle, then peel them, cut into quarters and remove the cores.

Push the quince flesh through a sieve and weigh the resulting purée, then transfer it to a pan and add an equal weight of sugar. Stir well and add the juice of 1 lemon. Stir constantly over a medium heat until the mixture boils. Cook for a few minutes, to thicken, but without letting it caramelise. Remove from the heat and pour into a mould or dish. Cool, then put into the fridge for a day or two to dry out.

When the paste is almost dry to the touch, it is ready. Loosen it from the mould and turn it out. Wrapped in greaseproof paper it will keep for a couple of weeks in the fridge. Slice and serve with cheese.

Throughout mainland Italy, every mountain and every valley has a different, special style of cheese, because there is so much variation in microclimatic conditions, but what I feel about Sicily is that you have far fewer of these differences, and so you tend to find very similar kinds of cheese all through the island – that is, wherever it is even possible to make cheese, because in some areas there is so little grass for the animals. This aridity is one of the reasons that most of the cheeses are made with sheep's milk, since sheep are able to survive in the most difficult territories.

Apart from ricotta (see page 190), caciocavallo (see page 242), *tuma*, *primosale*, and pecorino or *canestrato* (see page 242), these last three made with sheep's cheese (pecorino comes from pecora, the word for sheep), you also find *tuma* made with cow's milk.

The next stage on from *tuma* is *primosale*, which means first salt, and whereas once you could buy the cheese at this stage, a new EU ruling doesn't allow this. So, what people do is buy the unsalted *tuma*, and salt it themselves, with Trapani sea salt, at home. You would be amazed how much moisture the salt draws out of it. After 12 hours it is totally wet, but after three or four days it has become quite dry and ready to eat.

Aged cow's milk is known as *tumazzu* (though just to be confusing, *tumazzu* is also used to refer to aged pecorino or *canestrato*).

You will also find small producers making local cheeses, such as the goat's cheese of Santo Stefano di Quisquina in the province of Agrigento; Fiore Sicanu, a kind of pecorino; Cofanetto, made in the Valle dei Belice, a fresh cheese, made with a mixture of cow's milk and sheep's milk; Maiorchino, sheep's milk cheese, made all around the Monti Peloritani; or the round Padduni, a fresh goat's cheese made in central Sicily. Some of the most amazing goat's cheeses are made with milk from the rare breed Girgentana goats, with their long white hair and extraordinary twisted horns on the top of their heads – which make them look as if their hair is in curlers. Their milk is very special, light and digestible, and the cheeses they make are often made using a crushed fig rennet, and wrapped in fig leaves.

These are the best known cheeses that you are likely to come across:

*Formaggio*
Cheese

### Piacentinu

Piacentinu is famous around Enna and dates from Norman times. It is made with sheep's milk which has had a little saffron and black pepper added to it, and has quite a delicate flavour.

### Provola

This is made from whole cow's milk, and is very like caciocavallo. As it ages it becomes a deep yellow colour and has quite a sharp, tangy flavour. Sometimes it is also smoked. The two best-known cheeses are the Provola of Nebrodi, which has the same bulb shape as caciocavallo, and Madonie, which has more of a rounded pear shape, but is tied in pairs, then hung over a pole to mature in the same way as caciocavallo.

### Ragusano DOP

This has been made in Ragusa for centuries, traditionally from the milk of Modicana cows, and is now being supported by Slow Food, as well as having its own DOP (*Denominazione di Origine Protetta*, or 'Protected Designation of Origin'). I have seen the cows around Modica, where they graze on the Iblei meadows. They are really healthy-looking, red-coated animals which are sadly in danger of disappearing, mainly because they deliver only about half the quantity of milk of other modern breeds of dairy cows. The cheese is also similar to caciocavallo, but is made into blocks, known as *scaluni*, or 'steps' in dialect, which are tied with cords and hung up to age. Although Ragusano can be eaten after a week, it is also aged (*stagionato*), when it forms a golden crust and begins to taste more tangy, and can be sliced or grated.

### Vastedda del Belìce

This is the cheese they make in Agrigento, Trapani and Palermo, where the producers are supported by a Slow Food Presidium. It is a fresh, spun-curd cheese, made with milk from the native Belìce sheep, which graze on meadow flowers. It is moulded by hand into balls and there is no ageing process – the cheese is meant to be eaten any time from an hour after it is made, up to about three days. My son, Jack, and I love Vastedda; and Margherita likes it if I pan-fry it for her and put it on top of some wilted spinach with olive oil and garlic.

Wine-making is very, very important to Sicily because it gives work to so many people, and it is currently having a big renaissance. There is an idea that most of the wines the island produces are big, red, full-bodied and fruit driven, but the reality is that of the 150,000 or so hectares of vineyards, 77 per cent are planted with white grapes – mostly on the western side of the island, with the smaller production of red grapes on the eastern side. The white grape Catarratto alone, which is the third most widely planted variety in Italy after Sangiovese and Trebbiano, accounts for about 40 per cent of the total Sicilian production. Of course Sicily grows some international varietals such as Chardonnay, Merlot and Cabernet Sauvignon, which have their own particular Sicilian character, but alongside them, and often blended with them, are indigenous varieties that have flourished in the Sicilian soil and climate for centuries, including some old varietals that were almost lost, but were identified in 2005 by Attilio Scienza, Professor of Viticulture at the University of Milan, and are now being saved from extinction by dedicated producers.

Our wine director at Locanda, Virgilio Gennaro, has compiled the following notes on the varieties you might come across on labels.

## Whites

Albanello: mainly planted in Siracusa province, though some is found in Ragusa. Produces wine that is usually blended with other varieties, and that is slightly aromatic and light, with a touch of toasted almonds on the finish.

Carricante: planted around Catania, especially on Mount Etna, this produces wine with lemony, greenish, floral, herbaceous notes, and plenty of minerality and structure. Good wines for ageing.

Catarratto: planted everywhere in Sicily with the exception of Enna province. Produces rich, golden-coloured wine, lacking a little in aroma, but big in structure and alcohol. It can be part of the Marsala blend.

Damaschino: imported by the Arabs, this is planted in the provinces of Trapani and Agrigento, and makes a light wine that is usually blended and is designed to be drunk early.

Grecanico: planted over a large area covering Trapani, Palermo and Agrigento, some research suggests that this is a natural mutation of the Greco grape, which is typical of Campania. The wines are often rich in colour and structure.

Grillo: this is the main grape used in the production of Marsala. It is planted across Trapani province, Palermo, Agrigento and in smaller quantities in Siracusa too. Grillo is structurally one of the richest Sicilian white grapes, delivering deep yellow to gold-coloured wines that age well.

Inzolia or Ansonica: mainly planted in the province of Catania but found in the rest of Sicily too, this grape produces wine with a medium yellow colour, greenish highlights and a herbaceous aroma; it can also be part of the Marsala blend.

Malvasia di Lipari: part of the big family of Malvasia, the grapes are usually dried to produce a dessert wine with ripe apricot flavours. As well as Lipari, some is planted in the provinces of Messina and Catania.

Minnella Bianca: the name derives from *minna*, which in dialect means 'the breast of a woman', and refers to the shape of the grape. It is planted in Catania province and is often found in the Etna area, where it is used as part of a blend (sometimes of red grapes) and adds a touch of finesse and crispness.

Moscato Bianco: part of the Moscato family, this clone has been the main grape used for sweet wine production in the province of Siracusa since ancient times (when it was apparently known as Pollio di Siracusa), and has been revived largely thanks to the producers Azienda Agricola Pupillo. One of the best examples is Moscato di Noto Naturale, but some dry versions can also be found.

Moscato di Pantelleria or Zibibbo: this clone of the Moscato family originates in Alexandria in Egypt and was brought to Sicily by the Romans. Generally known on the island as Zibibbo (from the Arab word *zibibb*, meaning dried grapes), it is grown mainly on the island of Pantelleria, where it is made into the world-famous luscious dessert wine Passito di Pantelleria. Some plantings can be found in the province of Trapani too.

## Reds

Corinto Nero: planted by the Greeks, and mainly found in Greece and Turkey, this is planted on the Aeolian islands (especially Lipari and Salina). The grapes are generally dried and used for sweet wines – one of the most famous is Malvasia delle Lipari – or used in Sicilian recipes.

Frappato: planted mainly in the provinces of Ragusa and Siracusa, this grape adds a touch of cherry flavour and freshness to blends, the most notable being Cerasuolo di Vittoria, the island's unique DOCG (*Denominazione di Origine Controllata e Garantita*, or 'Controlled Designation of Origin Guaranteed'), in which it is combined with Nero d'Avola.

Nerello Cappuccio or Nerello Mantellato: planted in the provinces of Catania, Messina, Agrigento and Enna. Often used as a blend with Nerello Mascalese in the Etna area to produce the Etna Rosso DOC (*Denominazione di Origine Controllata* or 'Controlled Designation of Origin').

Nerello Mascalese: planted mainly in Catania province but found in Messina, Agrigento and Enna too. It is the main grape for the pale and vibrant wine Etna Rosso DOC.

Nero d'Avola: the most planted red grape in Sicily, which is found everywhere. Its origins are still not certain, but the wines are full-bodied, with flavours reminiscent of Shiraz, and they have made Sicilian wine famous worldwide. It is also part of a blend with Frappato in Cerasuolo di Vittoria DOCG (see entry for Frappato, opposite).

Nocera: mainly found in the province of Messina and sometimes in Catania and Siracusa. In Roman times the grapes were used to make the famous Mamertino wine, which Julius Caesar is said to have drunk, and today it produces wines similar in style to the Nerello.

Perricone: the most planted grape in the western part of Sicily, generally found in the provinces of Palermo, Trapani and Agrigento. The wines have medium body and red cherry flavours, and are generally designed for early drinking.

# Acknowledgements

To Plaxy, who has held my hand in amazement on my journey of discovery around Sicily, and to Dita and Jack, who have shared everything with us. To my mum, Giuseppina, my dad, Ferruccio, and brother, Roberto, who have backed me all the way in everything I have done, and to my grandmother, Vincenzina, and grandfather, Mario, who gave me my first food education. To Mara, who always gives me moral support, and Clive, whom I miss a lot.

At Locanda: a big thank you to Ivan Icra Salicru (my right-hand man) and Rino Bono (our head chef from Sciacca) for the immense work they put into committing the recipes in this book to paper, on top of everything else they do every day at Locanda. Thanks, too, to all the Sicilian boys in the kitchen, always on hand to settle an argument over a traditional dish, or the endless names for every ingredient in dialect. And to Virgilio Gennaro, who has always been my walking 'wine bible' Nikki Morris (my ears) and Roberto Veneruzzo (my eyes). And of course to Alessandra Pino, my 'un-substitutable' assistant, who makes impossible things look simple every day.

To Lisa Linder, who captured the brilliance of Sicily, its food and its people so beautifully, and has been a friend of our family, through Plaxy, for years. To Sheila Keating, without whom this book simply wouldn't be here. To Joby Barnard, who patiently put up with everybody's ideas on how it should look, and channelled them all into the design. To Annie Lee, who edited the text so cheerfully even into the early hours of the morning, and to Rachel Smyth, who put the jigsaw of text and pictures together so speedily.

At Fourth Estate: to Louise Haines, who steered everything with her usual vision and calm, Georgia Mason, who worked tirelessly to pull everything together, and Louise Tucker, who jumped in to help everyone out.

In Sicily: a big thanks to my good friend Alessio Planeta, without whom my relationship with the island may never have happened, and to the incomparable Vittorio, his wife Francesca and his family, especially his son Michelangelo, and son-in-law Ignazio, a chef I really respect. Vittorio is a truly larger than life character who welcomed me warmly from the first time I set foot in his restaurant in Porto Palo. So many of the people I have met, the ingredients I have discovered, and the places I have been to in Sicily have Vittorio as their starting point.

To John Dickie, who wrote *Cosa Nostra*, the first book I read on the Mafia, and Matthew Fort, whose understanding and love of the food and the island shines from every page of *Sweet Honey and Bitter Lemons*. Both have fed my love of Sicily every time I have met up with them or read their words. Peter Robb's *Midnight in Sicily* is a compelling mix of Mafia history and food, and thank you, Saverio Lodato, Leonardo Sciascia; and, of course, Andrea Camilleri, for giving the world the great food-loving Inspector Montalbano. I am also indebted to Mary Taylor Simeti, whose book *Sicilian Food* is such an incredible work of research, beautifully woven together; while Giuseppe Tomasi di Lampedusa's mournful *Il Gattopardo* (*The Leopard*) is a novel I grew up with, but only fully understood when I began to get to know Sicily. Finally, thanks to the Accademia Italiana della Cucina, whose collections of traditional recipes and opinions of various academics form such a solid base for any research on Italian food – especially Benito Fiore, head of the Accademia's base in London, who has always encouraged my love of Sicily.

# Index